Designing & Implementing

MICROSOFT®

PROXY SERVER

David Wolfe

201 West 103rd Street
Indianapolis, IN 46290

Publisher and President	*Richard K. Swadley*
Publishing Manager	*Rosemarie Graham*
Director of Editorial Services	*Cindy Morrow*
Managing Editor	*Kitty Jarrett*
Assistant Marketing Managers	*Kristina Perry* *Rachel Wolfe*

Acquisitions Editor
Steve Straiger

Development Editors
Todd Bumbalough, Kristi Asher

Production Editor
Mary Ann Abramson

Indexer
Cheryl Dietsch

Technical Reviewer
Bret Bonenberger

Editorial Coordinator
Katie Wise

Technical Edit Coordinator
Lorraine Schaffer

Editorial Assistants
Carol Ackerman, Andi Richter, Rhonda Tinch-Mize

Cover Designer
Tim Amrhein

Book Designer
Allyssa Yesh

Copy Writer
Peter Fuller

Production Team Supervisors
Brad Chinn, Charlotte Clapp

Production
Jenaffer Brandt, Jeanne Clark, Rebekah Stutzman, Mark Walchle

Overview

Contents

Part IV Use   137

9 Concepts and Realities of Name Resolution with Proxy Server   139

10 Proxy Server Performance Issues   159

Acknowledgments

I would like to be able to thank a bunch of people for helping me on this book, but I can't because no one did. Microsoft is notorious for hanging beta users out on their own, no matter how much they happen to like their product or what they happen to be doing in relation to that product. The only person I do want to thank is Steve Straiger, my liaison at Sams. When deadlines came and went, I expected Steve to show up on my doorstep with a gun screaming, "Write faster, damn you!" He never did. He didn't even yell. For this, I thank him. I also thank him for doing his best to get me the material and information I needed. As project managers go, Steve ranks at the top. Steve, I think I should buy *you* lunch.

About the Author

David Wolfe. What can be said about this world-renowned humanitarian? If he's not helping the sick and dying in India, he's working on his computers. Come to think of it, he hasn't been helping the sick and dying in India much lately, so he's been spending more time than is healthy in front of a computer (David's head glows brighter than a 75 watt bulb these days...). To make money, he likes to shake down old ladies who aren't armed, but because most of them are, he also works as a DeskTop Support Specialist at DowElanco in Indianapolis. While at work, he spends his time pestering the LAN guys to convert all the Novell servers into NT servers and to stop using UNIX as their Internet gateway, but no one ever listens to him. His house is filled with boxes of technical books (a lot of them written by him), and he is the leading dial-in user on at least two Internet providers in Indianapolis. But what he really enjoys most of all is writing about himself in the third person.

Tell Us What You Think!

As a reader, you are the most important critic and commentator of our books. We value your opinion and want to know what we're doing right, what we could do better, what areas you'd like to see us publish in, and any other words of wisdom you're willing to pass our way. You can help us make strong books that meet your needs and give you the computer guidance you require.

Do you have access to CompuServe or the World Wide Web? Then check out our CompuServe forum by typing **GO SAMS** at any prompt. If you prefer the World Wide Web, check out our site at http://www.mcp.com.

Note: If you have a technical question about this book, call the technical support line at (800) 571-5840, ext. 3668.

As the publishing manager of the group that created this book, I welcome your comments. You can fax, e-mail, or write me directly to let me know what you did or didn't like about this book—as well as what we can do to make our books stronger. Here's the information:

FAX: 317/581-4669

E-mail: enterprise_mgr@sams.mcp.com

Mail: Rosemarie Graham
         Sams.net Publishing
         201 W. 103rd Street
         Indianapolis, IN 46290

Introduction

The Internet is becoming more than just a playground of the technically minded. It's becoming a place where many people and companies conduct daily business. Many individuals are looking for ways of connecting their networks to the Internet in a simple manner, and companies small and large are looking for ways to cut down on the costs of providing Internet access to their employees while at the same time increasing the overall control they have over the sites on the Internet their employees have access to.

The solution these individuals and companies are turning to is known as a proxy server. For years, UNIX users have enjoyed the flexibility that a proxy server could bring to a network, and recently many smaller companies have been developing proxy servers for the Windows environment. Now, Microsoft has developed its own high-powered proxy server for Windows NT 4.0 known as the Microsoft Proxy Server.

Microsoft Proxy Server allows an entire network to have access to the Internet through a single connection point even if this connection point is as simple as a dial-up connection to an Internet Provider. This book will give you as a network administrator the information you need to set up and run Microsoft Proxy Server to its fullest capabilities. Inside, you will find complete information on the principles behind setting up a proxy server for any size network as well as detailed discussion on how to configure Microsoft Proxy Server to do the job it was intended to do.

Microsoft Proxy Server has features which no other proxy server for Windows can currently claim. Microsoft Proxy Server can provide Windows for Workgroups machines, Windows 95 machines, Windows NT workstations, UNIX machines, OS/2 machines, and Macintosh machines with CERN- compliant proxy services which will allow such Internet client software as Microsoft Internet Explorer and Netscape Navigator to connect to the Internet with changes to just a few internal configuration settings. As well as CERN-compliant proxy services, Microsoft Proxy Server can bring to Windows workstations the ability to allow nearly *any* Internet client to connect to the Internet through a proxy connection without any special configuration to the Internet clients. Windows workstations can have special client software installed on them which will allow popular Internet client applications such as Eudora, WinVN, WS_FTP, and nearly any other to use Microsoft Proxy Server to connect to the Internet.

If you are a network administrator or just an individual looking for an Internet connection solution for connecting your network to the Internet in an economical and highly controllable manner, Microsoft Proxy Server is likely to be the answer you are looking for.

PART I

Learn

CHAPTER 1

Proxy Server Overview

The Internet has grown from a relatively small network used by a few egg-head types like myself into a global system of information distribution linking all types of users. Businesses, universities, government agencies, and private individuals all use the Internet today in growing numbers. The Internet has become as important to some users as their own private LANs (Local Area Networks). As the Internet grows in its number of users and its scope of use, more people are looking for simple, cost-effective ways of linking their own LANs to the Internet.

Installing a full-fledged connection to the Internet can cost quite a bit. Even though hardware costs for Internet routers and CSU/DSU (Channel Service Unit/Digital Service Unit) units are coming down, proper Internet connections are still beyond the reach of most small businesses and private users. This being the case, people have been searching for solutions that will provide LAN-wide access to the Internet through a smaller connection which does not require all the fancy hardware that installing a large connection, such as a T1 line, requires. Modem speeds are increasing at a rate of about one jump every eight months, and ISDN (Integrated Services Digital Network) may take hold as a standard for data communication in the near future. These two forms of data communication are far cheaper than installing a T1 line and are used by millions of people.

The nature of a TCP/IP (Transmission Control Protocol/Internet Protocol) network also makes it impossible for a private, non-sanctioned LAN to have a legitimate connection to the Internet with typical dialup-type connections. The addressing scheme used requires all IP addresses to be unique. Many private networks using the TCP/IP protocol are set up using IP (Internet Protocol) addresses that may already be in use by other Internet sites. Connecting a private network with repeated IP addresses will cause serious problems. There is also the issue of routing. Unless the entire Internet is aware of a block of addresses (known as *subnet*), data will not be routed correctly to a site. That's where the InterNIC comes in. The InterNIC governs the Internet and issues addresses to sites wanting a legitimate presence on the Internet. Once a site has a valid set of addresses, the core routers are informed of the new addresses, and data will flow correctly to and from the new site.

The process of getting a valid subnet and a connection can take many weeks, cost several thousand dollars in hardware, and cost between $1000 and $2000 a month in access charges. In contrast, a single user dialup connection to an ISP (Internet Service Provider) through a modem takes no time to obtain, averages about $20 a month, and requires little more than a $120 28.8 Kbps modem. ISDN access to a provider (if it's available) can run in the neighborhood of $20 to $70 a month plus metered charges and about $300 in hardware. If a valid connection to the Internet is beyond your price range right now, you're in luck. Microsoft has developed Microsoft Proxy Server, an NT server application that makes it possible for an entire LAN with non-sanctioned IP addresses to have access to the Internet through a typical dialup link to an ISP. Microsoft Proxy Server will work with any valid link to the Internet: Analog Dial Up, ISDN, T1 and beyond.

In some situations, using Microsoft Proxy Server will be a better choice than actually giving workstations full access to the Internet with valid IP addresses. Microsoft Proxy Server is easier to set up and has security features that make it easy to control the type of Internet access client workstations have. Controlling access to the Internet on a LAN with a legitimate connection is tough to do, because each workstation on the LAN can have its own valid presence on the Internet. When workstations connect through Microsoft Proxy Server, they rely on its presence on the Internet for their connection.

Microsoft Proxy Server Web Proxy Is an IIS Web Server Sub-Service

In order for Microsoft Proxy Server to be installed, the Microsoft IIS Server must first be installed. The only element of IIS that must be enabled is the Web server element. The Microsoft Proxy Server Web Proxy runs as an aspect of the IIS Web server and operates by using the IIS Web server to listen to TCP port 80 traffic. It is the job of Microsoft Proxy Server Web Proxy to determine if it is to be remoted to the outside or whether it is to remain locally serviced by the IIS Web server (or another Web server operating on the local LAN). HTTP, FTP, and Gopher requests can all be handled through port 80. Microsoft Proxy Server is actually two services in one. The first part, the Web Proxy, handles CERN-compliant proxy requests through port 80 on the TCP/IP protocol. CERN, Conseil Europeen pour la Recherche Nucleair (European Laboratory for Particle Physics), developed many UNIX-based Internet communications standards. Among these standards was a proxy service protocol that allowed for remoting Internet requests through a dedicated connection point.

The CERN-compatible proxy server element of Microsoft Proxy Server supports communications through port 80 of HTTP, FTP, and Gopher requests. These services all obtain data through the Internet using similar means. In order for CERN-compatible proxying to function correctly, clients must be able to interact with a proxy server. This approach is OK for compliant applications, such as IE (Internet Explorer) and Netscape, but there are many other Internet applications that do not have built-in proxying capabilities.

Many Internet applications simply communicate with the Windows Socket interface (WinSock), which in turn communicates with the rest of the network, internal or external. For these applications, another proxy method must be used to give them access to the outside Internet. The second element of Microsoft Proxy Server is known as the WinSock Proxy server. For those applications that do not support CERN-compliant proxying, the WinSock Proxy server can intercept their WinSock calls and remote them to Microsoft Proxy Server for external processing. This necessitates the installation of special WinSock Proxy client software, which can intercept a client's WinSock call and redirect it correctly. The difference between the Web Proxy and the WinSock Proxy is covered later in this chapter.

What Is a Proxy Server?

Catapult was the code name Microsoft gave to its proxy server. Like everything Microsoft produces, it was renamed Microsoft Proxy Server upon release. Proxy servers have been around in the UNIX world for a while now, but Microsoft Proxy Server is Microsoft's first attempt at creating a proxy server for the NT environment.

The actual definition of a proxy server is a server that performs an action for another computer that cannot perform the action for itself. A real-world analogy for a proxy can be seen at high-priced art auctions. Many bidders at art auctions will not attend the auction themselves, for whatever reason. Some of the actual bidders at the auction are the *proxies* for the real buyers. The proxy acts for the buyer and relays the status of the proceedings to the buyer over the telephone. If you watch CNN coverage of important art auctions, you'll see proxies all over the bidding hall talking to their buyers over land line or cellular phones. The proxy acts only when instructed to do so, and anything that the buyer could do in person, the buyer can do through his proxy.

In the world of computers and the Internet, workstations behind the proxy do not have valid Internet connections and therefore cannot talk to the Internet on their own. The proxy sits at the juncture of the Internet connection and the local LAN connection (typically an NT machine with two network interface cards (NICs) or with one network card and a RAS connection to the Internet) and routes local LAN requests to the Internet as though Microsoft Proxy Server itself were requesting the information. On LANs that do not have valid subnets issued from the InterNIC, workstations cannot route data through an NT machine that does have a connection to the Internet.

The following is a small diagram of my own scenario:

Figure 1.1.
The author's network.

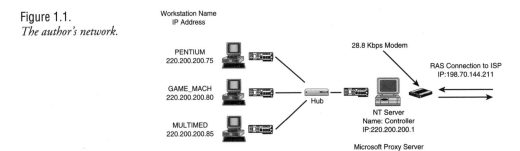

I am working on the machine named PENTIUM. The IP addresses given to all of my workstations and server are on the 220.200.200 subnet. This selection of a subnet was a fairly random process. I selected it because it fell within the Class C subnet range and was easy to remember. Most network administrators implementing the TCP/IP protocol on a non-Internet connection LAN will select a subnet in a similar manner. When a LAN is not connected to the Internet, network administrators have few restrictions when selecting the addressing scheme to be used. If a LAN is to be legitimately connected to the Internet, the LAN must be configured with IP addresses issued by the InterNIC.

There are sets of private IP subnets that private LAN administrators can use for their own internal TCP/IP networks. These private subnets were set aside by the InterNIC and will never be used openly on the Internet. These addresses should be the ones given to private TCP/IP networks that will not be directly participating on the Internet. I actually chose my addresses in the 220.200.200 subnet poorly, without doing enough research. When a private LAN uses addresses for the Internet that are already taken, Microsoft Proxy Server will keep all traffic directed to those addresses local, which will cut off a large chunk of the Internet from your LAN users. Microsoft Proxy Server determines what is local and what is external. When the internal addresses overlap external addresses, Microsoft Proxy Server will keep traffic for those addresses as local-only traffic. Chapter 4, "Planning Your Installation and Configuration," will cover the reserved IP addresses in more detail.

The diagram in Figure 1.1 shows my simple 10BaseT network of three Win95 workstations and one NT server. The server is connected to the LAN via a standard network card and to the Internet through a 28.8-Kbps modem connected via RAS. When Microsoft Proxy Server is installed on the NT server and properly configured, all workstations may connect to the Internet through Microsoft Proxy Server as though they themselves were connected. Of course, each workstation must be specially configured to connect to a proxy server, rather than the actual Internet. Setting up a proxy requires a little more effort that just installing and setting up the software on the server. Fear not however—client-side configuration is very simple, because all Microsoft Internet applications rely on a centralized configuration point in the control panel for proxy settings. Most non-Microsoft Internet applications can be easily configured individually to communicate through a proxy. Because the use of proxy servers is becoming common, most Internet application programmers are incorporating the capability for their software to communicate with the Internet through a proxy server. In the future, a majority of Internet applications will have the capability to use a proxy server for their connection. Even if an Internet application does not have the capability to communicate through a proxy, special client-side software can be installed that will allow nearly all Internet applications to talk properly with Microsoft Proxy Server.

How Microsoft Proxy Server Serves a Network

The primary use of the Internet these days is World Wide Web (WWW) access. Whether your network uses Microsoft Internet Explorer or Netscape Navigator, LAN users will be able to "surf the net" through Microsoft Proxy Server as though they were connected directly to the Internet via Dial Up Networking. If you have ever tried other proxy servers, such as WinGate or NetProxy, you'll find that Microsoft Proxy Server's performance exceeds their performance by quite a bit. Having tried both WinGate and NetProxy, I can attest that Microsoft Proxy Server's performance is nearly identical to actually being connected with a local workstation connection to the Internet via Dial-Up Networking. Both WinGate and NetProxy, while fine applications in their own right, did not compare to Microsoft Proxy Server's performance with any client, such as IE 3.0, Netscape 3.0, Eudora, WinVN, or WS_FTP32.

Microsoft Proxy Server supports nearly any type of Internet client, from WWW client to FTP client to Newsgroup client. Win95 workstations work best through Microsoft Proxy Server, but almost any TCP/IP client (such as OS/2 and Windows for Workgroups) can access the Internet through an NT machine running Microsoft Proxy Server. There are some limitations to 16-bit clients using Microsoft Proxy Server, but this topic will be covered in greater detail in Chapter 11, "Proxy Server and Client Applications."

Users of a LAN can access the Internet through a personal dialup account, connected by RAS on the NT machine running Microsoft Proxy Server. This means that users on a LAN will not have personal e-mail accounts on the ISP providing the connection. Most ISPs give only one e-mail account for each dial-in account. Most companies in this situation will opt to use the provided e-mail account as a company-wide account. Privacy is one of the concessions necessary when using Microsoft Proxy Server through a dial-in account.

Microsoft Proxy Server's purpose is to provide LAN access to the Internet, not vice versa. In other words, outside Internet users will not be able to access LAN workstations through Microsoft Proxy Server. Microsoft Proxy Server only listens to internal network requests for outside information.

Microsoft Proxy Server can also provide a very high level of security for controlling which LAN users have access to the Internet connection and exactly what those users can access. Because Microsoft Proxy Server is an integrated NT application, it can draw on NT's internal security systems for LAN user authorization. All Internet protocols can be separately configured for different security levels. Different users or groups of users can be authorized for each type of Internet connection (such as HTTP, FTP, and NNTP). Microsoft Proxy Server also has the capability to limit the sites where LAN users can connect. If you need a secure Internet access point, Microsoft Proxy Server is your best choice.

Web Proxy Versus WinSock Proxy

As previously mentioned, Microsoft Proxy Server consists of two separate servers. The first is the Web Proxy server and the second is the WinSock Proxy server. Both are installed when Microsoft Proxy Server is installed, and each runs as a separate service under NT. Each service can be controlled and configured through the Internet Service Manager found in either the Microsoft Proxy Server folder or the Microsoft Internet Server folder in the Programs group on the Start menu.

The Basics of TCP/IP

All communication which takes place over the TCP/IP protocol is done through ports. The IP address, combined with a port number, is known as a *socket*. Servers that communicate via TCP/IP do so through predefined ports, depending on which type of server they are. For example, the WWW server communicates with the HTTP protocol. This protocol uses port 80. FTP servers listen to port 21 for their traffic. Telnet communications take place over port 23. The NNTP protocol (Newsgroup communications) uses port 119, while SMTP (Mail) uses port 25. These ports are virtual channels of communication, used between servers of clients using the same protocol.

The most confusing part of this discussion is the term *protocol*. Protocol is used at every level of networking to describe the procedure two applications (server/client) or devices (network interfaces) use to talk to one another. Network protocols are used by two network cards to communicate, while server and client applications communicate using software protocols. Take the following arrangement of protocols, for example:

- PPP is used to transport network protocols over an asynchronous link, such as a modem.
- A network protocol such as TCP/IP can be carried by PPP.
- An Internet protocol such as HTTP is carried by TCP/IP protocol along TCP port 80.

It gets very confusing at times when the word protocol is used to describe so many different levels of networking.

TCP/IP packets have a header. This header has information such as destination IP address and destination port. Two types of packets can pass over the TCP/IP protocol: TCP and UDP (User Datagram Protocol). The primary difference between TCP and UDP packets is that TCP packets contain header information in them that indicates the sequence of the packets and UDP packets do not. Most Internet protocols use TCP packets to communicate. Because sequencing (making sure the order of received packets is the same on the receiving end as it was on the sending end) requires slightly more overhead, UDP communication is used by servers requiring the highest level of efficiency, but at the slight cost of data integrity. Servers such as Real Audio and VDO Live use UDP communications because their data is transmitted in real time and requires the fastest possible communication.

TCP packet transmissions are known as *stream-oriented*, while UDP packet transmissions are known as *datagram-oriented*. Both use the TCP/IP protocol and are nearly identical, except for the differences mentioned earlier.

The Web Proxy Server

The Web Proxy server element of Microsoft Proxy Server is a CERN-compliant proxy server that operates by listening to TCP/IP port 80 for traffic. It must use the IIS Web server as its listening mechanism, because port 80 is the WWW port. The Microsoft Proxy Server Web Proxy server is incorporated into the IIS Web server once it is installed.

The Microsoft Proxy Server Web Proxy consists of two parts: the filter and the application. Clients properly set to talk to a proxy server send their requests out on port 80 in a different request format than they would if they were communicating with the actual destination server on their own. This alteration of request format is done so the proxy server will know exactly what kind of request it is being sent—HTTP, FTP, or Gopher. When browsers are not set to talk to a proxy, they make the correct type of request to the destination server, depending on the format of the user-entered request.

For example, when a non-proxy-enabled browser gets a user request for:

`http://www.pandy.com/index.htm`

the browser knows that the protocol to be used is HTTP from the format of the command. The browser then sends the following request to the WWW server `pandy.com`:

`GET ./index.htm`

`GET` is a standard command for obtaining Internet objects such as files, HTML documents, and imbedded objects. This command is implemented in different ways, depending on which protocol is using `GET`.

If a browser that is not configured for proxy use sends `GET ./index.htm` to a proxy server, the proxy server would not know which protocol to use nor the location of the object to `GET`. Therefore, when browsers are configured to send proxy-formatted commands to a proxy server, the requests look like this:

`GET http://www.pandy.com/index.htm`

The browser assumes that the proxy server will correctly parse the command and issue it to the correct site in the correct format. Keep in mind that FTP clients configured for CERN-compliant proxy interfacing use the same format and port (80) as Web clients, even though FTP clients use port 21 when talking to servers on their own.

Once the proxy server receives the properly formatted request, it sends the request to the actual destination in the same format the browser would have, had the browser not been configured for proxy interface. If the request for data was an FTP request, the proxy server would have initiated communications to the destination FTP server on port 21. Once the proxy server receives a reply from the destination, it sends the data on to the requesting workstation on the LAN, and the cycle is complete.

The job of the proxy filter is to determine if the received HTTP request is in proxy format or in local request format. If the filter determines that the HTTP request is in standard format (`GET ./index.htm`), it assumes the request is to be handled by the local WWW server. If the HTTP request is in proxy format, it will pass the request on to the proxy application, where it will be reformatted and reissued to the correct destination.

The proxy application performs many operations on the request before it actually sends it out. The proxy application is responsible for looking in the local proxy cache to see if the data requested is already present. If the data is present, its Time To Live (TTL) has not expired, and the object has not been changed on the destination server, the proxy application will pull the object from the cache and send it to the requester, without having to go out to the Internet to get it. This process of holding a certain amount of information in a local cache can greatly increase Microsoft Proxy Server's perceived performance, especially when a smaller connection to the Internet is being used by many people. Caching is discussed in greater detail in Chapter 12, "Controlling the Proxy Server Cache."

The proxy application is also responsible for authenticating the requester and ensuring that he has authorization both to use the protocol and to obtain information from the requested destination. Client authentication takes place before any other action.

Once the requested information has been obtained, either from the local cache or from the Internet, the proxy server will send the information to the requester via the HTTP protocol on port 80.

The WinSock Proxy Server

The WinSock Proxy server works quite differently from the Web Proxy server. In order for the WinSock Proxy server to function correctly, special WinSock Proxy client software must be installed on each workstation needing WinSock Proxy support. When Microsoft Proxy Server is installed, a special network share is created that contains the WinSock Proxy client installation files. Workstations can link to this shared resource and run the SETUP file found there to correctly install the WinSock Proxy client software.

When Internet clients such as Eudora (a popular e-mail client) request data from a TCP/IP network, they make WinSock calls to the local WinSock DLLs (Dynamic Link Libraries). The WinSock DLLs then process the request via the TCP/IP protocol. In order for applications such as Eudora (which has no special proxy configurability) to work correctly in a proxy environment, the WinSock layer on a workstation must be able to forward or remote the request to the WinSock Proxy server that performs the action on behalf of the requester.

For this to happen, the client WinSock DLLs must be renamed and new WinSock Proxy DLLs must be put in their place. In a 16-bit environment, the WinSock DLL is WINSOCK.DLL. In a 32-bit environment, such as Win95, the WinSock DLL is WSOCK32.DLL. These original DLLs are not overwritten by the new DLLs, but are renamed something different. Once the WinSock Proxy client software is in place, all Internet clients on workstations will function as they always did for local LAN traffic.

During the installation of Microsoft Proxy Server, Microsoft Proxy Server will examine your private LAN and determine which set of local addresses is used by your network. These addresses are contained in the LAT (Local Address Table). This information is kept in the file \MSP\CLIENTS\MSPLAT.TXT. This is a very important file that will be discussed later.

Once the WinSock Proxy client software is installed, any Internet application requesting data does so to the new WinSock Proxy DLLs. Once the WinSock Proxy DLLs get a request, they open a control channel to the WinSock Proxy server on port 1745 and download a copy of the LAT. The address of the requested destination is compared to the contents of the LAT. If the address is found to be local, the WinSock Proxy DLLs simply relay the request to the legitimate WinSock DLLs on the workstation, and the request is processed as any other local request.

If the request is found to be an external request, the WinSock Proxy DLLs remote the request to the WinSock Proxy server for processing. The WinSock Proxy server establishes a link on the client's original request port (for example, port 119 for Telnet clients) to both the client and the Internet destination. The WinSock Proxy client DLLs from that point on forward all data to the original WinSock DLLs for standard processing. The original DLLs simply communicate on a given port at this time and not to a specific IP address. Because the WinSock Proxy server has been initialized by the WinSock Proxy client, the WinSock Proxy server will be responding on that port for the client. The client will see the WinSock Proxy server as the final destination and the WinSock Proxy server will be talking to the originally requested destination and relaying information to the client.

Several clients, such as FTP clients, send out their local IP address in a handshaking packet, so that the Internet server they are attempting to connect with will be able to open a connection back to the requester. The WinSock Proxy server is responsible for removing the local IP address used by the client and replacing it with the WinSock Proxy server's Internet IP. This means the contacted server will open a backward connection to the WinSock Proxy server rather than attempting to open a connection with the originally indicated IP address. Keep in mind that the local IP addresses used on a private network are not valid, and the WinSock Proxy server must use the IP issued to it from the ISP giving the Internet connection.

Once the Internet server correctly establishes a return connection to the WinSock Proxy server, the WinSock Proxy server in turn establishes a return connection to its own client on the same port. The client lets the WinSock Proxy server know that it is expecting a return connection by listening to the proxy server's IP address for a return connection. Remember that when the client makes a connection, it actually makes it with the IP address of the WinSock Proxy server. The WinSock Proxy DLLs determine if the original request was local or remote. If local, the request was already passed to the real WinSock DLLs. If the request was remote, the WinSock Proxy WinSock DLLs would instruct the client to talk to the WinSock Proxy server IP as though it were the final destination. If the client is listening for a return connection to come from the IP of the WinSock Proxy server, the WinSock Proxy server knows to expect a return connection from the destination Internet site.

IP-less Listening

There are some rare situations where a client application might issue out a TCP/IP listen command to the WinSock DLL without a destination IP address. When these situations occur—and the WinSock Proxy DLL cannot determine if the listen request is to be kept local or remoted to the Internet—the request will remain local. This is done for security reasons.

Web Proxy and WinSock Proxy Working Together

The combination of the Web Proxy server and the WinSock Proxy server allows Microsoft Proxy Server to service nearly any WinSock 1.1-compliant client application. Those clients that have the internal capability to talk directly to a CERN-compatible proxy have that capability, and those clients that do not can still get Internet access via the WinSock Proxy server.

The WinSock Proxy server can handle the traffic of Web browsers, FTP clients, and Gopher clients on its own, if those browsers do not have the capability or are not set to use a proxy server. There are no drawbacks to using WinSock Proxy with these types of clients. The primary edge the proxy server has over the WinSock Proxy server is that no special client software must be installed in order for it to work. This means that non-Windows operating systems can take advantage of a Windows NT Microsoft Proxy Server Web Proxy server via the TCP/IP protocol.

Using IPX/SPX

It is possible to use the IPX/SPX protocol as the only protocol installed on workstations and still be able to access the Internet with clients via the WinSock Proxy server. The WinSock Proxy client software has the ability to use IPX to transport Internet requests and responses to and from clients to the WinSock Proxy server. This ability allows a network administrator to have full control over Internet traffic.

When IPX is used as the only network protocol on a LAN, any request made by a TCP/IP client will be considered a remote request. The replacement WinSock Proxy DLLs will remote the request to the WinSock Proxy server, which will use IPX to respond to the client.

Obviously, the TCP/IP protocol must be installed on the NT server that is connected to the Internet, in order for a legitimate TCP/IP connection to be established between the NT machine and the ISP.

The Microsoft Proxy Server will perform a protocol translation between TCP/IP and IPX. The IPX protocol is similar in nature to the TCP/IP protocol in that each workstation on the LAN has a unique node ID, and IPX packets can be routed to specific destinations.

Summary

This introduction to Microsoft Proxy Server gave you a clear idea of Microsoft Proxy Server's purpose and capabilities. As Microsoft gets deeper and deeper into the Internet market, you are going to see more and more applications like Microsoft Proxy Server. Microsoft Proxy Server can be used as a cheap, efficient alternative to real connections to the Internet. Because Microsoft Proxy Server can provide all the services an actual connection to the Internet could, I have a feeling more people will be looking to Microsoft Proxy Server as the best solution.

CHAPTER 2

Proxy Server, IIS, and Windows NT

As most people know by now, Microsoft is making a great push toward the Internet. Most applications released by Microsoft deal directly with the Internet in some way. Microsoft has tried to design Windows NT 4.0 to be the platform of choice for all types of Internet servers and applications. It's taken a little while for Microsoft to get up a full head of steam down the Internet road, but they're now going full tilt. Microsoft Proxy Server is part of a global package of Internet-oriented applications. Each of these applications in turn is designed to work as an extension of the NT operating system. Each element, including Microsoft Proxy Server, IIS Web server, IIS FTP server, and IIS Gopher server, uses such NT subservices as security and network channels to work together as seamless applications.

This integrated approach has been common in the UNIX environment for a while, but is just now becoming the standard for Windows NT. For a long time, Internet applications and servers in the Windows NT, Windows 95, or Windows 3.x environments have been a hodge podge of stand-alone systems that relied on their own security and separate TCP/IP stacks. There are a couple of reasons for this fact. The first reason is that Microsoft was not headed in the direction of the Internet. In the world of the Internet, Microsoft is a newcomer. Granted, Microsoft can devote far more development resources to Internet applications and servers than any other software company, but the UNIX crowd has had a big head start. Because Microsoft's attention to Internet development has been slight until now, previous versions of Windows were not well suited for use as Internet platforms.

Because of this, third-party Internet software developers had to create their own security systems and protocol layers for use in Windows environments. Naturally, it was rare that any two server-side applications would work in tandem unless they were developed by the same company. The effort involved in creating a complete Internet site in the Windows environment was a pretty daunting task. Windows had a bad reputation as an Internet platform and justifiably so.

Windows NT 4.0

I attended World Wide Alive in Indianapolis in July of 1996. World Wide Alive was a live, one day seminar by Microsoft, which was transmitted to approximately 90 locations around the country and a few international sites. Not only was this seminar designed to showcase upcoming Microsoft products, such as Microsoft Proxy Server and Windows NT 4.0, but it also detailed Microsoft's dedicated direction toward the Internet in most of its future software plans. For example, the scheduled 1997/1998 (you know Microsoft's famous timetables) revision of Windows 95 is supposed to change Windows 95 into a completely HTML-based environment. This means that the Windows 95 desktop will be nothing more than an actual HTML document. The Control Panel will also be HTML-based in much the same way.

Those folks who are good at managing HTML Web documents now will be right at home with Microsoft applications in the future. Imagine being able to use your desktop to simply link to a friend's desktop via a dial-up link, such as the one many people have to an ISP today.

Windows NT 4.0 is the first step toward this type of environment. Obviously the Windows NT 4.0 desktop is not HTML-based, but many of its subservices have been redesigned to offer greater flexibility with the Internet and Internet-related servers.

The NT Internet Interface

Access to the Internet can be gained in several different ways with NT. The two most common ways are:

- Multiple NICs (network interface cards) where at least one card is physically linked to an Internet line (such as an ISDN line or a T1 line)
- The second and more common form of Internet connection, and the one I believe will be most applicable to readers of this book is through RAS (remote access services) via a modem

NT treats each form of connection the same way, although at a substantially different connection speed. This book is written with the network administrator in mind. It's assumed that you have an adequate understanding of the networking terms and concepts that will be addressed in this book. Installation and use of Microsoft Proxy Server to facilitate global LAN access to the Internet is a pretty straightforward process. However, no two LANs are ever set up identically, so it can sometimes get confusing when trying to describe certain scenarios in which Microsoft Proxy Server can be useful.

The most common network arrangement for most private individuals and companies who use NT is as an isolated LAN with periodic dial-up connections to the Internet, for those people on the LAN who need Internet access (see Figure 2.1).

Figure 2.1.
A typical network with independent periodic Internet connections.

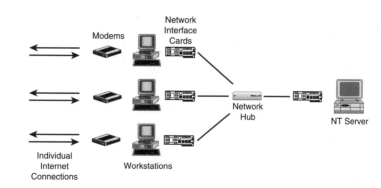

This arrangement means that Internet users on a LAN must have a separate phone line to each computer that needs Internet access and a modem. Each individual LAN user may also need separate dial-in accounts with a provider. However, this is not always true because some providers do allow multiple simultaneous dial-ins on the same account. This can be pretty expensive if a LAN has many users who need Internet access. There are ways to work around this, such as using a modem pool on a central server to eliminate the need for individual phone lines and modems at network workstations, but this type of solution can be expensive because most modem pooling software doesn't come cheap (see Figure 2.2).

Figure 2.2.
Internet connections to workstations through a modem pool.

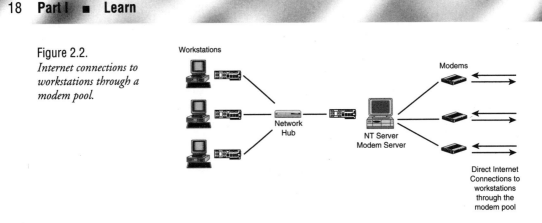

Modem pooling can also be flaky at times and place extra overhead on network workstations. It still does not eliminate the possible need for individual ISP (Internet Service Provider) accounts for each LAN users needing Internet dial-out access. Modem pooling does reduce the number of individual dial-out lines and modems though. However, modem pooling software for NT runs around $300 on average for a five-user license, and the cost goes up for each line added to the system. If you are thinking about Microsoft Proxy Server for your LAN, I assume one of the main reasons for this is to keep the cost of Internet access as low as possible. Of all Internet access scenarios, using Microsoft Proxy Server is the cheapest and offers the highest performance for multiple users.

NT Server Access to the Internet

As already mentioned, NT can access the Internet in several ways. The most convenient way is to have access to a dedicated line of some form. However, if a LAN has access to a dedicated line, it is most likely that all network workstations will already be set up to access the Internet themselves without the need of Microsoft Proxy Server. Figure 2.3 diagrams a typical network with LAN-wide Internet access.

Figure 2.3.
A LAN with a permanent Internet connection.

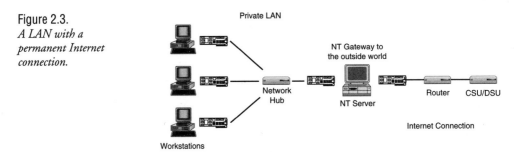

Under this scenario, network workstations may have direct access to the Internet. Full LAN access to the Internet requires more than just the correct hardware. The second element necessary for full Internet access is a valid set of addresses for each workstation on a network. If a LAN has a dedicated line, such as a T1 or higher, the provider giving such access will almost certainly have allocated a subnet of valid Internet addresses for the LAN. It is therefore un-likely that a LAN in this scenario will need the services of Microsoft Proxy Server. However, it is possible that for some strange reason workstations of this type of LAN are prevented from having fully qualified Internet addresses. If, for example, the private LAN only operated via the IPX or NetBEUI protocols, access to the Internet would not be directly possible. Microsoft Proxy Server can provide access to the Internet if the TCP/IP protocol is not supported or used on the workstations, but the IPX protocol is. Microsoft Proxy Server can use IPX as a transport protocol when TCP/IP is not available or supported. The use of IPX is discussed in greater detail in Chapter 6, "Configuring Proxy Server."

Microsoft Proxy Server will most likely be used when an NT server on a LAN has a periodic connection to the Internet. This usually comes in the form of either an ISDN connection or a modem connection to an ISP (see Figure 2.4).

Figure 2.4.
A periodic connection to the Internet.

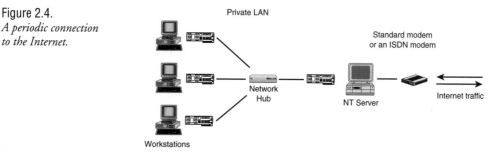

In this scenario, only the NT server itself will normally have access to the Internet via the dial-up connection. Because the workstations on the private network do not have their own valid IP addresses, they cannot access the Internet through the dial-up connection on the NT server. NT 4.0 does have the physical ability to route IP packets correctly through RAS, whereas NT 3.51 did not. As a result, RAS is no longer limited as a network interface. As long as RIP (Routing for Internet Protocol) is installed as a service on the NT server with the Internet ac-cess, TCP/IP packets will be correctly routed if they originate from valid addresses, no matter which NIC they pass through. The problem is getting a range of valid Internet addresses when the form of connection is only a periodic dial-up. Most ISPs will not give out more than one address to an ISP customer. Some ISPs do have forms of dedicated dial-up access that provide more than one address.

The largest ISP in Indianapolis offers dedicated dial-up access for $100 a month. With this level of service, customers also get six valid IP addresses to use on their own LAN. This allows a private network to have access to the Internet for up to six individual workstations, under the right conditions. If there are no more than six workstations on the network then the arrange-ment will work out quite well. If there are more than six workstations on a network that need access to the Internet, a DHCP server will need to be available on the LAN to hand out those six IP addresses only when needed.

Internet Versus Intranet

The world seems to revolve around catch words and phrases. One of the latest to dominate the chatter about computers is the word intranet. Because the Internet has been such a large part of computers, a word had to be created to distinguish the outside world from the inside world. That word is *intranet*.

The difficult thing with setting up a private LAN with the TCP/IP protocol is that the LAN is normally set up with invalid IP addresses. On my home network, I picked out an IP subnet of `220.200.200.*`. No real reason for this range, that's just the one I chose. Most network administrators do the same thing with their own networks. In actuality, another site on the Internet may already be validly using the 220.200.200.* subnet. Routers on the Internet would go crazy trying to route packets from Internet sites using an invalid set of addresses. Consult Chapter 4, "Planning Your Installation and Configuration," for full details on properly selecting a subnet for a private LAN. My choice of `220.200.200.*`. is not the best choice.

When a LAN is not connected to the outside world, the IP addresses used on the LAN are meaningless. This can cause problems later if a permanent connection to the Internet is obtained. It means long hours of reconfiguring all workstations on the network for the new set of addresses.

One of the simplest elements that can be added to a network which can greatly reduce reconfiguration time is a DHCP server. A DHCP server or Dynamic Host Configuration Protocol server is an NT service that hands out TCP/IP configuration information to workstations on a network. A DHCP server can hand out all necessary protocol information a TCP/IP workstation might need when starting up. Such things as IP address, DNS location, and subnet mask can be passed out by a DHCP server on a network.

For example, if a LAN has 100 workstations, each with preset IP addresses, and those 100 workstations have to be reconfigured because of a change of some sort, you're looking at a couple days work just plugging in new numbers. A DHCP server can turn a two-day project into a two-minute project. But of course, there is a drawback to workstations with dynamic addresses. However, with such NT services as WINS, the drawbacks can be greatly reduced or completely nullified.

It's important to have a clear understanding of possible future needs of a LAN when setting it up. It's also important to understand some of the vital NT services, such as WINS and DHCP, if you're planning on adding Internet-type services to an intranet. WINS is similar in action to DNS, except its main purpose is to resolve NetBIOS names as opposed to Internet names. When used in conjunction with DHCP, the dynamic addresses which the DHCP server passes out to new machines on a network are automatically registered with WINS. Therefore, an up-to-date database of local IP addresses to NetBIOS machine names is available for network use. This ensures continued proper network operation when IP addresses for a LAN change (among other possible changes).

Internet Servers

Many companies are beginning to use Web servers to manage internal company information. The point-and-click nature of the Web makes it very simple for computer novice employees to perform their jobs. Also, a Web interface is the perfect environment for disseminating information. Opening a Web server, or any Internet server (such as FTP and Telnet) to the outside world when the network where the server resides does not have valid Internet addresses is a tricky task.

The purpose of Microsoft Proxy Server is to deny outside Internet users access to the resources of a private LAN. Therefore, unless Internet servers are on the NT machines with the Internet connections, access to these servers will not be possible from the outside. Even though general access to a LAN is not normally possible from the outside through Microsoft Proxy Server, it is possible that experienced hackers could gain access in rare situations. Microsoft recommends disabling IP forwarding on Microsoft Proxy Server to ensure that the NT machine itself does not propagate outside packets into the private LAN.

Keep in mind that Microsoft Proxy Server does not require any form of IP forwarding on the server on which it is running in order to function normally. Microsoft Proxy Server handles its own delivery of IP packets to and from the outside connection. Disabling IP routing is covered in greater detail in Chapter 6.

Most arrangements of Microsoft Proxy Server will be such that it will be running on the same machine as Internet server applications. This poses no problem as long as the Web server in use is the Microsoft IIS Web server. The Microsoft IIS Web server is the only application that is required by Microsoft Proxy Server. This is because Microsoft Proxy Server "piggy-backs" on the listening services of the IIS Web server on port 80 in order to pick up on LAN requests that are destined for the outside world. Any other Internet server applications can be run on an NT machine that also runs Microsoft Proxy Server. Microsoft Proxy Server's Web Proxy and WinSock Proxy services are implemented so that port conflicts are not an issue on the server.

Other proxy servers, such as WinGate, operate by listening to ports that other server applications listen to. This causes a conflict because no two applications can respond to the same TCP/IP port traffic. In cases where proxy servers such as WinGate are used on machines with other Internet applications, the Internet applications must have their listening ports altered to ports on which the proxy server itself is not listening.

Microsoft Proxy Server circumvents such conflicts in two ways. With standard proxy requests (WWW, FTP, and Gopher), the IIS Web server first fields all traffic through a special filter DLL that determines whether the traffic is local or destined for the outside. If the traffic is not to be picked up by the WWW server itself, Microsoft Proxy Server takes over the traffic and passes it outside. TCP/IP traffic that is not covered by the Microsoft Proxy Server Web Proxy server (any traffic on a port other than 80) is handled by the Microsoft Proxy Server WinSock Proxy service.

The WinSock Proxy server works in tandem with the WinSock Proxy client on the workstations. The WinSock Proxy client software fields any local TCP/IP requests, translating the traffic to the port that the WinSock Proxy server is listening to. This means that the WinSock Proxy server can handle nearly any type of TCP/IP client, such as SMTP, NNTP, and Telnet, without a conflict with other Internet server software that may be running along side of Microsoft Proxy Server.

I have personally run non-Microsoft FTP servers, SMTP servers, and POP3 servers on the same system that runs Microsoft Proxy Server without encountering a problem. Chapter 1, "Proxy Server Overview," covers in greater detail how the Web Proxy server and the WinSock Proxy server operate.

NT Security

If you are only familiar with Windows 95 or Windows 3.*x*, you'll be unfamiliar with how NT deals with user security. NT's level of security far exceeds that of Windows 95 and Windows 3.*x*. In fact, one of NT's strongest points is its level of network security. As with all IIS applications, Microsoft Proxy Server directly uses NT's network security systems for its own security needs. Unlike other Internet server applications Microsoft has designed to use NT's security system to deal with outside users wanting access to a LAN, Microsoft Proxy Server uses NT's security systems to deal with internal LAN users needing access to the outside.

Microsoft Proxy Server fully utilizes all network security features of an NT-based network. When a LAN user attempts to access the Internet via Microsoft Proxy Server, whether by Web Proxy or WinSock Proxy (both types of servers can have their security configured independently), Microsoft Proxy Server authenticates their access against the NT user database.

When a user starts a Windows 95 or Windows for Workgroups (WFWG) workstation and logs in, that user can do so in one of two ways. A standard Windows login simply requires the user to indicate a name and a password. This information is not immediately validated by a domain controller (primary or backup), but is stored by Windows. This form of login to a workstation is a *basic login*. If a user then attempts to access a secured network resource, such as a server disk or a service such as Microsoft Proxy Server, the Windows workstation will present the login information to an available domain controller for validation. If the user information is not in the NT database of users or if the user is present but does not have sufficient access to use the requested resource, the server will deny access to the resource.

Windows workstations can also have a login name and password immediately validated by a domain controller if the workstation is configured for such a login.

Microsoft Proxy Server has a wide range of security options. As already mentioned, the Web Proxy server and the WinSock Proxy server can be configured independently. Each type of connection can also have independent security limitations placed on it. For example, Microsoft Proxy Server can permit only a certain network group to access WWW servers while allowing another network group to only have access to FTP servers. Microsoft Proxy Server can even go so far as to permit or deny access to Internet servers for individual LAN users.

Microsoft has devoted a great deal of development to the high-end security features of Microsoft Proxy Server. For my own needs and (in my opinion) for the needs of most private individuals and small to medium companies, the security features of Microsoft Proxy Server far exceed what is needed. Large companies will almost certainly have valid Internet connections for the workstations of their employees. However, Microsoft Proxy Server does offer a great deal of control to the outside Internet via a central authority. A great deal of control is lost when workstations have their own valid Internet access. For some companies, Microsoft Proxy Server is a better solution for Internet access than actually extending a valid Internet presence to individual workstations.

As well as controlling who can have access to the Internet through Microsoft Proxy Server, Microsoft Proxy Server can also control which sites on the Internet are accessible to LAN users. Yeah, it's a big brother approach, but if your employees spend all afternoon downloading dirty pictures from WWW.PLAYBOY.COM or WWW.PENTHOUSE.COM through an Internet connection you are paying for, you begin to want a little control over what your employees are accessing.

Microsoft Proxy Server also has outstanding logging features that help to track down misused Internet access. When workstations have their own valid Internet presence, users have much less restricted access to the outside, and the logging features of NT are not nearly as thorough at tracking that kind of activity. In the long run, it may be better for some companies to use Microsoft Proxy Server over full workstation Internet access. Chapter 8, "Configuring Proxy Server Security and Authentication," covers how to configure the security features of Microsoft Proxy Server.

NT Gateways

Access to the outside Internet is possible through more than just one point. In a completely valid arrangement, a LAN might have several gateway points through which to access the outside Internet. Workstations can be configured with a list of available network gateway points, which will each be tried in turn should the workstation need outside access. Figure 2.5 shows a possible network arrangement with multiple gateway points.

Figure 2.5.
*A possible network
with multiple gateway
points.*

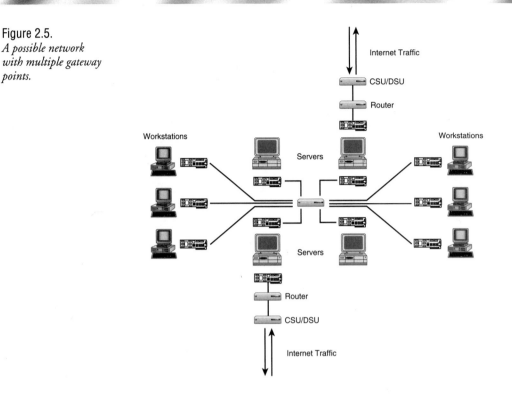

If a single gateway point is not sufficient to handle the amount of Internet traffic a LAN has, multiple gateway points can be used. However, most networks would simply increase the capacity of a single connection. Multiple gateways can also be used as a form of fault tolerance in case one connection fails.

The same approach can be used with multiple Microsoft Proxy Server gateways. Keep in mind that Microsoft Proxy Server gateways can be used just like normal gateways. Because most Microsoft Proxy Server gateways will be using smaller connections, such as analog modems or ISDN modems, scenarios involving multiple Microsoft Proxy Servers will be more common than gateways on LANs having valid Internet gateways.

An arrangement of which workstations access which Microsoft Proxy Server is a configuration element set up on each workstation. After installing Internet Explorer 3.0 or higher, a new control icon is placed in the Control Panel of Windows 95 machines. This icon is the access point to configuring all vital Internet settings for a Windows 95 workstation, including proxy settings. Figure 2.6 shows the Internet control applet of the Control Panel. The Connection tab is selected. This is the tab for controlling whether Windows 95 will use a proxy for its Internet connections.

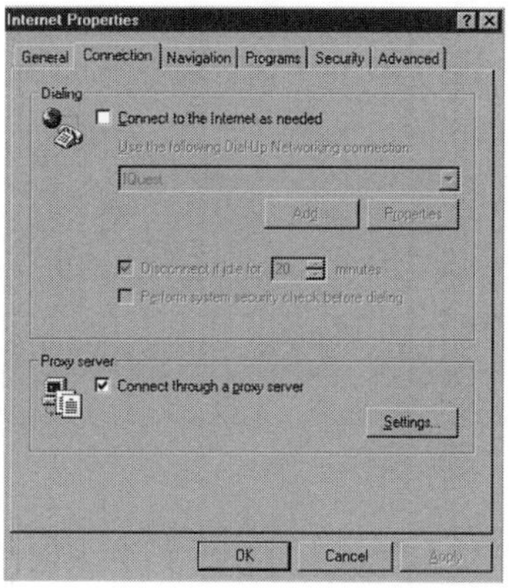

Figure 2.6.
The Internet applet of Control Panel.

The Settings button of this area allows for the specification of proxy server locations. Figure 2.7 shows the Settings dialog box.

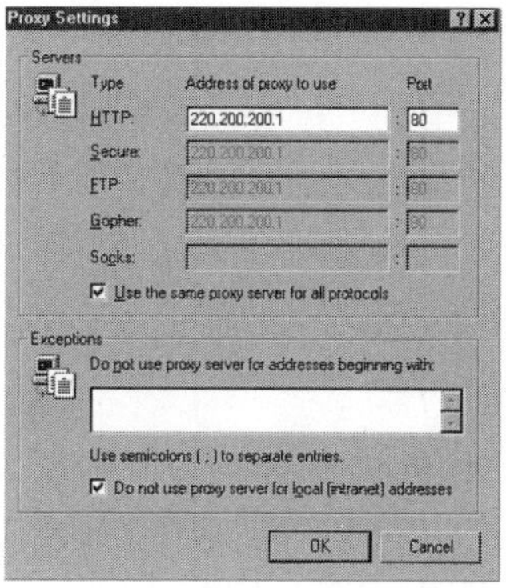

Figure 2.7.
The Settings area of the Internet control applet.

As you can see, Microsoft Proxy Server operates identically for WWW, FTP, and Gopher clients, passing all requests for such servers through port 80. The flexibility exists to configure each type of service differently should a different type of proxy server be used. Because the Microsoft Proxy Server Web Proxy listens for all requests on port 80, configuration is a simple task. The address 220.200.200.1 is the address of the NT server on my network that runs Microsoft Proxy Server. Chapter 11, "Proxy Server and Client Applications," deals with correctly setting up client applications, both standard Microsoft clients, such as Internet Explorer 3.0, and non-Microsoft clients such as Netscape and Eudora.

The WinSock Proxy portion of the client side is a little trickier than the Web Proxy side. With the proxy side of things, configuration consists of only a few settings in Control Panel. The WinSock Proxy client-side configuration requires installation of special client software. Enabling or disabling WinSock Proxy redirection is controlled via an INI file. Correctly configuring the WinSock Proxy client is also covered in Chapter 11.

In order to spread out the Internet access load on LANs with many Internet users, multiple Microsoft Proxy Server gateways should be used. The organization of such an arrangement depends on a network administrator's need. Each Microsoft Proxy server on a network can be dedicated to trafficking only a certain type of connection (FTP, for example). Another distribution method can set different groups of LAN users to use different Microsoft Proxy servers. Keep in mind that FTP access is more demanding of a connection than WWW access. Not only does FTP access involve lengthy file transfers, but the data that is transmitted is not stored in the Microsoft Proxy Server cache as it is with WWW information. Cached information can greatly improve the performance of Internet access through Microsoft Proxy Server.

Common Control Interface

When Microsoft Proxy Server is installed, it attaches itself to the same control interface used by other IIS servers. This control interface is accessed through one of two points. The Internet Service Manager can be started from either the Microsoft Internet Server folder or the Microsoft Proxy Server folder. Figure 2.8 shows the service manager.

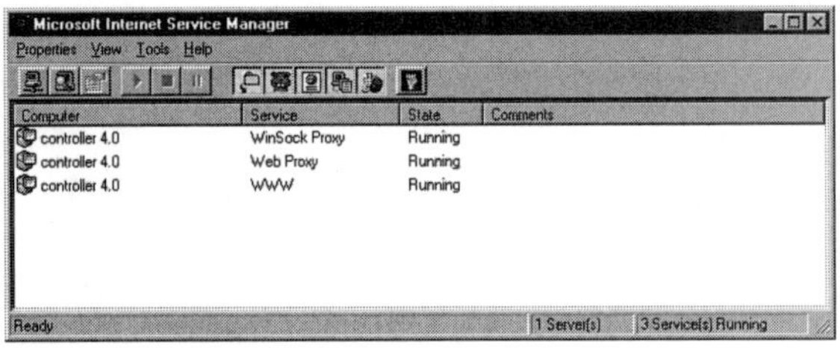

Figure 2.8.
The Internet Service Manager.

All Microsoft Internet servers will attach themselves to this common control interface. As you can see, both the Web Proxy server and the WinSock Proxy server show up as independent servers.

From this common interface, Microsoft Internet servers can be configured, stopped, started, or paused. As with most NT control interfaces, the Internet Service Manager can be used to view and control the status of Internet servers running on other NT machines. Details of how to use the Internet Service Manager can be found in Chapter 6.

Microsoft BackOffice

A lot of talk has been heard recently about the Microsoft BackOffice, but I've found that not very many people understand what it means. Simply put, BackOffice is a reference to what Microsoft considers to be essential elements of an operating system that do not normally come with the OS itself.

Over the years, Windows operating systems have been packed with more and more features that people had at one time considered to be add-on type elements. For example, in the days of

Windows 3.0, interoffice mail was not considered something that should be part of the operating system. Today, Exchange is shipped with both Windows 95 and Windows NT 4.0 as part of each operating system. Mail applications went from the back office to the front office.

Because Microsoft is beginning to focus heavily on Internet-oriented applications, software like Microsoft Proxy Server, IIS, and SQL Server are all now considered to be part of the Microsoft BackOffice family of products. As time goes by, these products are being woven more tightly into the OS. In a short while, elements that we now consider to be separate of the OS will be totally integrated. The following is a list of application packages that are considered to make up the Microsoft BackOffice family of servers:

- Microsoft Mail Server
- SQL (Structured Query Language) Server
- SNA (System Network Architecture) Server
- Systems Management Server
- IIS (Internet Information Server)
- Exchange Server

SQL Server is the database engine of choice by Microsoft. Many of the sites on the Internet that are powered by Windows NT use SQL servers for search engines, forms processing, and other functions. SQL Server is definitely a separate package that can cost a pretty penny. Microsoft is pushing hard to get SQL Server more widely accepted than it is currently.

The MS Mail Server is the old standby office mail server that has shipped with Windows NT, Windows 95, and Windows 3.x for many years now. The Exchange Server is an improved form of the Mail Server that can handle such things as file transfers and Internet mail gatewaying for networks.

IIS is of course made up of all the Microsoft Internet server applications, such as the WWW server, FTP server, Gopher server, Microsoft Proxy Server, and all of the others that may come along in the future.

The SNA server is a server package created by Microsoft to facilitate NT's ability to interface with IBM mainframes. The Systems Management Server is a server package created to help facilitate remote control of NT servers. One of the biggest advantages of NT is that it is designed to be able to be controlled remotely. In the growing world of the Internet, being able to control a server remotely is a vital element.

How Much Does Microsoft Proxy Server Cost?

Microsoft Proxy Server costs roughly $995 and can be purchased from most software vendors. Separate licenses for Microsoft Proxy Server must be purchased for each Microsoft Proxy server installed on a network. However, there is no need for connection licenses for Microsoft Proxy Server as is needed with NT Server itself.

Summary

Hopefully this chapter gave you an idea of how Microsoft Proxy Server fits in as a member of the Microsoft concept of a fully integrated OS that is designed as an Internet platform. As NT grows in strength and popularity, its Internet abilities will gain the respect that the UNIX operating system has basked in for years now. Getting a grip on NT at this stage of the Internet game (yes, it's still pretty early) can give you an advantage in the network administrator's employment market of the future.

Design

CHAPTER 3

System Requirements and Preparation for Proxy Server

The most difficult element when preparing to install Microsoft Proxy Server is the actual connection to the Internet that will be used. LAN users have a wide range of options to use to connect to the Internet. The connection can be as simple as a normal dial-up account to an ISP (Internet Service Provider), or it can be as complicated as a permanent connection with routers and CSU/DSU units. However, most people who have a permanent connection to the Internet will not need the services that Microsoft Proxy Server can provide, because a permanent connection usually includes LAN-wide access to the Internet.

The hardware and software requirements of Microsoft Proxy Server are not much more demanding than the requirements of Windows NT 4.0. However, this chapter gives a basic outline of the requirements of all forms of connections, from modems to ISDN lines to permanent connections, such as a T1 line. This chapter will also cover the basics of installing and setting up RAS (Remote Access Services), which the majority of Microsoft Proxy Server users will be using to connect the NT machine running Microsoft Proxy Server to the Internet.

Hardware Requirements

If your machine will run NT 4.0, it will run Microsoft Proxy Server. Keep in mind that, the more services that run on an NT machine, the stronger that NT machine is going to have to be to keep up with network traffic. The nature of a Microsoft Proxy Server machine is to handle the traffic of multiple LAN workstations through a single connection to the Internet. The two most important items that should be focused on are RAM and connection speed to the Internet.

In order to get the basics out of the way, I've made a list of basic requirements that need to be met before NT 4.0 will install:

- At least 12 megs of RAM. If an NT machine has only 12 or 16 megs of RAM, be prepared for a lot of disk accessing as NT uses the hard drive for a ton of virtual memory.

- A 486 or better CPU. The days of the 386 are history. NT no longer operates on any CPU lower than a 486. Stick with Intel. Though Cyrix and AMD CPUs are sound alternatives for Win95 or DOS, these chips are not good choices for NT systems.

- At least 100 to 120 megs of free hard drive space. NT needs this much for the operating system files alone. The swap file may take up another 35 to 100 or more megs of hard drive space. The installation routine may need up to another 120 megs of hard drive space for temporary files. NT is a very fat operating system.

- VGA or better resolution. Unless the NT system in question is going to be used for anything other than basic network serving, a small VGA card with little memory will do fine. In fact, the smaller the VGA card (256K of video RAM will be fine), the less overhead video will place on the operating system.

- A network card. Obviously if you are looking at the NT server as an office or home option, you have a need for a network interface. If many users will be accessing the NT server, a PCI network card will be the best choice. PCI cards place less strain on the motherboard than 16-bit ISA network cards do.

Microsoft Proxy Server requires nothing special in the way of hardware (outside of a connection method). Any connection method supported by NT can be used by Microsoft Proxy Server to route LAN Internet traffic to the outside.

Optimal Hardware

By far, the best thing a network administrator can do to improve the performance on any NT server is to get more RAM for it. Though NT can get by on 12 to 16 megs of memory, adding an additional 16 megs or more will improve NT's performance greatly (70 to 100 percent sometimes). Depending on the number of services an NT machine is running, 32 megs of memory may not be enough. NT will be very happy with 64 megs of memory. With the price of memory now dropping like a stone, it's a great idea to get as much memory as you can afford. When buying memory chips, remember to buy the biggest density you can afford. Don't fill out SIMM slots with a lot of low-density chips, or you will reduce your ability to upgrade at a later time. For example, if a motherboard has four SIMM slots, each with an 8-meg chip installed (for a total of 32 megs of memory), upgrading to 48 megs of memory means that you will have to buy two 16-meg chips and have no use for two of the 8-meg chips. If, on the other hand, the original 32 megs of memory were comprised of two 16-meg chips, no memory would be wasted when installing an additional 32 megs (two more 16-meg chips) into the two free SIMM slots. Make sure that a certain memory configuration will not waste chips if the system is later upgraded.

The number of internal connections Microsoft Proxy Server must support is also a factor in the amount of memory NT needs. The more connections Microsoft Proxy Server must maintain, the more memory is required. This is true for all forms of network connections. The TCP/IP protocol is a very memory-demanding protocol. Because Microsoft Proxy Server requires that the TCP/IP protocol be installed on the NT server it is running, 16 megs of memory will most likely be too little to provide adequate performance.

If the NT machine running Microsoft Proxy Server will be doing nothing but running Microsoft Proxy Server, a high-end 486, such as a DX4/100, will do fine. One factor in deciding CPU requirements is the speed of the Internet connection Microsoft Proxy Server is using. If the connection is a smaller one, such as a 28.8-Kbps modem or an ISDN link, a DX4/100 will be sufficient. If the connection is a high-speed permanent line, then a Pentium CPU should be used. If the CPU does not have to channel a large quantity of data between a few internal workstations and external Internet sites, a small CPU will work fine. If the CPU will have to channel large amounts of data between many internal workstations and external Internet sites, a small CPU will be overtaxed, no matter how much memory the system has.

Microsoft Proxy Server can cache most WWW objects (graphics, sound bytes, and HTML documents, for example). This means that Microsoft Proxy Server can draw from a local hard drive to serve out Internet data that it has already handled. This improves performance to workstations and reduces the use of the outside link. The larger the cache, the more data Microsoft Proxy Server can maintain. If your LAN has many users accessing many different sites throughout the day, Microsoft Proxy Server may be expiring cache data way too soon for the cache to be of any use. By default, Microsoft Proxy Server should use a cache of at least 100 megs. This is a dynamic cache and can be expanded if too small. If an NT machine is going to be dedicated only to running Microsoft Proxy Server, it is a great idea to expand the Microsoft Proxy Server cache to be as large as possible. This will ensure that cache objects are not expired because of an influx of new objects. If many users will be using Microsoft Proxy Server to access a multitude of different Web sites, objects in the cache could be flushed before they are ever called on again. This will nullify the use of the cache.

Hard drives, like memory, are dropping rapidly in price (thank you, Western Digital, for starting that little price war...). IDE drives topping 3.1 gig can be bought for about $300 today. SCSI drives are slightly more expensive, but have greater flexibility, access speed, and transfer rate. Installing a large drive with plenty of free space will allow Microsoft Proxy Server to have a sufficient cache to prevent possible future problems.

Do not worry about installing a high-end video card. High-end video cards place higher demands on a system than low-end cards do. The great thing about NT servers is that very few tasks are (or should be) executed on them locally. This means that there is little need for video resolution above 640×480, or a color depth greater than 16 colors. If an NT machine is going to be used to create HTML documents or handle other graphically oriented tasks, the color depth should reach 256, or better yet, 65,000 colors. Because the de facto graphics standard on the Internet is JPG, 65,000 colors should be used to view these images. *JPG* is a graphics format which displays 16 million colors per image. Personally, I have never been able to see the difference between 65,000 and 16 million colors. Setting an NT machine to display 16 million colors can really place a lot of overhead on the system.

The Internet Connection

Microsoft Proxy Server can use any valid connection method that is supported by NT to talk to the Internet. Most people will be using a simple modem to start off with, and some people will be using an ISDN connection. No matter which of these connection methods will be used, RAS will be the software portion of the equation. If an NT machine already has a permanent connection to the Internet, it is most likely that the LAN the NT machine is connected to already has workstation-level access to the Internet. However, there are some situations where using Microsoft Proxy Server is preferable to letting workstations have valid Internet connections on their own.

I can't stress enough how important it is to use external connection devices over internal devices. Granted, external analog modems and ISDN modems are slightly more expensive than their internal counterparts, but the flexibility external devices have over internal devices far outweighs the cost factor. The following is a short list of benefits external devices have over internal devices:

■ External devices do not consume independent system resources. External devices connect to existing ports. Internal devices require their own I/O ports and IRQ assignments. If an external device is hooked up to an existing serial port, no additional system resources are used.

■ External devices can be independently switched off and on should they lock up. If an internal device locks up during operation, the entire machine must be switched off and rebooted. The nature of network servers makes it difficult to find a free moment when they are not being accessed, to reboot. In a busy office environment, if the NT machine running Microsoft Proxy Server is also performing other vital network services, such as serving shared resources (disks, printers, and fax modems, for example) or acting as a DHCP or WINS server, it may not be possible to reset the machine until the end of the day.

■ The ability to accurately monitor device activity. Granted, RAS and Dial-Up Networking under NT provide simulated modem activity lights in the system tray (the sunken area in the lower right corner of the desktop), but these simulated lights are only partly accurate when displaying device activity. If you need to immediately see if a modem is experiencing activity, the simulated modem lights in the tray are pretty much useless. The simulated lights have a small lag time that makes them worthless for error debugging.

■ The ability to replace defective or outdated devices without downing the entire machine. It seems like modems are being improved almost monthly these days. The 28.8 standard has been out for little more than a year and already modem manufacturers are putting forth a 33.6-Kbps speed standard. As of right now, the 33.6 standard has not been ratified as a formal standard. This poses a big problem. Network administrators always want to have the faster hardware for LAN users. However, upgrading before ratification can be a waste of time and effort, because the non-ratified standard is rarely the one the people in charge settle on. It means a lot of swapping around or adding upgradable BIOS chips to modems until the dust clears. If you are buying a modem and want the most flexible kind available, make sure to inquire as to whether the modem is flash BIOS upgradable. Many modems still require the user to replace the BIOS chip in order to obtain a step-up upgrade (going from a 28.8-Kbps modem to a 33.6-Kbps modem is a step-up upgrade). External devices can be upgraded *much* easier than internal devices in this manner. However, if a modem or a device is flash upgradable, the device will require no hardware replacement, and a simple software patch will do. I wish my Practical Peripheral modems had a flash BIOS, but upgrading to 33.6 for me at this point takes $25 per modem and a three- to four-week stay at the Practical Peripheral factory.

The one drawback to having external devices rather than internal devices is that the ports the devices are connected to must be adequate to maintain the data passing through them.

Serial Port Hardware

Sadly, the device most computer manufacturers scrimp on is the serial port. Many serial ports installed in pre-made systems are substandard ports that are not suited for soundly passing large amounts of high-speed data through them. The primary element of concern when dealing with serial ports is the generation of its UART chip. A UART (Universal Asynchronous Receiver Transmitter) chip controls the flow of data passing through the port and ensures that what comes in from the outside (the device connected to the port) gets to the CPU in the same form it came in. Older UARTs are 8250 or 16540 generation, while newer UARTs are 16550AFN or 16650 chips. The 16550 UART had bugs in it in earlier incarnations and was updated a couple of times to worm those bugs out (ha ha ha... I kill myself sometimes.) The latest standard version of the debugged 16550 UART is the 16550AFN chip.

Advanced UART chips are very important, because they handle the flow of serial data over very high-speed connections. Port speeds of 115 Kbps are now standard for 28.8- or 33.6-Kbps modems. The importance of a high port speed cannot be stressed enough. Many people get confused about the difference between port speed and connect speed. Port speed is often referred to as DTE or Data Terminal Equipment speed (the speed at which the computer talks to the serial device or modem). The speed at which a modem connects to another modem is known as the DCE speed, or Data Carrier Equipment speed. Figure 3.1 shows the speed relationships:

Figure 3.1.
Port and device speed relationships.

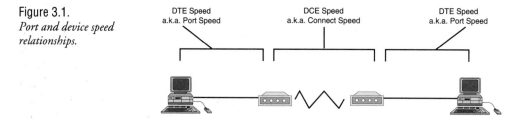

The main reason for needing a higher port speed than connect speed is the use of hardware data compression. Nearly all modems used today use some form of data compression to increase the amount of data that can be passed through a modem connection. The same principle used with compressing data for storage in archive files, such as ZIP or LZH files, applies to passing data between modems. Because modems used in a Microsoft Proxy Server scenario or for dial-up networking will be dealing with non-compressed data, a high port speed is essential. Take the following scenario, for example:

A Microsoft Proxy Server client is requesting a large HTML document of text from a Web site. The connect speed being used is a 28.8-Kbps connection. The sending end performs hardware data compression on it and achieves a compression ratio of 3:1. This ratio is not out of the question, and sometimes even higher compression ratios can be achieved on certain types of data. So, in essence, 86.4 Kbps worth of data (28.8×3) is passing between the modems. When the data arrives at the receiving end of the connection, the receiving modem expands the data to its original size. Basically, the receiving end is getting data at a rate of 86.4 Kbps. The receiving end must be able to offload that data as quickly (or hopefully more quickly) as the modem can spit it out. This is the need for a high port speed. If the port speed is not sufficient to handle the stream of data being received, the sending end will have to wait for the receiving end to process it, and that means a drop in performance and efficiency.

The same principles apply in reverse. If the sending end is unable to feed the sending modem fast enough, the data stream will not be as full as it could be, and again the performance will not be as high as it could be.

Hardware data compression is not very useful at increasing the speed at which already-compressed data is transmitted. Images in JPG format are already very highly compressed, and archive files such as ZIP, ARJ, and LZH files are also tightly compressed. Hardware compression done by modems will achieve very little additional compression, if any. However, much of the data transmitted from Web servers is not compressed.

Without advanced UART chips maintaining data integrity, data will be corrupted as it passes through the serial port. Because NT is a multitasking environment, the CPU is not constantly monitoring the serial ports and offloading the data as soon as it arrives. The data may have to wait a nanosecond or two before the CPU cycles around the serial port. *FIFO* chips refer to 16550 and 16650 UARTs. FIFO stands for First In/First Out. It's a reference to the manner in which UARTs ensure data integrity. The 16550 chip has an eight-byte buffer and the 16650 chip has a 32-byte buffer. These buffers are used to hold data until the CPU can cycle back around to the serial port to offload the data. Some non-standard UARTs may have expanded buffers, but the principles of data integrity are the same. UARTs prior to the 16550 did not have buffers.

As you can see, it is very important to have a port which is capable of supporting the amount of data a high-speed modem may be sending. When ISDN modems enter the picture, port speeds of 345 Kbps and 460 Kbps are necessary to ensure reliable data transfers. Special serial port hardware can be purchased that supports these tremendously high speeds, but most of these ports are not based on 16*xxx* UART technology. Without a high enough port speed, the performance of a modem will not be what it could be, and workstation users will not be getting the fastest performance they could.

Internal devices obviously do not hook up to a serial port. Internal analog modems and ISDN modems have their own onboard UART chips that handle the data which passes between the modems and the CPU. Internal devices, like external devices, have separate speeds at which they talk to the CPU. The same terminology of port speed and connect speed applies to internal devices as it does to external devices.

If you are looking at Microsoft Proxy Server as a possible LAN Internet solution, you are most likely looking at it for its cost-cutting capability. Don't make the mistake of not optimizing your connection. An inefficient connection can make your online time increase. Depending on the ISP you or your company uses, online time may be an expensive part of the access equation.

Modems

Not too many people like my advice when it comes to what types of modems they should use. I don't toe the US Robotics line nor have I ever been a Hayes lackey. I've had more experience with modems than most people, and I have come to a personal conclusion that the high-end modems are high only in price. I have tried all kinds of modems: cheap, mid-range, and expensive. I have always had the best luck with mid-range modems, such as Zoom, Cardinal, and Supra. High-end modems such as USR and Practical Peripheral are just not what people make them out to be. I get a full 28.8 connection nearly every time I dial my ISP with my Supra or Zoom modem. USR and Practical Peripheral modems will hardly ever connect at a full 28.8 Kbps with anything other than another of their own kind. I know there are going to be some people out there screaming that I'm nuts, but that has been my personal experience.

Many external modems these days are stripped down and do not have a full range of status lights. Make sure that any modem you are considering purchasing has the following lights:

- TX—Transmit Data.
- RX—Receive Data.
- OH—Off Hook. Indicates if the modem is off hook (line is busy) or on hook (line is clear).
- CD—Carrier Detect. Indicates that the modem is successfully connected to a remote end. This light will oftentimes blink rapidly if line quality degrades.
- HS—High Speed.
- TR—Terminal Ready. Indicates when the modem hears a ready signal from the computer.
- MR—Modem Ready. Indicates when the modem is in a ready state.

One element I have always admired in the Practical Peripheral modems has been a full four-line LCD display indicating the modem status. This feature is only available on the ProClass Practical Peripheral modems, but is a very handy element to have.

Without a full range of status lights, it is difficult to figure out if a problem is due to a connection problem or to a software configuration problem.

ISDN

My opinion of ISDN has never been very good. I have never been a big believer in ISDN, because in my area of the country it is prohibitively expensive and is metered (meaning you get charged by the minute for your online time). Also, few providers here in Indianapolis provide flexible and reliable ISDN service. However, I do realize that in other parts of the country ISDN is only slightly more expensive than regular phone service, and the metered rate is very reasonable. Also, ISDN hardware is becoming more affordable and easily obtained by the general public. Even Egghead Software now sells ISDN modems for around $300. So, who knows? I may be wrong about the future of ISDN.

ISDN is a digital interface. Digital is a faster and more reliable connection method. Standard modems communicate over analog links. Comparing analog to digital is like comparing vinyl albums to compact discs. The quality and capability of compact discs far exceed that of old vinyl records. ISDN as a connection format is available in two forms. The first is known as Basic Rate Interface ISDN (BRI ISDN) and is the most common form of ISDN. The second form of ISDN is known as Primary Rate Interface (PRI ISDN) and is harder to find.

BRI ISDN is a digital connection consisting of three channels. One is a 16-Kbps controller channel that the ISDN modems use to talk to each other (the D channel) and the two remaining

64-Kbps channels are used to carry data (the B channels). The B channels can be used together to reach a throughput of 128 Kbps, or they can be used separately for outbound or inbound data or voice lines. ISDN is handled much like regular telephone connections in that an ISDN line is assigned a telephone number and can be dialed up just like a regular telephone. The B channels can be used independently for bi-directional communication. They can be used for standard voice communication, as well. Many providers have various pricing schemes for utilizing ISDN channels together or one at a time.

In my area (one of the most expensive areas, so I've been told), ISDN service costs about $90 to $120 a month in service fees alone. Per-minute charges can run two or three cents, depending on the time of day.

PRI ISDN is equivalent in bandwidth to a full T1 line, but still has the flexibility of a periodic connection. PRI ISDN is broken up into 24 64-Kbps channels, 23 of which are used to carry data, and the 24th is reserved for communication between the two ISDN units. Hardware for PRI ISDN connections is different than BRI ISDN and is much more expensive, usually costing from $1000 to $1200 for an ISDN unit. PRI ISDN also cannot be carried over standard copper lines as BRI ISDN can, making the installation costs much higher. If finding a provider for BRI ISDN is hard, finding a provider that offers PRI ISDN service is nearly impossible. Most people who use PRI ISDN are doing so for connections that transmit a high volume of data between set points, rather than using PRI ISDN to link to the Internet.

If you are considering using PRI ISDN as your Internet connection, the better choice is committing to a T1 line. T1 access is a dedicated, 24-hours-a-day line of access which is not metered. Therefore, the amount of data passing over the line passes at one set cost.

Some providers can handle obtaining ISDN service for you, and others can't. You may need to work through your phone company to get BRI ISDN service, if you want to go that route. If you are setting up an ISDN connection that is far away from a phone company junction, you may be required to pay extra for the connection, because the phone company will need to put in a special high-speed loop from your office or home to the nearest junction. In this way, ISDN is similar to a T1 line, in that it needs a local loop to get to the nearest hookup point.

Dedicated Access (T1)

Getting dedicated access usually means that all the pieces are available for providing normal LAN-wide access to the Internet for all workstations on a network. This is usually the job of Microsoft Proxy Server through a smaller connection. However, there are ways of using Microsoft Proxy Server with a dedicated connection that provides greater control over how network users access the Internet.

Dedicated access usually involves working directly with a provider to get a dedicated digital line of some kind (such as a DDS, Fractional T1, or a Full T1). With this dedicated access usually comes a set of valid addresses to distribute to all workstations on the network, so that each workstation can have a valid presence on the Internet and route correctly through the connection point. Figure 3.2 shows a diagram of a possible dedicated connection using a T1 line.

Figure 3.2.
A possible dedicated connection arrangement.

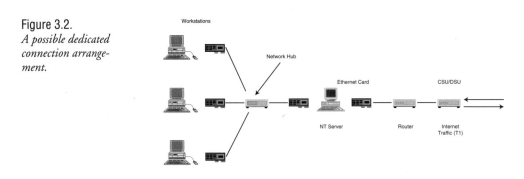

A CSU/DSU unit is a termination unit that converts the digital signal which passes along a T1 line into an Ethernet-compatible signal. A router is also capable of communicating via an Ethernet signal. Routers can cost between $1500 and $2500, and CSU/DSU units can cost between $1000 and $1500. Installation charges can also be fairly expensive for T1-level access, costing anywhere from $900 to $1500.

I've heard a wide range of monthly T1 charges, anywhere from $900 to $2000. Generally a T1 will cost at least $1200. That includes the charge for a local loop connection from your location to your provider's location and the bandwidth charge you will use from your provider's site to the Internet.

With the connection and hardware comes a subnet of addresses that can be used by all machines on a network for authentic Internet access through the connection point. A subnet consists of 254 addresses. Microsoft Proxy Server can be used in place of issuing valid addresses to all workstations. Microsoft Proxy Server can sit at the connection point and route local invalid Internet-addressed traffic out through the connection point. This offers a level of control over the traffic that passes through the connection point that a network administrator cannot get if all workstations on the network are valid Internet workstations.

The decision to get a dedicated access line is one that many companies are making these days. The use of the Internet is becoming more and more common for businesses and private individuals. This book does not focus on those scenarios that have a dedicated connection, because it is assumed that the majority of readers of this book are looking for a solution to provide a cheaper alternative to LAN-wide Internet access.

Software Requirements

There are two major software requirements that must be met before Microsoft Proxy Server will run correctly. The first is that the Internet Information Server must be running. The only component of this that must be installed is the Web server. The second software requirement is that a connection method must be used. This usually comes from RAS connecting to an ISP through an analog modem or ISDN modem. There are a couple of other minor points which will also be discussed in the following section.

Removing Any Previous Microsoft Proxy Server Beta

With anything of this nature, any previous beta should be removed before installing a release version of the software. Beta software has a nasty tendency sometimes to use slightly different filenames for DLLs and configuration files. The release copy of software sometimes does not remove the references to these beta files. The end result is the release copy of the software sometimes still looks for beta filenames. Removing these beta files before installing the release copy of the software will ensure that only the correct files are used.

To remove a beta version of Microsoft Proxy Server (known as Catapult), follow these steps:

1. Open the IIS Service Manager.
2. Stop the Proxy, WinSock Proxy, and WWW services.
3. Exit the IIS Service Manager.
4. Start the Microsoft Proxy Server Setup program, found in the Catapult Server folder. If this is not present in the Catapult Server folder, you may need to re-expand the archive that you obtained Catapult in, and run the setup.exe program in that archive. Remember to expand the catapult.exe file with the -d parameter, in order to recreate the proper directory structure for Setup.
5. Select Remove All from the Setup menu. See Figure 3.3.
6. Restart the WWW service via the IIS Service Manager.

Figure 3.3.
The Catapult Setup
menu.

Once any previous beta copies of Microsoft Proxy Server have been removed, you can install the release version of Microsoft Proxy Server.

The IIS Web Server

The IIS Web server is required for Microsoft Proxy Server to operate properly. Microsoft Proxy Server relies on the IIS Web server to provide its listening capabilities for LAN requests for outside connections. Microsoft Proxy Server Web Proxy runs as a sub-service of the IIS Web server and has no ability to operate on its own. Installation of the IIS Web server can be done during the installation of NT 4.0, or it can be done at a later time.

To install the IIS server after NT 4.0 has been installed, you must have the NT 4.0 installation CD. The installation routine for the IIS server is found in the \i386\inetserv directory. Running INETSTP.EXE in this directory will begin the installation process. The only element necessary for Microsoft Proxy Server is the WWW server. Consult the NT online help for further information about installing IIS.

Remote Access Service

RAS can be installed during the installation of NT, or it can be installed later as a standard network service. It is sometimes difficult to install RAS during the original installation of NT, if the modems that RAS will use are connected to non-standard serial ports. At no time during NT's original installation does the administrator have the ability to configure RAS to talk to non-standard serial ports. Non-standard serial ports must be configured after NT has been successfully installed. If all modems that RAS will use are on standard serial ports, RAS can be installed with NT without too much trouble. However, because RAS relies on so many other NT services, I tend to like to install it after NT is up and running.

To install RAS as an NT service, complete the following steps:

1. Open the NT Control Panel.
2. Select the Network icon.
3. Select the Services tab.
4. Select the Add button. A list of NT services will appear.
5. Select Remote Access Service and select OK.
6. NT will ask for the location of the setup files. Enter the drive letter of your CD-ROM and then \i386 (for example, e:\i386). Setup will now install RAS service.
7. If you have already set up modems under NT via the Modems icon in Control Panel, these modems will be available as possible RAS devices. However, if there are no modems installed, NT will begin the Modem Installation Wizard and allow you to search for modems connected to the computer.
8. Once modems have been installed, they can be added to RAS as RAS devices. Once at least one device has been installed for RAS to use, the Remote Access Setup dialog appears. See Figure 3.4.

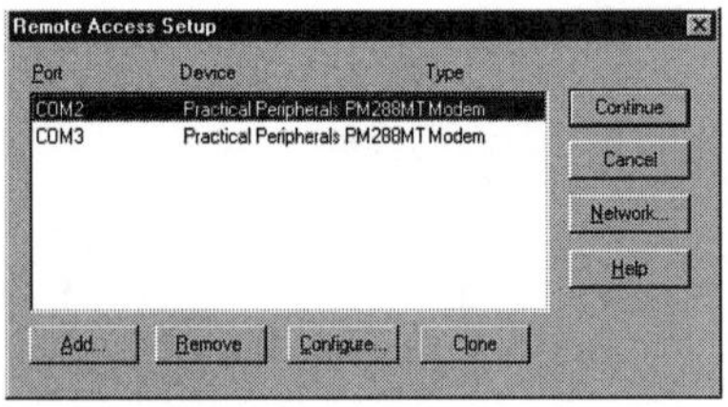

Figure 3.4.
*The Remote Access
Setup dialog.*

The primary purpose for RAS is to provide a dial-in feature for outside users of a network. However, it can also operate as a dial-out service for local users to connect to other networks. RAS can also be used to dial out and connect to the Internet. Under NT 4.0, the outbound capability of RAS is found in the Accessories folder as Dial-Up Networking. This has been done to more closely parallel the look and feel of Windows 95.

By default, all RAS devices are set as inbound-only devices. To set a RAS device as an outbound and/or an inbound device, highlight the device in the RAS list and select Configure. The following dialog box will allow you to set in which direction a RAS device will operate.

Selecting the Network button will allow you to configure which network protocols will be bound to RAS for both inbound and outbound traffic. For Microsoft Proxy Server, RAS only needs to be enabled for outbound traffic, and only the TCP/IP protocol needs to be active on the RAS service. See Figure 3.5.

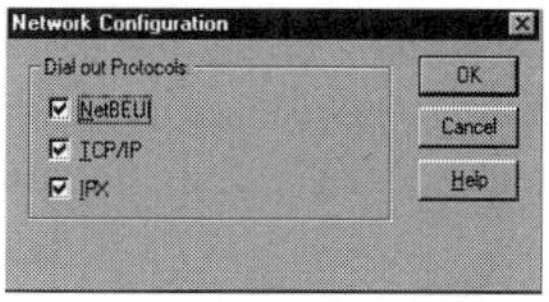

Figure 3.5.
The Network setup
portion of RAS.

If any of the RAS devices are set for inbound connections, the dialog box you will see for setting up the network options of RAS will be an expanded version of what you see in Figure 3.5. The inbound setup of RAS is not the focus of this section and will not be covered. Deselect all protocols except TCP/IP. Select OK.

Once the TCP/IP protocol has been set as the only protocol for outbound use, select OK at the Remote Access Setup dialog, and the installation of RAS will be finalized. The NT server will need to be restarted before a dial-out connection can be made.

Dial-Up Networking

Once RAS is installed and the system rebooted, a new item will be available in the Accessories folder. This is the Dial-Up Networking applet. With this application, a valid Internet connection to an ISP can be achieved, as long as you have an account with the ISP. Start the Dial-Up Networking applet.

The first time it is executed, the applet will prompt you to create a new entry to dial. A wizard will start that will prompt you for all the entry items needed to complete the dialing directory entry. If you choose, you can indicate that you are familiar with dial-up networking settings and you would like to enter them manually. Figure 3.6 shows a dialing directory entry.

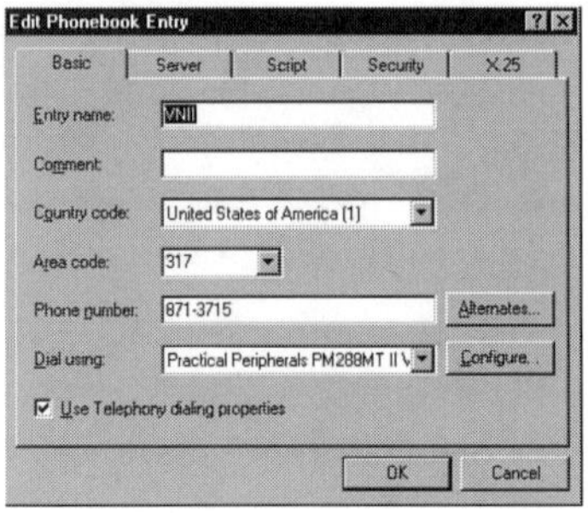

Figure 3.6.
*A dialing directory
entry in Dial-Up
Networking.*

The important items for a dialing directory entry are as follows:

■ Basic tab—Entry name.

■ Basic tab—Phone number. This is the data phone number of the provider you use.

■ Basic tab—Use Telephony dialing properties. This check box determines whether
Dial-Up Networking consults the internal NT telephony settings for controlling how
the phone number is dialed. Unchecked, Dial-Up Networking will dial the number
exactly as entered.

■ Server tab—Dial-Up Server Type. Indicates what type of server Dial-Up Networking
will be calling for this entry. Most providers use a standard PPP protocol connection,
so the default will work for most providers.

■ Server tab—Network Protocols. Indicates which protocols this entry requires. Only
TCP/IP should be selected.

■ Security tab—Authentication and Encryption policy. Most providers are UNIX
systems and as such may accept only clear text authentication attempts. Select the first
option, Accept any authentication including clear text, to make certain you can log in
to the provider.

On the Server tab, next to the TCP/IP protocol check box, there is a TCP/IP Settings button.
This allows you to manually enter some important number your provider may have given you.
See Figure 3.7.

Most providers will assign an IP address to you dynamically. This means that you will be given
a different IP address every time you log in to the provider. If you are lucky enough to have a
static IP address, select the Specify an IP address option and enter the IP address your provider
should already have given you.

The next section, concerning DNS resolution, may need to be filled in. Depending on the version of UNIX OS that your provider is running, it may pass out DNS location information
when logging on. If it does not, you will need to know what the address of the DNS server is
that your provider uses to perform name resolutions. If the provider's system passes out DNS
information at login, leave the default of Server assigned name resolution alone. WINS resolution is a NetBIOS name resolution service that is applied only under an NT network and is
therefore not necessary for NT to UNIX connections.

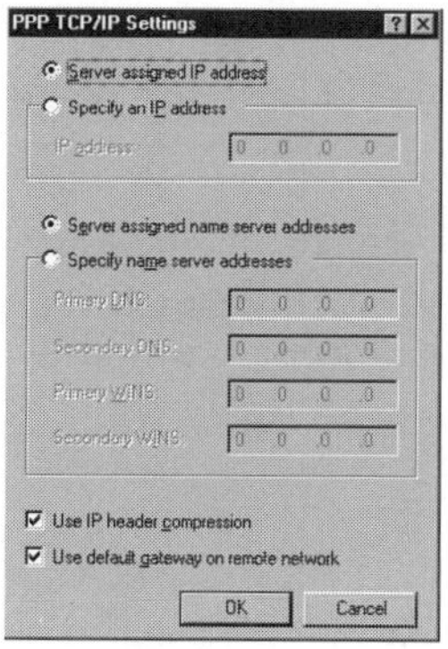

Figure 3.7.
The TCP/IP Settings
button is located on the
Server Tab.

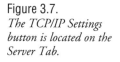

The remaining two options can be left alone, because if they are not options with your provider, they will not be correctly negotiated at connect, but will not interfere with the process of connecting.

Once the vital elements of an entry have been set, select OK and the entry will be saved and ready to dial. Figure 3.8 shows the primary Dial-Up Networking interface, which will be shown after the first dial-up entry is created.

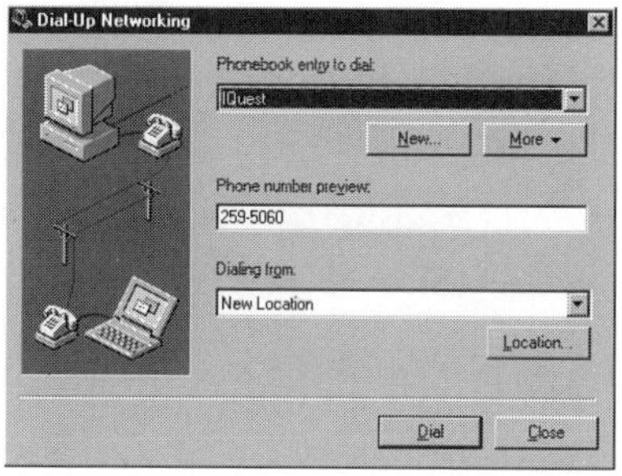

Figure 3.8.
The main Dial-Up
Networking Interface.

Select the Dial button to begin a dialout to the provider. If this is the first dial, NT will display a dialog similar to the one shown in Figure 3.9.

Figure 3.9.
Entering a username
and password.

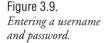

By default, NT pulls up the username with which you are logged in to NT. This name is rarely the name your provider needs you to log in with. Enter your ISP login name and password. The Domain field is needed only for connecting to another NT machine and should be cleared.

NT will not correctly connect to a UNIX-based ISP if there is an entry in the Domain field. Check the Save password check box if you do not want to continually enter the password before dialing this ISP.

Click OK, and Dial-Up Networking should dial the ISP and connect. From this point on, the NT machine will have a valid connection to both the local LAN and the Internet. When Microsoft Proxy Server is running on the NT machine, it will be able to route local traffic out to the Internet.

ISP Account

Getting an account with an ISP is a fairly simple task. Most often it takes just a call and a credit card number. Some providers take 24 hours before an account is fully set up, while others are able to get an account ready in one hour. Some questions to ask your provider are:

- Does their system pass DNS location information out at login?
- If the answer to the first question is no, what is the IP address of the primary DNS server?
- Does the provider have a backup DNS server? If so, what is its IP address?
- Does the ISP have an inactivity timeout? Meaning, if there is no activity on the connection for a certain time period, will the provider disconnect the call? This will be covered in greater detail, shortly.
- Does the provider use standard PPP for its user connections?

Once these questions are answered, you should have enough information to complete configuring your end to connect to the provider.

Connection Inactivity

Many providers will disconnect a connection if it has been inactive for a certain amount of time. This is usually 10 or 15 minutes. In order to keep a connection alive when there may not be activity on the connection for a long time, you may find you need a simple program that goes out and passes a small amount of data through the connection at regular intervals, just to keep it alive. Many of these types of programs exist and can be found on various Internet sites.

> **Note:** One of the best sites for finding Windows 95 and Windows NT software is www.windows95.com.

A utility I use to keep connections to my ISP open is called Ponger32. This utility can be used to ping a site at regular intervals or request a time response (where your system basically asks the host "what time is it?"). This will keep a connection open and prevent an ISP from shutting it down. Look around your favorite file sites and you should be able to find Ponger32, or something similar to it.

Auto Dial

Microsoft Proxy Server has the capability to automatically dial a provider if the Internet connection is not currently available when a proxy client requests a connection. This is known as Auto Dial. Configuring Auto Dial is done through an external application found in the Microsoft Proxy Server folder. This application can be used to configure which ISP is dialed and what times of the day the ISP can be dialed. By default, Auto Dial is not enabled, and the administrator is responsible for making the connection from the Microsoft Proxy Server to the Internet. Appendix B, "Auto Dial," covers setting up Auto Dial and the issues involved with it.

Disabling the RAS Timeout

Just as ISPs have timeout periods, NT also has its own timeout period. By default, if a RAS connection is not used within 20 minutes, NT will shut it down. If your ISP does not have a timeout value, you can turn off NT's timeout value, so you will not need a utility such as Ponger32 to keep the NT side of the connection alive. The NT timeout value can be disabled by editing a key in the Registry.

To start the NT Registry Editor, open a command prompt and enter the command REGEDT32.EXE. Locate the following key:

```
HKEY_LOCAL_MACHINE
 System
 CurrentControlSet
  Services
  RemoteAccess
   Parameters
   Autodisconnect
```

The Autodisconnect key is a hexadecimal key and is set to 14 (14 in hexidecimal notation = 20 in standard decimal notation). Editing this value and setting it to 0 will disable the timeout value for RAS connections. Be careful when editing the registry. Making incorrect changes will sometimes render NT unbootable, and only a reinstallation of the system will take care of the problem.

Network Protocol Requirements

Microsoft Proxy Server requires that the TCP/IP protocol be installed on the NT machine on which it is running. Obviously, to make a successful connection to a TCP/IP UNIX host, the TCP/IP protocol must be installed first. Connections to LAN workstations do not have to be through the TCP/IP protocol. Microsoft Proxy Server WinSock Proxy will function via the IPX/SPX protocol. The Web Proxy portion of Microsoft Proxy Server will function correctly only via the TCP/IP protocol. When IPX is the transport protocol between workstations and Microsoft Proxy Server, all Internet requests from workstations are handled as though they are external requests, and WinSock Proxy server will manage them all.

In order for IPX/SPX to be successfully used as the primary workstation transport method, the WinSock Proxy client software (provided with Microsoft Proxy Server) must be installed on all workstations wanting access to the Internet. Applications that would normally use the Web Proxy server (such as Netscape, IE 3.0, CERN proxy-compatible FTP clients) will have to use the WinSock Proxy server instead, because the Web Proxy server can communicate with clients only via a direct TCP/IP link.

Other than those minor points, Microsoft Proxy Server is very flexible when it comes to operating via either the TCP/IP or IPX/SPX protocols.

Disabling IP Forwarding

Under rare conditions, it is possible for outside packets to slip into a LAN that is connected to the Internet. This opens up the possibility for outsiders to have access to resources within the network. The following conditions at the least would have to be met before LAN security would be compromised. Keep in mind this issue has nothing to do with Microsoft Proxy Server, because Microsoft Proxy Server only directs internal traffic outward.

■ Outsiders have to send directed packets into the LAN and know ahead of time the actual IP address of the system to connect to.

■ The target system must be running a server application that the outsider is attempting to connect to. Remember that Windows 95 is a network server that can serve out connections to valid Microsoft Network clients.

■ Network security must be breached. If the resource that is attempting to be accessed has a password assigned to it (in the case of a Windows 95 or Windows for Workgroups system), the outsider must know the password. If the target resource is an NT resource, the outsider will be challenged to provide valid NT security credentials.

■ IP Forwarding on the NT machine connected to the Internet must be enabled.

As you can see, it's not very likely that a breach of security will ever occur. However, Microsoft has never been accused of under-doing something.

The last item in the list can be the total stopping point for all inbound TCP/IP accesses to the LAN. When IP Forwarding is disabled, the NT machine connected to the Internet and the LAN will not pass IP packets between NICs. To disable IP Forwarding, complete the following steps:

1. Open Control Panel.
2. Select the Network icon.
3. Select the Protocols tab.
4. Select the TCP/IP protocol.
5. Select Properties.
6. Select the Routing tab.
7. Uncheck Enable IP Forwarding.

There, your LAN is ultimately secure. The NT machine will need to be restarted before the change takes effect.

Don't think that by disabling IP Forwarding you are preventing Microsoft Proxy Server from doing its job. Microsoft Proxy Server does its own separate, secure routing of LAN traffic out to the Internet.

NTFS File System

One of the most secure actions you can take to make certain that your system is never compromised is to use NTFS (NT File System) on all important disk drives. NTFS is an alternate file system to FAT and has many advanced security and performance enhancements that will make Microsoft Proxy Server run more smoothly and allow you as network administrator to control just who has access to what on the server, right down to the file level.

Access Control Lists can be created for individual directories that control which users have access to the files held within. Consult the online NT help for more details concerning how to implement ACLs.

When installing NT for the first time, you have the option of converting the NT boot partition to NTFS format. This is a non-destructive conversion from FAT and takes very little time to complete. A disk can also be converted to NTFS at a later time by using the CONVERT.EXE utility found in the \WINNT directory. The command is used in this manner:

```
CONVERT D:
```

Conversions will take place immediately, unless the NT boot partition is being converted. If the boot partition is being converted, the system will need to be restarted in order for the conversion to take place.

Summary

Hopefully, this chapter gave you an understanding of the hardware and requirements needed by Microsoft Proxy Server to operate correctly and to the best of its ability. This chapter covered connection issues that will give you a clearer understanding of how Microsoft Proxy Server talks to the Internet and the costs involved.

CHAPTER 4

Planning Your Installation and Configuration

Designing a network architecture for a LAN that will use Microsoft Proxy Server as its primary Internet gateway is one of the most important steps you will take. Microsoft Proxy Server can always be reconfigured pretty easily, but once the topology of a network is set, it is sometimes very difficult and time-consuming to change. This is especially true of medium or large networks. If you have the luxury of designing your network before it is used by tens or hundreds of users, you will be able to carefully plan out most of the foreseeable situations you might encounter. Unfortunately, most network administrators do not have the luxury of building a network before users become active on it.

Most networks come into being a piece at a time, and the design process is an ongoing chore, which is more of a problem-solving task than actual topography design. Most network administrators will inherit a network from a previous administrator. This means that the new administrator will not only have the job of trying to understand what has already been done, but also must figure out how to improve the network and upgrade it to current standards. Networking is one of the fastest growing segments of computer technology, and with the onset of the Internet as a daily business tool, learning how to properly integrate the two will ensure that your network has the capabilities that are needed in business.

This chapter discusses the issues of setting up a network for use with Microsoft Proxy Server and how to best implement Microsoft Proxy Server itself. This chapter obviously cannot possibly cover all the network scenarios that a network administrator will encounter. Hopefully there is enough information presented to enable you to deal with most situations that you may encounter and understand how best to deal with them.

In this chapter, I deal almost exclusively with Microsoft networking architecture and tools. While Novell still commands the majority of the networking market, NT and Windows 95 are making strong inroads on Novell's hold on the networking arena. Even if Novell servers and NDS (Network Directory Service) are used on a network which is partly Microsoft in design, they should not conflict with anything related to NT servers. In reality, NT servers and Novell servers get along quite nicely on a network, when properly configured. Windows 95 machines can utilize both Microsoft Network client software and Novell Networking client software simultaneously to access both types of servers.

Designing the Network

This section discusses how a network should best be designed if a network administrator could have every wish granted. Obviously some of the topics discussed here can be optionally implemented, or implemented in an alternate manner to suit the specific needs of your own network. There are always multiple ways of getting something done, and not everyone has the same opinion on the best way to do a task. I don't claim that the advice given in this chapter has been clinically proven to be the best and voted as such by four out of five network administrators. However, I also don't believe I'm a dunce when it comes to network design, having installed more than my fair share over the past few years. The discussion presented in this chapter is my own personal opinion and should be taken as such.

The first decision that must be made is what network protocol will be used as the primary transport method for Microsoft Proxy Server. Microsoft Proxy Server can use either TCP/IP or IPX between workstations and the NT server running Microsoft Proxy Server. The NT server that runs Microsoft Proxy Server must have TCP/IP installed and working properly, but the workstations can use IPX exclusively.

Using TCP/IP or IPX

The TCP/IP protocol is the native protocol used on the Internet and has some advantages over using just IPX. Keep in mind that there are two components to Microsoft Proxy Server: the Web Proxy and the WinSock Proxy. The WinSock Proxy requires special client software to be installed on each workstation that will allow nearly any Windows socket application to communicate with the Internet through Microsoft Proxy Server. This client software simply renames the existing WinSock DLLs and replaces them with new ones that are designed to forward TCP/IP traffic to the WinSock Proxy server, if the TCP/IP traffic is destined for the outside world. If the traffic is to be kept local, the original WinSock DLLs take over and the WinSock Proxy server is not hampered by routing local traffic. Figure 4.1 shows a possible network architecture with TCP/IP.

Figure 4.1.
A network with TCP/IP and Microsoft Proxy Server.

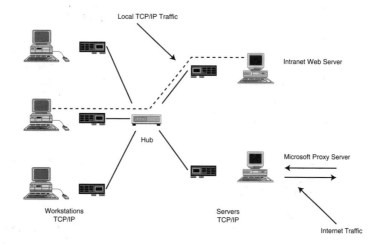

The figure shows that local TCP/IP traffic will be routed directly to any local Web servers that may be accessed by users of a network. Many businesses today are using intranet web servers for a wide range of business needs. Operations such as information distribution, database searching, and forms processing can all be handled via a well-set-up web server. Figure 4.2 shows a possible network architecture using only IPX on the workstations and IPX and TCP/IP on the servers.

Figure 4.2.
A network with IPX, TCP/IP, and Microsoft Proxy Server.

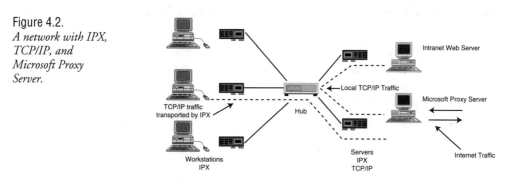

If IPX is the only network protocol available to the workstations, the WinSock Proxy will be required to handle all WinSock traffic, both local and external. As you can see in Figure 4.2, even if a workstation is connected to a local web server, the WinSock Proxy will be required to act as an intermediary between the workstation and the web server. The web server and the WinSock Proxy server will communicate with each other via the TCP/IP protocol, but the workstations will communicate with the WinSock Proxy server via the IPX protocol. This will add more stress to the Microsoft Proxy server if any local intranet servers are accessed frequently by LAN users.

A huge drawback to using only the IPX protocol as the transport method between workstations and Microsoft Proxy Server is that the Web Proxy portion of Microsoft Proxy Server will be completely unused. The Web Proxy requires workstations to use the TCP/IP protocol. If only IPX is used, the WinSock Proxy will be handling all traffic. The WinSock Proxy can handle all traffic that the Web Proxy can, but it does so through other methods. Keep in mind that the WinSock Proxy does *not* cache any information passing through it, like the Web Proxy does. This means a greater amount of work will be placed on the WinSock Proxy, because it will have to go out to the Internet for all data requests. The Web Proxy caches information which passes through it and will use this cached data whenever possible to cut down on the amount of time it has to go out to the Internet for information.

A benefit to using only the IPX protocol is enhanced security and less configuration time. Admittedly, the TCP/IP protocol requires more network configuration than does the IPX protocol. Also, when IPX is used, network administrators can be certain that all LAN Internet traffic is being handled through one service (the WinSock Proxy). If you have a high-speed connection to the Internet and do not need to provide caching services to workstations, using the IPX protocol between workstations and Microsoft Proxy Server will eliminate the need to configure two proxy servers. It will also allow you to prevent LAN users from doing things such as setting up their own FTP or WWW servers. I know many large companies want to restrict LAN users from setting up their systems to operate as servers, even though this is a built-in feature of Windows 95. Imagine a network with 500 or more computers all showing up in the Network Neighborhood when users go browsing. Network performance would drop dramatically and users would be swapping files without having to go through a network server.

A new generation of semi-literate computer users who have the knowledge to circumvent network security by doing things such as running their own FTP servers or WWW servers is evolving. By using only the IPX protocol, you can prevent clever LAN users from getting around company policies.

The benefits of the caching services built into the Web Proxy are hard to let go if your connection to the Internet is a small one compared to the number of users accessing the Internet from your LAN. My advice is to use the TCP/IP protocol, which will enable the use of both the Web Proxy and WinSock Proxy servers. A network will always have security problems from internal network users. Vigilant monitoring of network activity is the best way to ensure proper use of network services. As a network administrator, you can always limit problem users to just the IPX protocol. There is no configuration issue which limits the entire network to just one of the transport methods Microsoft Proxy Server supports. The two can be used in concert with each other to achieve the desired results.

Private Versus Registered IP Addresses

The next most important issue to discuss when dealing with network setup is what IP address range should be used with a network. This discussion is only relevant when the TCP/IP protocol is used.

The InterNic has set aside several address ranges that can be used by private networks for their own TCP/IP configuration. These address ranges will never be found on the Internet and were set aside so that private networks could use the TCP/IP protocol and not conflict with any other site found on the Internet. The private addresses are as follows:

- Class A subnet: 10.0.0.0
- Class B subnets: 172.16.0.0 to 172.31.255.255
- Class C subnets: 192.168.0.0 to 192.168.255.255

Throughout this book, you see my own personal examples of my network setup. You will note that the address range I have selected is the 220.200.200 class C subnet range. This is *not* a private address range, and as such may already be registered to a site on the Internet. When I initially set up my own network, I just selected 220.200.200 because it was easy to type. Because this address range may already exist on the Internet, I have created a problem for Microsoft Proxy Server. If one of my workstations attempts to contact a server on the Internet within the 220.200.200 address range, Microsoft Proxy Server will consider this to be a local address and bounce the request back to the local network. I have in essence cut off part of the Internet from my own workstations. If you have done something similar, you would be well advised to take the time to reconfigure your network for one of the private address subnets mentioned previously.

If you are not familiar with subnets, I'll give you a quick definition. *Class A subnets* are subnets of 16 million addresses. Any IP address starting with a number between 0 and 126 is a class A subnet. These subnets are all taken by large companies such as IBM. *Class B subnets* contain 65,000 addresses and are any IP address starting with a number between 128 and 191. Class B subnets are also all spoken for. *Class C subnets* contain 254 addresses and are any IP address starting with a number between 192 and 223. It has been estimated that the InterNic has enough class C subnets to hand out for another four or five years. After that, the addressing scheme of the Internet will have to be altered to handle the ever-increasing growth rate.

The 127 subnet range is a special subnet range reserved for local addressing only. If you are an experienced network administrator, you will know that the IP address 127.0.0.1 is always a reference to the local host (computer). If you perform a ping on 127.0.0.1, and TCP/IP is configured correctly on your network, the local workstation should immediately respond to the ping request.

If you are like most people thinking about using Microsoft Proxy Server to service the Internet needs of your network, you will not have a dedicated connection and will be relying on a periodic dialup link via a modem (or set of modems) or ISDN. These periodic connections do not provide you with a permanent subnet of valid Internet IP addresses, so you will need to set up your network with one of the previously mentioned subnets. If you do have a dedicated connection of some kind, you will most likely have been given a valid class C subnet (or multiple subnets) address from the InterNIC to use. If you have a dedicated connection and the know-how to correctly configure an NT server to act as the official gateway between your LAN and the Internet, each workstation on the network can have a valid presence on the Internet and not need to go through Microsoft Proxy Server for its connection.

When each workstation on a network has a valid Internet address, you as network administrator lose a great deal of access control. Workstations with their own valid Internet presence have a virtually free reign over Internet access. NT is not designed to monitor or restrict TCP/IP access in valid network arrangements. Microsoft Proxy Server, on the other hand, is heavily designed to monitor and restrict the activities of clients to the Internet. It is for this reason that Microsoft Proxy Server is sometimes the best choice for network users to use to access the Internet.

If you do have a dedicated connection to the Internet and have been given a valid class C subnet or subnets, it is a good idea to just shelve those addresses and use a reserved address, listed previously in this chapter. A huge advantage to this approach is that you can use the class A subnet, or one of the class B subnets, if your network will need to support more than 254 network workstations. Large networks that are forced to use multiple class C subnets to cover the number of workstations on the network are much more difficult to administer, due to the routing problems that isolated class C subnets cause. When you have the ability to use a larger subnet, administering a large network becomes much easier.

Other NT Services

Once you have decided what protocol and IP subnet to use (if you will be using TCP/IP), the next step is to decide whether DHCP (Dynamic Host Configuration Protocol) will be used and what form of name resolution (if any) will be used on your network.

DHCP is an NT service which is designed to hand out IP configurations to workstations on a network. When workstations are set to use DHCP for their IP configuration, they will broadcast a datagram requesting configuration information from the network when they start up. DHCP servers are designed to hear these datagram broadcasts and respond with setup information pertinent to the network architecture. DHCP greatly cuts down on the amount of administration work an administrator must do for each workstation on a network. Imagine having a 200-workstation network and having to manually configure the IP address for each workstation. It would be not only time-consuming, but also very inflexible. Should something change on the network, it would be a huge task to alter the IP address scheme. Using DHCP gives the network administrator the ability to centralize the TCP/IP configuration of all workstations. Should the TCP/IP arrangement of a network change, only the DHCP server needs to be reconfigured.

The Microsoft DHCP service is an NT service that can run on any NT server. It does not have to be running on the primary domain controller or a backup domain controller. It cannot be separated from a portion of the network by a router. Routers do not forward broadcast packets. Therefore, new workstations that are booting up and looking for a DHCP server which happens to be across a router will never find the server, because the router will not forward on the broadcast information they generate.

If you are unfamiliar with the Microsoft DHCP service, there is a great deal of help on it in the internal NT help system. By default, it is not installed as a service. There should be only one DHCP server for a network.

Another network element that must be considered is a name resolution mechanism. In NT 4.0 two name resolution mechanisms are available: WINS (Windows Internet Naming Service) and DNS (Domain Name Service). WINS is a Microsoft-only name resolution service that performs both NetBIOS name resolution and Internet-style name resolution, but only to Microsoft clients. WINS is only supported by Microsoft operating systems. It is not supported by UNIX, Macintosh, or OS/2 systems. These systems must rely on the globally-accepted DNS resolution method.

The ability to resolve Internet-style names to IP addresses is a function that will add a high level of flexibility to your network. When Internet clients attempt to contact Microsoft Proxy Server (either the Web Proxy or WinSock Proxy services), they can do so either directly by IP address, or by NetBIOS or Internet-style name. If all workstations are set to address Microsoft Proxy Server via a static IP, changing the location of Microsoft Proxy Server can be a tough task. In these cases, all workstations would have to be manually altered to address the new IP address. On large networks, this can be a very time-consuming task.

When clients are set to access Microsoft Proxy Server via a name, the location of Microsoft Proxy Server can easily be changed by altering the IP address that is resolved to the name in question. For example, a static mapping in the WINS server can be established for PROXY at 192.168.10.101. Should the location of Microsoft Proxy Server change, the static mapping for PROXY can be edited to point to the new IP location. All workstations would immediately begin to resolve the name "PROXY" to the new address.

If your network must support workstations of other platforms, such as UNIX or Macintosh, you will need to provide DNS resolution capabilities. NT 4.0 does ship with an available DNS service that can run along side of the WINS service without conflict. By default, Windows workstations will attempt to access a WINS server before they will attempt to contact DNS servers (if workstations are configured to look for both types of name servers). Entire books have been written on the topic of WINS and DNS, and it's not the purpose of this book to describe how to set them up. Their basic functionality requires little extra networking knowledge, and their presence on a network can greatly enhance the functionality of services such as Microsoft Proxy Server or other Internet-style servers.

Using Web Proxy, WinSock Proxy, or Both

By now you should understand that Microsoft Proxy Server is actually two separate services running along side of each other. The Web Proxy server is a CERN-compliant proxy server that provides cross-platform proxy services to any client that is capable of interacting with a CERN-compliant proxy. The Web Proxy can handle HTTP, FTP, and Gopher traffic from clients all through TCP/IP port 80. (This is a default, but this port can be changed.) Clients such as Internet Explorer and Netscape Navigator all have the built-in ability to communicate with a CERN-compliant proxy server. Other Internet clients, such as WS_FTP, also have the ability to communicate via CERN proxy standards.

The WinSock Proxy is very new and is currently only supported by Windows environments. The WinSock Proxy involves special client software, which takes traffic that is destined to the outside Internet and redirects it through the WinSock Proxy server. When the WinSock Proxy client software is installed on Windows systems, nearly any WinSock application can have access to the Internet, even if it does not have built-in CERN proxy communication ability.

Benefits of using the Web Proxy are:

■ Cross-platform support. Mac clients, UNIX clients, and OS/2 clients can all access the Microsoft Proxy Server Web Proxy via the TCP/IP protocol without any special software.

■ High-level data caching services. Most information that passes through the Web Proxy gets cached, to be used later to help cut down on the amount of external traffic the Web Proxy generates to the Internet.

■ Support by the major Web browsers, such as Netscape Navigator and Internet Explorer. Since 95 percent of all the Internet activities LAN users will do will be through a Web browser, the Web Proxy server may be all you need for your network.

Benefits of using the WinSock Proxy are:

■ Support for nearly any WinSock 1.1–compliant client application. Some workstations may need support for Internet applications, such as a newsgroup reader, a mail client, or RealAudio. The WinSock Proxy provides support for these protocols.

■ The ability to manually configure support for a protocol not currently configured. The WinSock Proxy comes preconfigured to support a wide range of Internet protocols, such as NNTP, SMTP, and Telnet. If you need to add client support for another protocol, the WinSock Proxy has this flexibility.

Both servers can be highly configured for security and site restrictions. If you do not want to provide support for any client other than a Web browser, you will not need to worry about dealing with the WinSock Proxy. This will cut your configuration chores by at least half. Using the Web Proxy will also ensure that the special WinSock Proxy client software does not cause any configuration problems on workstations. I have not seen the WinSock Proxy client software cause any problems to date, and I have put it through its paces enough to be comfortable with it. However, I also know that my network does not encompass all possible scenarios either.

Most small networks will need the services of both servers. I say this because most small networks will not have high-end NT services such as an Exchange gateway available to them. The only major thing lacking in the Web Proxy is the ability to support mail clients. If your network users use a mail program such as Eudora to retrieve their mail from an Internet host, the Web Proxy alone will not be able to give them this access. On medium or large networks, it is more common to find an Exchange server available. An Exchange server is another Microsoft product which provides network and Internet mail services to LAN users. The Exchange client is commonly accessed by workstations as the Inbox icon found on the desktop. When an Exchange server is available, the only part of Microsoft Proxy Server that is normally needed is the Web Proxy. However, some WWW functionality may be lost if only the Web Proxy is used. It is becoming more common for Web browsers to execute hidden client applications such as Shockwave and RealAudio player without the knowledge of the user. These kinds of clients do require the WinSock Proxy, because they do not communicate via CERN standards. Again, it may be better not to support these kinds of clients, because they are exceedingly high bandwidth consumption clients. Shockwave and RealAudio are clients which involve high-volume data transfers of sound, video, and animation information. These kinds of clients can quickly drag down the performance of an entire network's Internet connection.

Physical Distribution

The most common use of Microsoft Proxy Server will be through small Internet connections. If you have only one large dedicated connection Microsoft Proxy Server will be using, the physical setup is simple. However, if you will be using multiple smaller connections, you have some decisions to make as to how Microsoft Proxy Server will be used on each connection.

A WINS server or a DNS server can be used to daisy chain multiple Web Proxy servers together. Don't confuse this with multiple Web Proxy servers working together as one unit. This is not a feature of the current release (1.0) of Microsoft Proxy Server. A WINS server can be easily configured to resolve names for a multi-homed group. A static mapping can be added to a WINS database that represents all available Web Proxy servers on the network. For example, a multi-homed group called WEBPROXIES can be added to the WINS database. This group would list the IP addresses of the participating members of the group. When referenced by a client, the WINS server would select the IP of a member of the group to resolve the name to. The selection criteria is based on the proximity of the group member to the client asking for name resolution. Members of the group within the same subnet as the client will be resolved to the name before groups outside the subnet. If there are no close candidates within the group, the WINS server will select a member at random.

Through this method, you can set up a group of Web Proxy servers that will be used by users of a network addressing a proxy server named WEBPROXIES (for example). Figure 4.3 shows this possible arrangement.

Figure 4.3.
*Multiple Web Proxy
servers cascaded by a
WINS server.*

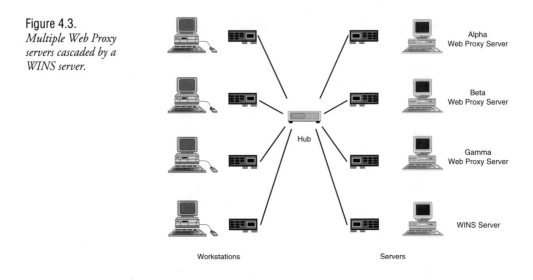

Workstations   Servers

In this example, we can assume that a multi-homed group called WEBPROXIES has been set up on the WINS server. In this group, the IP addresses for Alpha, Beta, and Gamma have been established. When any of the workstations attempts to address WEBPROXIES, the WINS server will pick the best candidate out of the group and resolve the name request to that IP address. If the requesting workstation had been outside the subnet, the WINS server would have resolved the address to a randomly selected member of the group.

Through this name resolution method, you can set up a group of cascading Web Proxy servers for a network, so that the work load of Internet traffic will be spread out among multiple Web Proxy servers. However, you are not required to use a WINS server. You can manually configure each workstation to access a specific Web Proxy server. If you have multiple Internet channels, you should do your best to distribute the work load equally among them.

WinSock Proxy servers should not be arranged in this manner. A workstation should be specifically configured to access one WinSock Proxy server. If WinSock Proxy servers are arranged in a cascading group, Internet clients will not function properly. WinSock Proxy clients must have a constant connection to a single WinSock Proxy server to operate correctly.

User Groups Versus Task Groups

When you are configuring members of your network to access specific Web Proxy servers, you have two choices to consider. In the proxy configuration area of the Internet control panel, you can specify the address to be used for the HTTP proxy, the FTP proxy, and the Gopher proxy. To spread out the traffic load among multiple Web Proxy servers, you can opt to divide your LAN users into groups assigned to each available Web Proxy server, or you can set all users to access a separate Web Proxy server for each type of connection they need to make.

Since FTP traffic will cause the most stress on a connection, you might want to assign all Web Proxy users to access a dedicated FTP Proxy server, and leave another Web Proxy server dedicated to only serve out HTTP connections. The Web Proxy server serving out FTP connections should have the largest available connection. This approach may help increase the contentment your network users have with your proxy arrangement. Because access to the Web is generally more interactive than downloading files via FTP, you want to make sure your users are not staring blankly at their screens, waiting for an HTML document to pop up.

Unfortunately, the protocols supported by the WinSock Proxy server cannot be split up like the protocols supported by the Web Proxy server can. When a workstation is configured to access a WinSock Proxy server, that server will be used for all protocols supported. This being the case, you might want to be thorough when understanding what activities your network users will be doing through the available WinSock Proxy servers. Users who will be accessing a WinSock Proxy server just to retrieve e-mail will be causing far less of a work load on the server than those users drawing a RealAudio feed. Spread out users evenly, based on the amount of traffic they will be generating for each WinSock Proxy server.

Site Filtering

By far, the most powerful feature Microsoft Proxy Server has for controlling the amount of Internet traffic caused by LAN users is the ability to filter out access to specific sites on the Internet. Both the Web Proxy and the WinSock Proxy can be set to filter out access to all or just some sites on the Internet. By default, there is no filtering policy set for either server. However, it is a simple task to add a filter for certain sites, or you can set a general no-access policy for the entire Internet and set exceptions to the rule.

There are many distractions on the Internet, and one of the biggest problems a company has, once network users have desktop access to the Internet, is wandering minds. One of the more popular office distractions these days is a software package known as the Pointcast screen saver. The Pointcast screen saver is a Windows 95 screen saver that goes out to the Internet to the Pointcast site and transfers all manner of news and information back to the user's machine, where it is displayed throughout the day whenever the screen saver kicks in. When you have hundreds of LAN users all generating Internet traffic for a screen saver, your Internet bill might be an ugly thing. I happen to know that the Pointcast screen saver will operate through the Web Proxy server, so the information that comes into the network will be cached and usable by other network users. However, the range of information the Pointcast screen saver can retrieve is very wide, and the information is updated many times a day. While the caching element of the Web Proxy server will help, LAN users will still generate a lot of Internet traffic.

In this example, the Pointcast site, `pointcast.com`, could be filtered from access by the network administrator. This would eliminate the traffic problem entirely. (It might make many of the network users mad, but what the hey. They're not paying the bill, are they?)

Unfortunately, site filtering is still rough around the edges and does not support many filter options. Site filtering is done on a yes or no basis only. Perhaps in future releases of Microsoft Proxy Server, site filtering will be able to take into account filtering for time of day and specific users. Currently though, the Web Proxy can only globally permit or deny access to filter sites.

If you need to really restrict access to the outside Internet, a global deny policy can be set, and a few exceptions to this rule can be defined. This basically controls which Internet sites your network users will have access to. Unfortunately, Microsoft Proxy Server does not have the ability to filter sites based on a user-by-user approach. This means that you cannot define filters for specific users. Perhaps this will be a feature in later releases of Microsoft Proxy Server, although I have not heard of this yet.

Granting Internet Access

Obviously, one of the strongest elements of Microsoft Proxy Server is its ability to utilize the internal security system of NT. You have to decide which of your network users will have access to the Internet and which will not. You should become familiar with the User Manager for Domains. This utility controls the user database of NT and can be used to define new security groups and set user access rights.

Before you set up Microsoft Proxy Server, you should take some time to decide how you are going to configure security groups. Working with groups of users who share common needs is far easier than trying to configure individual user access for each protocol supported by both the Web Proxy and the WinSock Proxy. Once you have defined a group or set of groups for Internet access, you can configure security for the Web and WinSock Proxy servers much more readily.

Unfortunately, Microsoft Proxy Server does not have the ability to configure access for specific times of the day and night. If you have a large network of users but a relatively small link to the Internet, it would be nice to have the ability to separate a morning group and an afternoon group of Internet users. This would go a long way to more evenly distributing the traffic load the Internet link sustains throughout the day. I have been in large network environments and I have found that the Internet connection is slowest about an hour after everyone arrives in the morning (after everyone has had a cup of coffee and talked with their cube mates) and about half an hour after lunch (when people really don't want to get back to work and would much rather go see what's new on their favorite Internet site).

Perhaps later releases of Microsoft Proxy Server will have a wider range of time-driven access controls. For right now, you'll have to make do with security groups defined within User Manager for Domains.

The Decision Process

The following is a suggested list of decisions you will need to make when setting up Microsoft Proxy Server:

1. Which network protocol will be used to transport data between workstations and Microsoft Proxy Server? TCP/IP or IPX? If IPX will be the protocol used, you will not need to worry about configuring the Web Proxy server.

2. What IP address range will your network be using? Will the addresses fall within the reserved ranges, or will you be using a set of valid addresses?

3. Does your network have all the desired services up and running to support name resolution (through WINS or DNS) and dynamic host configuration (through DHCP)?

4. Will you be using the Web Proxy server, the WinSock Proxy server, or both? Small networks will probably need to use both, while larger networks may only need to use the Web Proxy.

5. How will the physical layout of your proxy server(s) be set? If you will be using more than one Web Proxy, will you arrange your users into groups to access each Web Proxy, or will you set each Web Proxy to perform transport for a specific protocol?

6. If you have multiple WinSock Proxy servers, make sure to distribute the traffic load equally, not just spread your users out numerically equally.

7. If you have multiple Web Proxy servers, will you be using name resolution to cascade access to them?

8. Will you allow any access to the Internet, or will you filter access to certain sites? Will you deny access to the Internet as a general rule and then set exceptions to that rule?

9. If your Internet connection is relatively small for the number of users you have on your network, which users truly need Internet access and which ones simply want Internet access? Use the User Manager for Domains to configure security groups.

Summary

Do yourself a big favor and thoroughly think through the installation and implementation of Microsoft Proxy Server. Once Microsoft Proxy Server is in place, it's difficult to alter the architecture. Try to think of all the future possibilities you can, and make allowances for them. Many network administrators fail to look far enough down the road and cause a lot more work for themselves than is necessary. Hopefully this chapter gave you some food for thought about the setup process. I certainly didn't cover all the possibilities, but hopefully I covered enough to let you think of other things that might need to be considered.

PART III

Install

CHAPTER 5

Installing Proxy Server

Before reading this chapter and installing Microsoft Proxy Server, make sure you have read and understand all the requirements presented in Chapter 3 of this book, "System Requirements and Preparation for Proxy Server." Chapter 3 details the system requirements for Microsoft Proxy Server and other important issues, such as connection methods. This chapter will explain the installation process in detail.

Unlike many other Microsoft Internet products, Microsoft Proxy Server is not being distributed for free. Its estimated retail price is $995 per server, with no connection licenses required. Microsoft Proxy Server will only run under Windows NT 4.0 and may be obtained through many channels. The most common channel people will be using to get a copy of Microsoft Proxy Server is through the Internet. However, Microsoft may also be distributing Microsoft Proxy Server on an installation CD which may be obtained directly from Microsoft.

Getting a Copy of Microsoft Proxy Server

Microsoft Proxy Server can be downloaded from the Microsoft FTP site as a single installation archive. Many software vendors (this includes Microsoft) are distributing their "over the Internet" software in self-expanding archive files. Many novice users assume any file with an EXE extension that they download is the actual installation program. To make matters more confusing, some vendors do distribute their software in self-installing formats.

The way to test an EXE to find out if it is a self-extracting archive or an actual installation program is to use PKUNZIP.EXE to attempt to view the EXE as if it were a ZIP file. Most network administrators are familiar with ZIP and other archive file formats. ZIP files can be EXE files which can be run on their own without the main archive program (PKUNZIP.EXE) to extract the files contained inside. These EXE files can also be treated as though they were standard ZIP files. Microsoft Proxy Server is not distributed as such an EXE file. The file MSP.EXE is an NT installation application. However, the beta version of Microsoft Proxy Server was a self-extracting EXE file and was named CATAPULT.EXE. If you want to uninstall Catapult before installing Microsoft Proxy Server, you can unzip the archive CATAPULT.EXE as any other ZIP file. This will give you some practice at determining which EXE files are installation programs and which are self-extracting ZIP files. To test CATAPULT.EXE to ensure it is a self-extracting archive and not an installation program, run PKUNZIP.EXE on it like this:

```
PKUNZIP -v CATAPULT.EXE
```

The -v parameter of PKUNZIP.EXE will view the contents of the archive file without actually expanding it. This method can be used on any EXE file to test if it is a self-extracting archive. If the EXE is a normal program, PKUNZIP.EXE will report the following error:

```
PKUNZIP: (W04) Warning! XXXXXXXX.EXE - error in ZIP use PKZipFix
PKUNZIP: (E11) No file(s) found.
```

XXXXXXXX.EXE will be the program filename being tested. This error indicates that PKUNZIP.EXE believes there is an error in the archive and the EXE is therefore most likely a program of some kind. A normal display will show a list of all files contained in the archive as well as their imbedded pathnames.

MSP.EXE can be downloaded from ftp1.microsoft.com. It is located in the /msdownloads/proxy/ i386 directory (for the Intel platform version of Microsoft Proxy Server). The archive will be at least 8 megs. Unfortunately, Microsoft does not prepare several smaller archive files for distributing Microsoft Proxy Server. This can be a pain if you are having trouble with a connection and cannot stay online long enough to get the entire 8+ meg file. Unlike BBS file transfers using a protocol like Zmodem, FTP file transfers cannot normally be resumed after a partial transfer attempt. If a download of an 8-meg file from the Internet fails for some reason, you have to start all the way from the beginning. Transferring many smaller files allows you to keep what was transferred successfully.

MSP.EXE can also be downloaded from the Microsoft Web site, though it is significantly harder to find. At this time, Microsoft requires users to complete a questionnaire before being permitted to download Microsoft Proxy Server. Using the Microsoft FTP server avoids this questionnaire.

NT 4.0 Service Pack 1

Service Pack 1 for NT 4.0 must be installed before Microsoft Proxy Server can be installed. This service pack can be found on the Microsoft FTP site ftp.microsoft.com in the \softlib\mslfiles directory. The filename is nt4_sp1i.exe. This is the Intel version of the service pack, but other versions of the service pack can also be found in this location. This service pack is an installation application, not a self-extracting ZIP file. Grab this application, run it, and then reboot your NT server. The installation process for the service pack simply installs replacement files into the NT directories (\winnt and \winnt\system32) and then forces you to reboot the server. Microsoft Proxy Server will now install without complaining.

Installing Microsoft Proxy Server

Once an NT machine is ready for Microsoft Proxy Server, it can be installed by running MSP.EXE from the root directory of the Microsoft Proxy Server installation CD or by running the MSP.EXE application which was downloaded from Microsoft.

An initial licensing dialog box is displayed. Select Continue to proceed to the first installation dialog box, as shown in Figure 5.1.

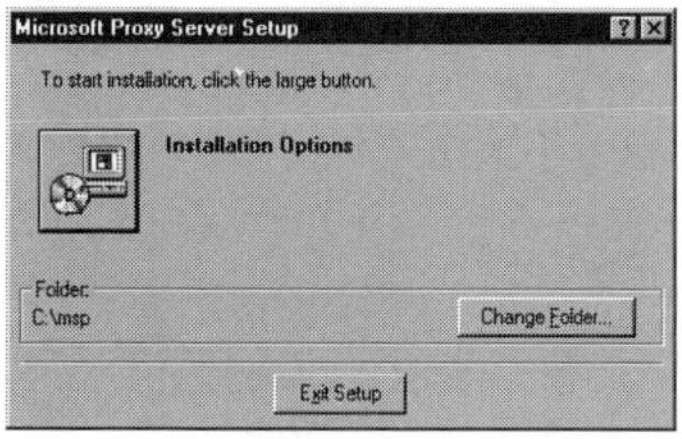

Figure 5.1.
The first Microsoft Proxy Server installation dialog box.

At this stage, you can alter the directory Microsoft Proxy Server will be installed into. If you need to install Microsoft Proxy Server into a directory other than C:\MSP, select the Change Folder button and then locate the directory you want to install Microsoft Proxy Server into. If the default directory is acceptable, selecting the Installation Options button will continue the installation procedure to the next step, as shown in Figure 5.2.

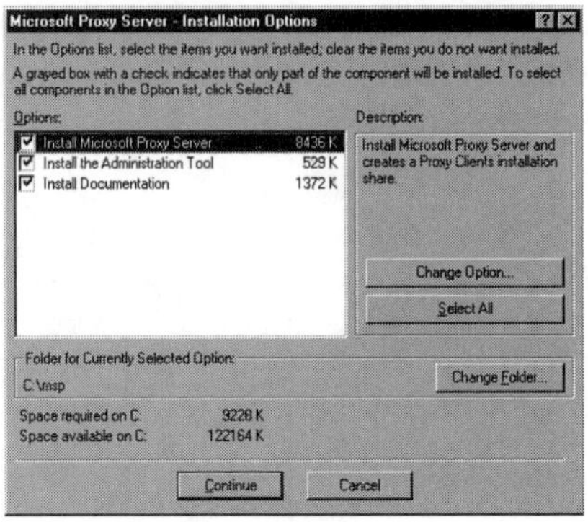

Figure 5.2.
Microsoft Proxy Server
installation options.

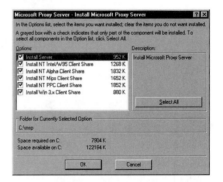

This stage lets you select whether or not to install the Server and Client files, the Administration tool, and Microsoft Proxy Server documentation. Microsoft has started a new approach to online documentation. The documentation for Microsoft Proxy Server is in HTML format and requires a Web browser to read. This is a very handy form of documentation because cross-references from one section to another can be easily embedded into the text.

The Install Microsoft Proxy Server check box allows you to set the installation of the Server and the Client share. Figure 5.3 shows the detailed view of the options of the check box. If any client files are installed, the installation routine will create a new network-shared resource on the server called MSPCLNT. This shared resource contains all the necessary files for installing the WinSock Proxy client software onto workstations. The WinSock Proxy client software is required for non-CERN, proxy-compatible software to function in a proxy environment. To determine on which platform client files will be installed, highlight the Install Microsoft Proxy Server option and select Change Option. The dialog box shown in Figure 5.3 is then displayed.

Figure 5.3.
The Install Server and
Client Installation
Share options.

You can cut down the amount of disk space used by the client share files by unchecking the system architectures that do not apply to your network. The Alpha, Mips, and PPC clients are NT-only clients. Microsoft only makes an NT OS version for these system architectures. Windows 95 is an Intel-only operating system. The Install Server check box controls whether or not the actual server software is installed. If you only need to install the WinSock Proxy client software, uncheck the Install Server check box. Uncheck all unneeded system architectures, select OK, and you will return to the main options dialog box.

You can always add support for clients of different platforms at a later time by rerunning the installation routine and selecting platforms again.

If you only want the HTML documentation portion of Microsoft Proxy Server, clear the other two options and leave the HTML Documentation checked.

The Administration tool is actually the IIS Manager. This application is the gateway for accessing all control interfaces for Microsoft Internet server applications, such as the IIS Web Server and the Microsoft Proxy Server. You can install the Administration tool application on other NT machines that will need to access the Microsoft Proxy Server for configuration needs. Since the IIS Manager is installed at the same time as the IIS Web Server, installing the Administration tool is not needed on the server that will be running Microsoft Proxy Server. This option is mainly for adding the IIS Manager to other NT machines that might need to control Microsoft Proxy Server.

Once you have selected all the appropriate options to install, select Continue to proceed with the installation. The Microsoft Proxy Server Cache Drives dialog box will be displayed, as shown in Figure 5.4.

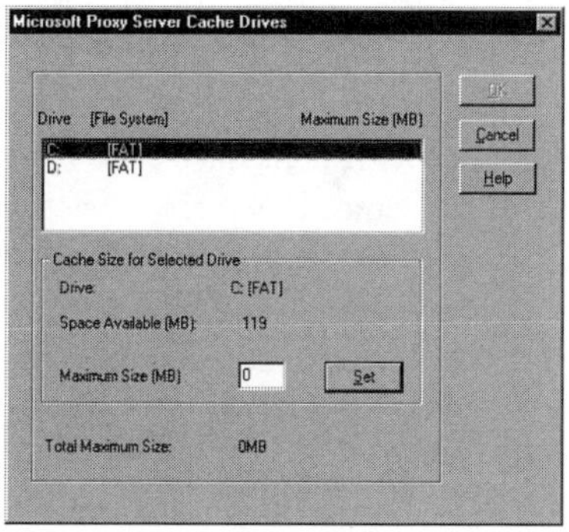

Figure 5.4.
The Microsoft Proxy
Server Cache Drives
dialog box.

This dialog box allows you to indicate which local hard drives should be used to hold Microsoft Proxy Server cached information. The Microsoft Proxy Server cache should be set to at least 100 megs, plus ½ meg per support proxy client. Allocate as many hard drives as you feel you can to hold Microsoft Proxy Server cached information. If one cache drive becomes too full, Microsoft Proxy Server will begin to use other allocated drives for cache data. Controlling the cache is discussed in greater detail in Chapter 12, "Controlling the Proxy Server Cache." Select the desired drive(s), indicate the cache space to allocate to that drive, and select the Set button. Try to arrange at least 100 megs of cache between drives. Once you have indicated the cache arrangement, click OK to continue. The Local Address Table Configuration dialog box is displayed next, as shown in Figure 5.5.

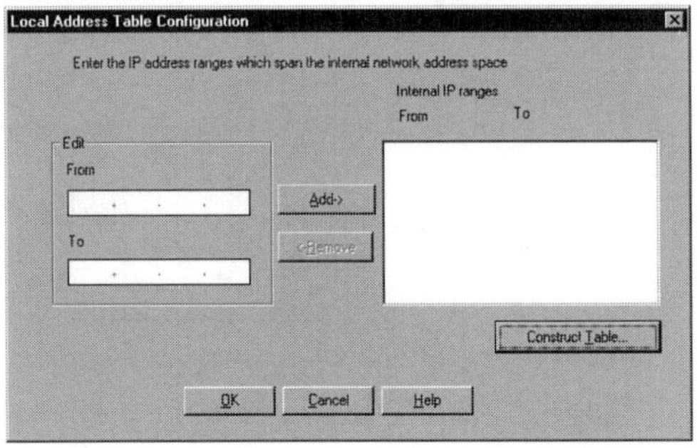

Figure 5.5.
The Local Address Table Configuration options.

This dialog box allows you to enter the IP addresses that should be considered local addresses for the private LAN. This should include the IP address of any NIC installed in the NT server, even NICs which are connected directly to the Internet. Contacting all addresses entered here will be handled by the internal WinSockets of each workstation, and will not be forwarded to the Web Proxy or WinSock Proxy servers for outside remoting.

Addresses are entered in pairs and indicate a range. If you wish to enter a single address, enter the same address as the From and To address. Select the Add button to add the new address range to the Local Address Table (known as the LAT). Highlight an entry in the LAT side of the dialog box, and select Remove to remove the address.

Select the Construct Table... button, and the installation routine will examine the routing table information stored by the NT server itself. This should adequately set up the LAT with the correct values for your network. The Construct Table... button will set the range of the subnet(s) the NT server is on into the LAT. This will also automatically set the range of private addresses which the InterNIC has set aside for private networks into the LAT. On my own network, I have chosen the subnet of 220.200.200. This is not a private subnet range and may already be allocated to another valid Internet site. This can cause problems. You should set up the IP subnet for your LAN from one of the reserved addresses.

On the off chance a workstation on my private LAN attempts to connect to a real Internet site on the 220.200.200 subnet, Microsoft Proxy Server will consider the site to be local and never remote the connection attempt to the outside. This essentially cuts off sites on the real 220.200.200 subnet from my own LAN. So far, I have never needed to access any site within the 220.200.200 subnet, and I don't even know if this subnet is in use yet.

The subnets that have been set aside by the InterNIC for use by private LANs to avoid Internet conflicts are:

- Class A subnet: 10.0.0.0
- Class B subnets: 172.16.0.0 to 172.31.255.255
- Class C subnets: 192.168.0.0 to 192.168.255.255

Using any of the above subnets for a private LAN will ensure that no problems will arise due to conflicts with real Internet sites.

Clicking the Construct Table… button will bring up the dialog box shown in Figure 5.6.

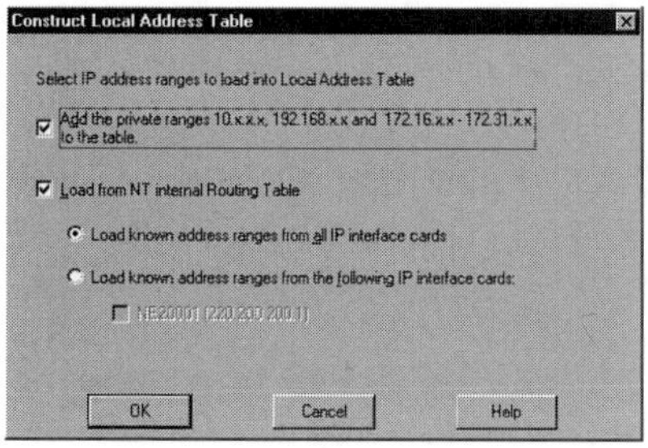

Figure 5.6.
The Construct
Local Address
Table dialog box.

You can optionally indicate whether or not to include the known private subnets in your LAT by checking the first option. The Load from NT internal Routing Table check box allows the installation routine to pull from the internal routing table maintained by NT. This routing table controls TCP/IP traffic between all networks interfaced on the NT server. You can indicate whether to pull subnets from all known interfaces or just from a single interface card. The default is to pull from all interfaces. NT supports multiple NICs and so can be part of several different subnets. You should let the installation routing construct the table from all subnets of which the NT server is a part. Clicking OK will return you to the main LAT table dialog box.

If a LAN uses both IPX/SPX and TCP/IP between workstations and servers, you may optionally choose to have no addresses considered to be local. This will force the WinSock Proxy client software to utilize IPX as a transport method, and all TCP/IP traffic will be handled through Microsoft Proxy Server, even if the destination is within the private LAN. If IPX/SPX is the only protocol used between client and server, the addresses entered here as local IP addresses will not matter because WinSock Proxy will have to pass all TCP/IP packets to Microsoft Proxy Server for processing.

Once you have added all necessary IP ranges, selecting OK will continue the installation routine. The next stage will allow you to indicate how client workstations access Microsoft Proxy Server. Figure 5.7 shows this setup stage.

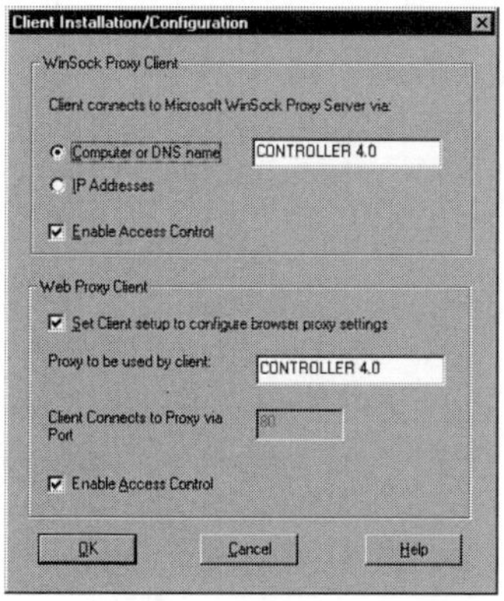

Figure 5.7.
Setting up how clients
access Microsoft Proxy
Server.

When the WinSock Proxy client software is installed on LAN workstations, the settings you indicate here will be used by clients. The top portion of this dialog box allows you to indicate how WinSock Proxy clients will access the WinSock Proxy server. When set to Computer or DNS name, the name you indicate in the entry field will by used by clients to access the WinSock Proxy server. This necessitates that your network have some form of name resolution capability, such as WINS or an internal DNS server available. If you do not use any internal name resolution service on your network, you will have to use the other option, IP Addresses, and indicate the IP address where Microsoft Proxy Server is running.

The figure shows the default setting of Computer or DNS name and my own NT server name loaded. Normal NT or Windows 95 machine names do not have a period (.) or a space in them, as does the one shown (Controller 4.0). This will cause problems with client setup: It isn't anything that can't be handled with a little manual editing, though. In order to alleviate client installation problems, it is best that the server name be a single word or a valid Internet-style name with no space. If a WINS server is running on the LAN, a static name entry can be added to the name database to represent Microsoft Proxy Server (such as MSP). If the machine name indicated at this point contains a space, the WinSock Proxy client software may only pick up the last part of the name. This will necessitate that the WinSock Proxy clients be manually configured for the correct machine name after installation.

One way around this problem is to use the IP address of Microsoft Proxy Server. This is the only choice if the LAN has no name resolution capability. It does cause extra configuration effort if Microsoft Proxy Server is ever moved to a different machine, because all client workstations will need to have their addresses modified. If Microsoft Proxy Server is accessed via a machine name, client workstations will simply resolve the name to a new address if the location of Microsoft Proxy Server changes (provided the machine name can follow the Microsoft Proxy Server to a new machine). This is where a WINS server comes in very handy. If a static entry is added to represent Microsoft Proxy Server, this is the only element that must be changed if the Microsoft Proxy Server changes IP locations and clients are set to look for Microsoft Proxy Server via a network name.

The Enable Access Control check box controls how the WinSock Proxy server grants Internet access to clients. If this box is checked, the WinSock Proxy server will follow the access restrictions placed on individual protocols controlled by the WinSock Proxy. If this check box is unchecked, any WinSock Proxy client will be granted a connection to the Internet. If internal security is not an issue for your network, unchecking this option will save you some time in configuring access permissions. By default, no one has permission to use any protocols through the WinSock Proxy server.

The bottom portion of this dialog box allows you to indicate whether, when installing the WinSock Proxy client software, the workstation proxy settings should be altered as well. The Web Proxy element of workstation connections to Microsoft Proxy Server do not require any special client software, as WinSock Proxy connections do. However, they do need to have the proxy settings enabled in order to work correctly via proxy. The WinSock Proxy client installation routine can set these settings during installation if the Set Client setup to configure browser proxy settings check box is checked. The WinSock Proxy client setup routine can configure both internal Windows 95 Internet settings for Web Proxy use, as well as older versions of Internet Explorer and Netscape Navigator, which do not rely on the internal Internet settings maintained by Windows 95.

The Proxy to be used by client entry field allows you to indicate the proxy name or address the WinSock Proxy client installation routine should set the Web Proxy clients to communicate with. Again, the same precautions taken with naming conventions with the WinSock Proxy server name should be taken with the proxy server name.

The Client Connects to Proxy via ## Port field is unchangeable. It indicates the TCP port that Microsoft Proxy Server will listen to for proxy traffic. This can only be changed by altering the port the IIS Web Server listens to and is done through the Web Server properties dialog box.

When the Enable Access Control check box of this area is checked, the Web Proxy will follow the security settings for client access. When this check box is not checked, any Web proxy client will be permitted access. If you do not have need for high security, you can uncheck this box.

Once these options have been set, select OK. The Microsoft Proxy Server installation routine will begin to install all necessary files. Once all files have been copied and installed, the IIS server will be restarted and Microsoft Proxy Server along with it. Microsoft Proxy Server is now running and listening for LAN traffic needing to get to the Internet. The NT server itself does not need to be restarted in order for Microsoft Proxy Server to be up and running correctly.

How to Read the Documentation

The default location of Microsoft Proxy Server is C:\MSP. Two subdirectories branch off this directory. These are the C:\MSP\DOCS and C:\MSP\CLIENTS directories. The DOCS directory contains all of the HTML documentation files for Microsoft Proxy Server. Microsoft Proxy Server documentation can be read by selecting the Microsoft Proxy Server Documentation entry in the Microsoft Proxy Server folder (Start button, Programs, Microsoft Proxy Server folder). Figure 5.8 shows the path to the documentation.

In order to read the documentation, you must have a Web browser installed on the NT machine that Microsoft Proxy Server is installed on. NT 4.0 installs IE 2.0, but you should obtain the most recent version of IE that is available.

The Microsoft Proxy Server Documentation entry simply starts up the default Web browser on the system and loads the TOC_CAT.HTM. This is the Table of Contents document that links all chapters of the Microsoft Proxy Server Documentation.

Figure 5.8.
*How to read the
Microsoft Proxy Server
documentation.*

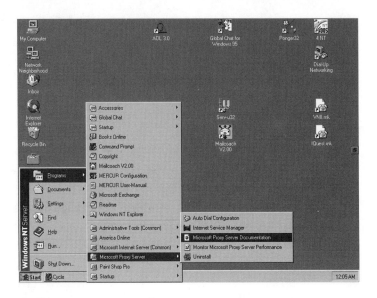

The MSPCLNT Share

As already mentioned, the Microsoft Proxy Server setup routine, if allowed, will create a new shared resource on the NT server called MSPCLNT. This is where the shared resource workstations should connect to in order to install the WinSock Proxy client software. Workstations do not need to map a network drive letter to this shared resource in order for the WinSock Proxy client installation software to run correctly. Some applications cannot be executed over a UNC (Universal Naming Convention) link. Instead, they must be run from a valid drive letter. Obviously most software created by Microsoft does not fall into this category. This means that the Network Neighborhood or the Windows Explorer can be used to run the WinSock Proxy client installation program. Figure 5.9 shows the Windows 95 Explorer with the MSPCLNT folder open without drive letter mapping.

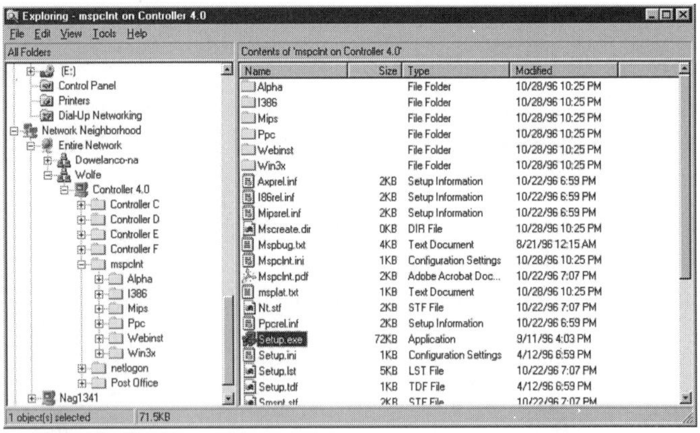

Figure 5.9.
*Using the Windows 95
Explorer to run the
WinSock Proxy client
installation.*

The Microsoft Proxy Server installation routine sets the MSPCLNT share to be accessible to everyone on the network. Unfortunately, the share is also set to grant everyone full control over this resource, which means that workstations can modify or delete files contained in this share. It's advisable to modify the access permissions for this share on the NT server to make the share accessible to everyone, but only in read-only mode. This can be done through the NT Explorer. Open the NT Explorer, locate the C:\MSP\CLIENTS directory, and right-click on it. A pop-up list will be displayed. Select the Sharing option. Figure 5.10 shows the dialog box for Sharing properties.

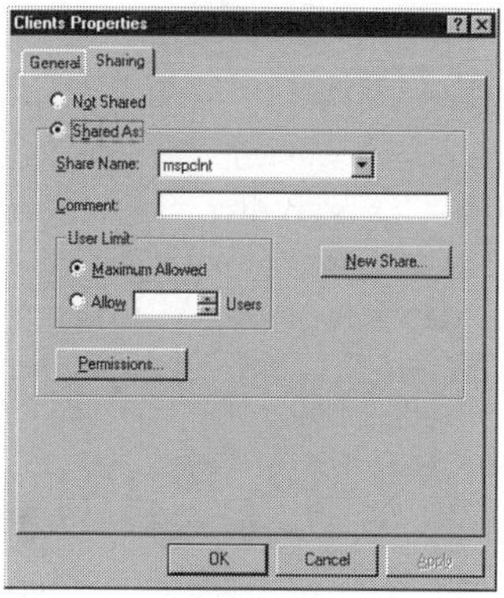

Figure 5.10.
Modifying the MSPCLNT
share properties.

At this point, select the Permissions… button. A new dialog box will appear, as shown in Figure 5.11.

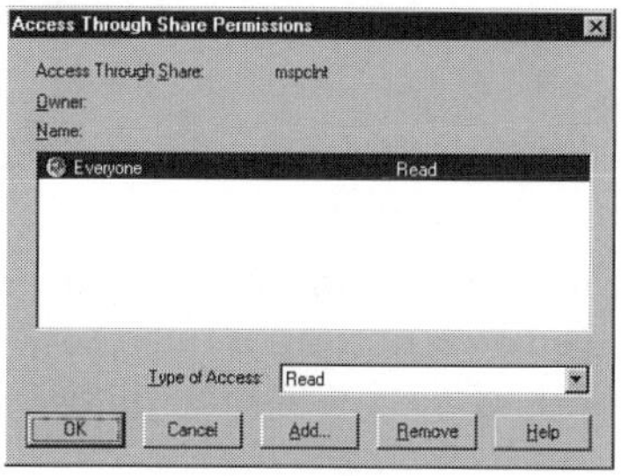

Figure 5.11.
Changing MSPCLNT
share permissions.

You should change the Type of Access for Everyone for the MSPCLNT share from Full to Read. This will ensure that no client workstation on your LAN will inadvertently modify or delete files in this shared directory. Select OK until you return to the main NT Explorer display. If you later need to reinstall Microsoft Proxy Server for some reason, be sure and check to see if the installation routine has reset the permissions for the MSPCLNT share.

Altering Microsoft Proxy Server After Installation

Microsoft Proxy Server can be reinstalled to modify some of the installation settings when needed. SETUP.EXE, found in the C:\MSP\SETUPBIN directory, can be run to alter the installation settings of Microsoft Proxy Server. Running the installation routine again will preserve all settings that do not change. This is a simple way of altering such things as location of the client share and which client platforms are supported.

Altering Microsoft Proxy Server Installation Settings

Running setup one more time will allow you to reconfigure the options you originally set during first installation. This is an easy way to modify such things as the Local Address Table and cache drive locations without having to go into the NT Registry Editor. Some of these settings can only be modified by reinstalling Microsoft Proxy Server. Luckily, permissions are preserved during a reinstall. Figure 5.12 shows the introductory dialog box after Microsoft Proxy Server has already been installed.

Figure 5.12.
Setup options after Microsoft Proxy Server has already been installed.

Selecting the Reinstall button will allow you to run through the installation process again, and reset any option you need to change. If the Local Address Table is modified, the machine will need to be restarted before the changes will take effect.

Adding/Removing Components

Components can be added or removed after the initial installation by selecting the Add/Remove button. If you need to reinstall components for WinSock Proxy clients because a network machine of a different architecture has been added, this is how to do it.

Removing Microsoft Proxy Server

Microsoft Proxy Server can be removed by selecting the Remove All button from the Setup dialog box. Microsoft Proxy Server can be removed successfully without having to restart the NT server it is running on.

Reinstallation Problems

There may be situations in which Microsoft Proxy Server will not reinstall after a crash or other problem has arisen. Sometimes either the WinSock Proxy server or the proxy server will simply stop responding during startup and a reinstallation will not fix the problem. In these situations, you may need to remove the IIS Web server and reinstall it first before reinstalling Microsoft Proxy Server.

Summary

Microsoft Proxy Server is actually very resilient, if it must be installed many times. I have played around with some software that pukes after just two installations. For the task Microsoft Proxy Server does, it is actually a very simple sub-service of the IIS Web server. The largest part of it is made up of the client installation files for the multitude of system architectures that NT can operate on. Once Microsoft Proxy Server is installed, the job of configuring it begins.

CHAPTER 6

Configuring Proxy Server

For the complicated job Microsoft Proxy Server performs, its setup is very easy and straightforward. The complicated part of Microsoft Proxy Server is understanding the principle behind what Microsoft Proxy Server does. The first thing you should have a clear understanding of before you attempt to configure Microsoft Proxy Server is that Microsoft Proxy Server is actually two separate servers working together to perform similar tasks. These servers are separate services under NT, but are both controlled through the IIS Service Manager. The first part of Microsoft Proxy Server is the Web Proxy server. This is a fully CERN-compatible Web Proxy server, meaning that any client that adheres to CERN Web Proxy standards can use the Microsoft Proxy Server Web Proxy to talk to the Internet. Web Proxy clients do not just have to be Windows-based clients. There are no proprietary elements to the Microsoft Proxy Server Web Proxy. In fact, there is no special software that must be installed on client workstations for them to be able to see the Microsoft Proxy Server Web Proxy.

For example, UNIX-based systems connected to an NT server running Microsoft Proxy Server by the TCP/IP protocol can run the UNIX version of Netscape and see the Internet through the Microsoft Proxy Server Web Proxy server. All flavors of Netscape can be internally configured to see any standard CERN Web Proxy via the TCP/IP protocol. Chapter 1, "Proxy Server Overview," covers the principles behind Web Proxy connections.

The second part of Microsoft Proxy Server is known as the WinSock Proxy server. This part of Microsoft Proxy Server is proprietary to the Windows environment, because special WinSock Proxy client software must be installed on workstations in order for them to access the WinSock Proxy server. Rumor has it that Microsoft is planning to release WinSock Proxy client software for other platforms (UNIX, Apple, OS/2), but I haven't had confirmation on this from any source.

WinSock Proxy works by replacing the local workstation WinSock DLLs with special DLLs that either keep TCP/IP traffic local or remote it over the WinSock Proxy server for transport to the Internet, depending on where it is destined for. Only WinSock communications version 1.1 is supported by the WinSock Proxy server. Microsoft will be updating Microsoft Proxy Server to support WinSock 2.0 communications as soon as it can. When support for WinSock 2.0 standards will be incorporated into Microsoft Proxy Server is hard to say, because WinSock 2.0 standards themselves have not been set. It may be that Microsoft Proxy Server 2.0 will still only support WinSock 1.1 standards if WinSock 2.0 standards have not yet been agreed upon. By adding a new WinSock layer to a system, the WinSock Proxy client software communicates to the WinSock Proxy server via a special control channel. This avoids TCP/IP port conflicts on the NT server running Microsoft Proxy Server. Any Internet server software can be run on the NT machine running Microsoft Proxy Server, because the WinSock Proxy server itself does not perform broadband TCP/IP port listening, as smaller third-party WinSock Proxy software such as WinGate does. With these third-party software packages, the server side runs by listening to all applicable TCP/IP ports for traffic. The Microsoft Proxy Server WinSock Proxy server communicates with clients via a single control channel. The WinSock Proxy client-side software is responsible for listening to specific TCP/IP ports.

By using WinSock Proxy on client workstations, nearly any Internet application (such as e-mail, Newsgroup reader, and FTP client) can operate locally, just as if it were directly connected to the Internet. Because the communication control takes place at the WinSock level, client applications using the WinSock Proxy interface normally need very little if any special configuration to work correctly.

Once you have a grasp of the two faces of Microsoft Proxy Server, you will know how to best make use of each element on your private LAN. Accessing the configuring controls for both elements is as easy as opening the IIS Service Manager.

The IIS Service Manager

The only major prerequisite for being able to install Microsoft Proxy Server is to have the IIS server installed. The Web Proxy part of Microsoft Proxy Server runs as a subservice of the WWW service, and therefore requires it to be functioning. Microsoft Proxy Server also makes use of the IIS Service Manager to provide an interface for controlling both the Microsoft Proxy Server Web Proxy and WinSock Proxy. The IIS Service Manager can be found in both the Microsoft Internet Server and Microsoft Proxy Server folders. Once started, the interface looks like Figure 6.1.

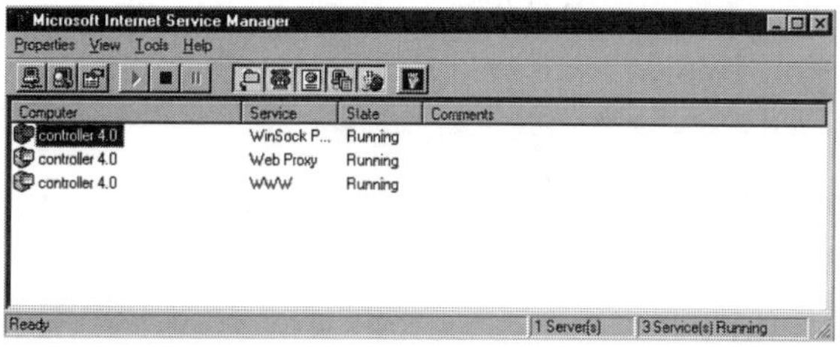

Figure 6.1.
The IIS Service Manager.

You may have more Internet services running on your system. By default, all three IIS services, WWW, FTP, and Gopher, are installed when IIS is installed. Figure 6.1 shows only the WWW server installed. I have no use for the Gopher server, and I think the IIS FTP server stinks. Gopher is an Internet server which is used to search multiple FTP sites for files. Its use (in my opinion) is negligible, because you can only search on specific filenames and not on descriptions. The IIS FTP server (again, in my opinion) is substandard in features and flexibility. As you can see in Figure 6.1, the IIS Service Manager has a very simple interface. Nearly every action that might need to be performed on a service can be accomplished through the toolbar buttons.

Starting/Stopping/Pausing Services

The middle set of buttons on the toolbar are the controls for starting, stopping, and pausing services (they appear on the bar in that order). Starting and stopping services is simple enough to understand. All you need to do is highlight one of the services listed in the service list and click the start or stop button.

Pausing a service is different than stopping a service. When a service is paused, current connections to that service will remain active, but new connections will not be accepted. Pausing a service is best used when the service needs to be fully stopped, but can't because of active connections. A service can be paused first and then fully stopped after all active connections end.

Filtering/Sorting the Service List

If there are many Internet services running on one machine, it may be convenient to filter out unneeded ones, or sort them for easier viewing. The last five buttons on the toolbar control the list filter. Figure 6.1 shows them all depressed, meaning all services are shown. The buttons from right to left are: FTP, Gopher, WWW, Web Proxy, and WinSock Proxy. The display area can show services running on other NT servers on the LAN. By default, only local services are shown. To filter out certain services, simply un-depress the desired filter button.

The service list can be sorted by NT Server, Service, Comment, or State. Click the View menu and select the appropriate sort method. The default sort order is by Server. The view mode of the service list area can also be changed to Server-oriented mode, a Service-oriented mode, or a Report-oriented mode. The default is a Report-oriented mode. The view mode can be changed through the View menu.

Connecting to Other Servers

NT is a fantastic environment for being able to fully control services running on other NT machines. The IIS Service Manager can be used to control any valid Microsoft Internet service running on another NT machine on the local LAN, or even over the Internet. In fact, the Microsoft Proxy Server installation routine can be used on NT workstations for just installing the Administration tool, which is just another name for the IIS Service Manager. By installing the Administration tool on an NT workstation, that workstation can be used to control the Internet services running on NT servers anywhere on the network. However, the WinSock Proxy cannot be used to remote NetBIOS traffic, which is what is used to control remote NT services. This means that Microsoft Proxy Server cannot be used to allow LAN workstations to perform network type activities, such as mapping drives or printing to systems on the Internet. Microsoft Proxy Server does not currently remote NetBIOS traffic.

The first two buttons on the toolbar are Connect to Server and Search Servers. The Search button will locate only IIS servers running on other NT machines on the private LAN. It won't search the Internet, obviously.

The Connect button can be used to connect to other servers, either by machine name or by IP address. Figure 6.2 shows the Connect To Server dialog box.

Figure 6.2.
*The Connect To
Server dialog box.*

A NetBIOS (machine) name or the actual IP address to connect to can be entered here. Once connected, the service display area will list all services running on the other machine, as well as services running on the local machine. From that point, all services can be controlled in any way.

Configuring Service Properties

The third button on the toolbar is used to configure service properties. Highlight the service to configure, and click this button. As with all Windows 95 and Windows NT 4.0 elements, this can also be done by right-clicking on the service and then selecting Properties from the pop-up list.

Authentication Principles

A large part of configuring both the Web Proxy and WinSock Proxy servers deals with setting up security. This section will give a brief overview of how Microsoft Proxy Server deals with security. For a full account of Microsoft Proxy Server security, please read Chapter 8, "Configuring Proxy Server Security and Authentication."

The Web Proxy service uses two levels of security, whereas the WinSock Proxy service uses only one.

The first level of authentication used by the Web Proxy service is login authentication. Because other operating systems can access a Microsoft Proxy Server Web Proxy, don't rely on the internal Windows login security. CERN authentication is built into the Web Proxy standard. When a client attempts to use the Microsoft Proxy Server Web Proxy service, it must send a standard HTTP request for access over port 80. Upon receiving this, the Web Proxy server returns an authentication challenge to the client. Clients that adhere to CERN authentication (such as Netscape and IE 3.0 or higher) should see a login prompt displayed. Some clients may be configurable to send an authentication name and password directly to the Web Proxy without prompting the user. The client must log in with an anonymous login (if that is permitted) or provide a login name and password that is present in the NT user database.

If the Web Proxy login is permitted, then the authentication name and password used will be further used by Microsoft Proxy Server to determine which specific Web Proxy services the user can access (WWW, FTP, and/or Gopher). This is the second level of authentication: protocol-specific access.

The WinSock Proxy service, on the other hand, uses only protocol-specific authentication, because the WinSock Proxy client can run only on a Windows platform. It's assumed that the network itself has already taken care of login authentication. Therefore, the WinSock Proxy service can use the internal NT security layer to demand network identification from clients to find out exactly who they are. That information is then used to determine protocol-specific access permissions.

Using the WWW Service to Provide Login Access

Because the Web Proxy service runs as a subservice of the WWW service, the login configuration of the WWW server applies to the Web Proxy service. To examine the login setup of the WWW service:

1. Highlight the WWW service in the service list.
2. Click the Properties button. The WWW properties dialog box is displayed, as shown in Figure 6.3.

Figure 6.3.
The WWW Service Properties.

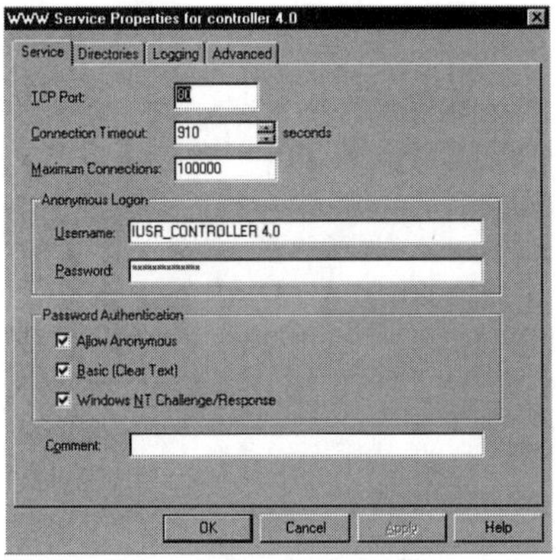

When the IIS server is installed, an NT user account is created to handle the rights given to anonymous logins. The name of this account is usually IUSR_servername, where servername is the name of your NT IIS server. As you can see in Figure 6.3, the username which controls access to anonymous logins for my system is IUSR_CONTROLLER 4.0. This account should not be assigned a password. If this account is given a password, anonymous logins must provide this password for access. The nature of the anonymous login is to use the e-mail address of the requesting user for a password. If you want to alter which account controls anonymous login permissions, enter a new user account name in the Username field of the Anonymous Logon section. Even if a password is blank, NT still displays a string of 14 asterisks for enhanced security.

Note the TCP Port field. This is the field for indicating which TCP port the WWW server listens to. This also affects which port Microsoft Proxy Server listens to and can be used to great effect when necessary. For example, if you want to run a completely separate WWW server, you can set the IIS Web server to listen to a port other than 80 (for example, 81) for network traffic. Another WWW server can be installed to listen to the traditional port of 80. Proxy clients on the LAN can configure their software to talk to port 81, leaving the other Web server to handle external connections on port 80. There is an option in the Web Proxy configuration for disabling external Web connections to the IIS server, though. When LAN workstations install the WinSock Proxy client software, they will automatically import the correct settings for whatever port you have set the IIS Web server to listen to.

Forms of Access

The WWW service supports three forms of login access. Any one of these forms can apply, or all three can be used simultaneously.

- Anonymous: When anonymous logins to the WWW service are permitted, anyone can log in without providing any form of authentication. Unlike FTP anonymous access, which requires a login name of ANONYMOUS and a valid e-mail address given as a password, WWW anonymous access requires no credentials. If the WWW service does not receive any user information upon client connection, it is assumed the connection should be extended anonymous login access permissions.

- Basic (Clear Text): When clear text logins are permitted, WWW clients can present their usernames and passwords in a standard, low-level encryption format. This form of authentication is fairly simple to break and should be avoided if possible.

- Windows NT Challenge/Response: This option is the highest form of security the WWW service supports. When a client attempts to access the WWW service, the WWW service demands the presentation of login credentials in Windows NT security encryption and format (NTLM C-R). In order for this form of login authentication to be available, the WinSock Proxy service must be present, and the client must have the WinSock Proxy client software loaded. Windows 95 and Windows NT support this form of authentication, but Windows 3.11 and Windows for Workgroups 3.11 do not. However, they can be upgraded to do so.

Obviously the WWW service itself is designed to field access requests from the outside Internet, and Microsoft Proxy Server is designed to field access requests from the inside. Keep in mind that a TCP/IP connection to the Internet is just another network connection. Login authentication can take place over a dialup link just as it can over a twisted pair cable.

Microsoft Proxy Server and NT Security

Microsoft Proxy Server runs as a standard NT service. As such, access by clients is controlled on a user-by-user basis. When a user attempts to connect, Microsoft Proxy Server consults the internal NT user database. Both the Web Proxy and the WinSock Proxy servers grant access to Internet protocols. A protocol is a TCP/IP virtual port and a standard form of communication between two applications: client and server side. For example, the NNTP protocol is a form of communication between a newsgroup server and a newsgroup reader. By convention, this communication is carried out over TCP port 119. Microsoft Proxy Server grants outside access on a protocol-by-protocol basis. All communication with the Web Proxy server happens over port 80, no matter if the client is a WWW client, an FTP client, or a Gopher client. The Web Proxy server determines the protocol request by the format of the data. The WinSock Proxy server determines the protocol by the port the client attempted to connect to.

Each protocol handled by the Web Proxy and WinSock Proxy servers has independent access permissions assigned to it. These permissions can be in the form of permission for specific users or permission for a group of LAN users. Microsoft Proxy Server can take full advantage of local NT security groups for assigning access to protocols. Out of the box, neither the Web Proxy nor the WinSock Proxy server has permissions assigned to any of the protocols it supports. Therefore, no one can use Microsoft Proxy Server until the administrator does some reconfiguring. The following configuration information will cover the basic steps needed, but Chapter 8 covers the in-depth issues associated with Microsoft Proxy Server security.

Configuring the Web Proxy Server

The first thing to do is open up the Web Proxy server configuration dialog box. To do this, follow these steps:

1. Open the IIS Service Manager.

2. Highlight the Web Proxy server in the service list.

3. Click the Properties button on the toolbar. Figure 6.4 shows the Web Proxy server configuration dialog box.

Figure 6.4.
*The Web Proxy
server configuration
dialog box.*

Conforming to the new configuration interface format, elements of the Web Proxy configuration are accessed via tabs at the top of the dialog box. The following is a basic description of the purpose of each tab.

■ Service: On this tab a basic description of the Web Proxy service can be added. If only a specific group of users is permitted to access the server, some comment to that effect would be a good idea. In a large environment of Internet servers, it makes it easier to know what each server does. This tab also allows you to access the LAT (Local Address Table) and edit it as needed.

■ Permissions: Access permissions for each protocol handled by the Web Proxy Server are configured on this tab.

■ Caching: This tab has settings which control the Microsoft Proxy Server Web Proxy cache.

- Logging: This tab has settings which control how the Microsoft Proxy Server Web Proxy logs activity information. Tracking access information is probably second in importance only to security.
- Filters: Microsoft Proxy Server controls which sites are being accessed, as well as who has permission to access them. Controlling access to specific sites is called filtering and is controlled on the Filter tab.

To select a tab, just click on it.

The Service Tab

The Web Proxy server comment will be displayed in the IIS Service Manager service display area. If there are many Internet services running on a network, using comments is important to keep things straight. This tab also allows you to view current connections and edit the LAT.

Viewing Current Sessions

At the bottom of this tab is a button for viewing online sessions to the Web Proxy server. Click this button to view current sessions. Figure 6.5 shows the Web Proxy Service User Sessions dialog box.

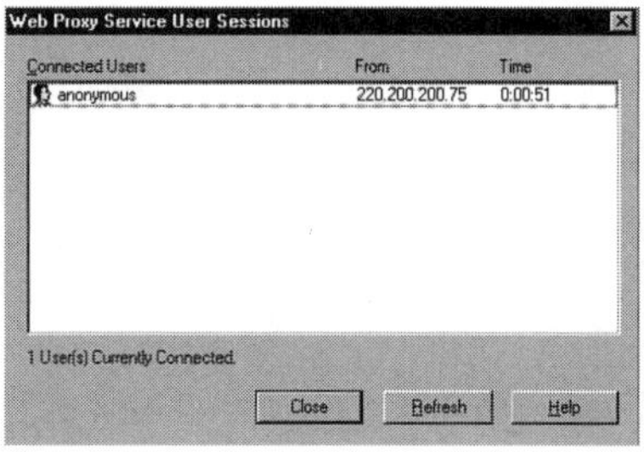

Figure 6.5.
Viewing online sessions to the Web Proxy server.

This dialog box shows the name of the user connected, the IP address that user comes from, and how long that user has been online. The username will be anonymous if no authentication information has been exchanged between the client and Microsoft Proxy Server. If anonymous access is not permitted, the username will be displayed. This dialog box does not dynamically refresh itself. To update the list, click the Refresh button. Click the Close button to return to the Web Proxy configuration dialog box.

Editing the LAT

The LAT is the table that indicates which addresses are local to the network. This is a text file stored in the MSPCLNT share and is transferred to WinSock Proxy clients when the WinSock Proxy client software is installed. This file is named MSPLAT.TXT. The Edit Local Address Table button calls up an editor that will allow you to make changes to the LAT, should your network arrangement change. The LAT is also dynamically sent to clients via the WinSock Proxy control channel. Figure 6.6 shows the LAT editor.

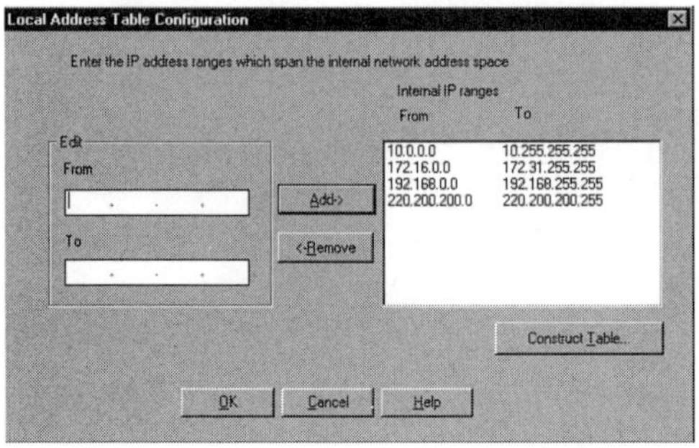

Figure 6.6.
The LAT editor.

You can make changes to the LAT in the same manner as when Microsoft Proxy Server was installed. If you need help editing the LAT, refer to Chapter 5, "Installing Proxy Server."

The Construct Table button in the LAT editor will call up another dialog box, shown in Figure 6.7.

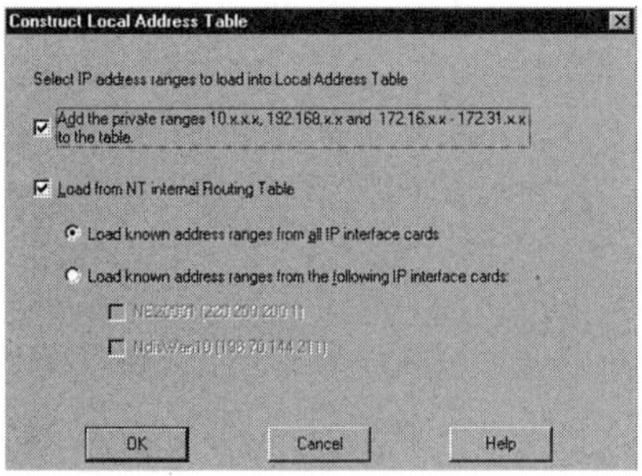

Figure 6.7.
*Constructing the LAT
from the internal NT
routing table.*

This dialog box allows you to import the values found in the NT routing table to create the LAT. The NT routing table contains all IP information about how to route TCP/IP packets between all network interfaces on the NT server. There are also options on this dialog box for creating entries in the LAT for the reserved local IP subnets. Chapter 5 covers the details of configuring this dialog box when installing Microsoft Proxy Server.

Note that the dialog box shows the RAS connection of my NT server as a valid network interface (it's greyed out near the bottom of the dialog box). If you have a static IP for your network connection to an ISP, that IP address should be part of the LAT.

Once the LAT has been edited correctly, the NT server should be rebooted in order for the changes to take effect.

The Permissions Tab

Configuring the permissions for the Web Proxy server protocols is simple, compared to configuring permissions for the WinSock Proxy server. With the Web Proxy server, only three protocols have to be dealt with. These three protocols also have nothing special to configure. With protocols handled by the WinSock Proxy server, many configuration elements are in the mix. Figure 6.8 shows the Permissions tab.

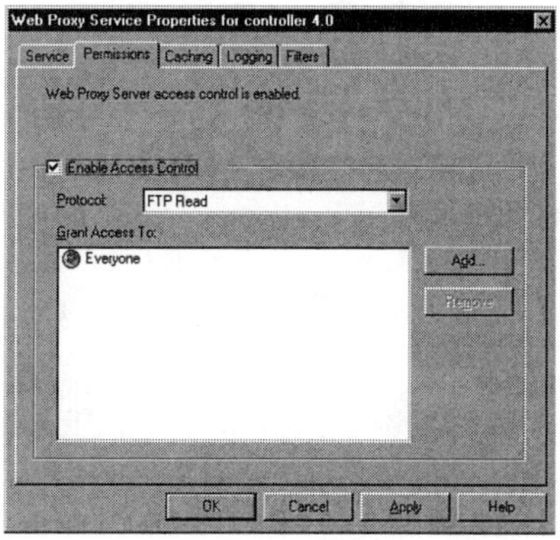

Figure 6.8.
The Permissions tab.

The Enable Access Control check box turns on and off all forms of access restrictions. When not checked, the Web Proxy will permit any connections, regardless of the credentials of the client needing access. When checked, the permissions settings that have been set will restrict client access accordingly.

The drop-down box allows you to select the protocol you wish to configure permissions for. Three Web Proxy protocols can be configured: HTTP, FTP, and Gopher. The display area shows which NT users or groups have permission to use the indicated protocol. The display area currently shows "Everyone" as having access. If you do not have a need for fancy security associated with each protocol, assigning Everyone as a permission to a protocol opens the protocol up for LAN-wide use.

You can also assign the Everyone group to the Unlimited Access protocol to open the Web Proxy up to unlimited access. Your Administrator group should be assigned to the Unlimited Access protocol. This will ensure that users with administrator privileges will not be hampered in any way.

Clicking the Add button will allow you to select NT users or groups who should have permission to use the protocol. Figure 6.9 shows the Add Users and Groups dialog box.

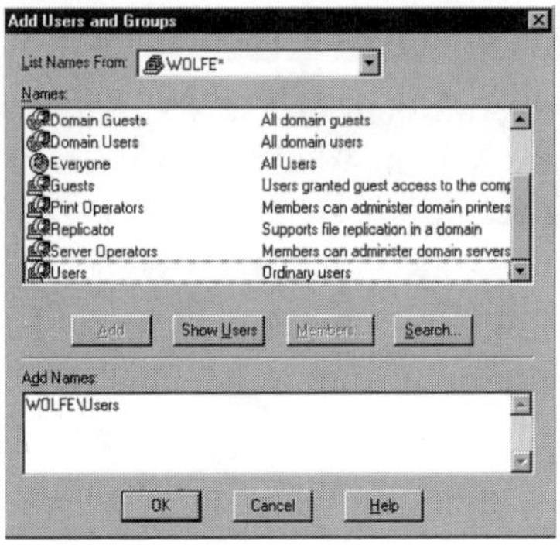

Figure 6.9.
The Add Users and
Groups dialog box.

If the current domain is in a trust relationship with another domain, you will have access to add users and groups from the other domain into the permission list for the protocol being configured. The List Names From drop-down list allows you to select the domain from which to draw users and groups. The default is the home domain of the Microsoft Proxy Server.

To add a user or group to the permission list for the protocol, follow these steps:

1. Highlight the group to add to the permission list. If you want to add a specific user, click the Show Users button, and Microsoft Proxy Server will pull in a list of all users of the selected domain. Figure 6.9 shows the dialog with this button.

2. Click the Add button. The user or group selected will show up in the Add Names display area.

3. Repeat the process and select all users and groups you wish to give permission to for this protocol.

4. Click OK, and those users and groups will now have permission to use this Web Proxy protocol.

The Show Users button will allow you to display exactly which NT users are members of a highlighted group. This is very handy to view just to whom you are granting Web Proxy permission.

The Search button will allow you to search for a user or a group within the current domain or selected domains, which is able to be contacted from the current domain. Multiple domains can be searched simultaneously. On large networks, this is a handy feature to have. Domains must be in a trust relationship before groups and users can be shared between them.

Back on the main Permissions tab, the Remove button will remove a highlighted user or group from the permission list of a protocol.

You may consider creating an Internet group, rather than relying on one of the existing NT groups for handling Internet access.

The Caching Tab

The Web Proxy service can cache objects which pass through it on their way to clients. These objects can be graphics, sound files, icons, or anything that would normally be part of a Web page. Currently, only WWW objects are cached. Files transferred by the FTP protocol through Microsoft Proxy Server are not cached, just as Gopher data is not cached. These stored objects can later be issued out to requesting clients on the private LAN, if the right conditions are met (such as object not expired or object unchanged on server). This reduces the amount of external traffic Microsoft Proxy Server has to maintain. The Web Proxy cache settings are controlled through this tab, shown in Figure 6.10.

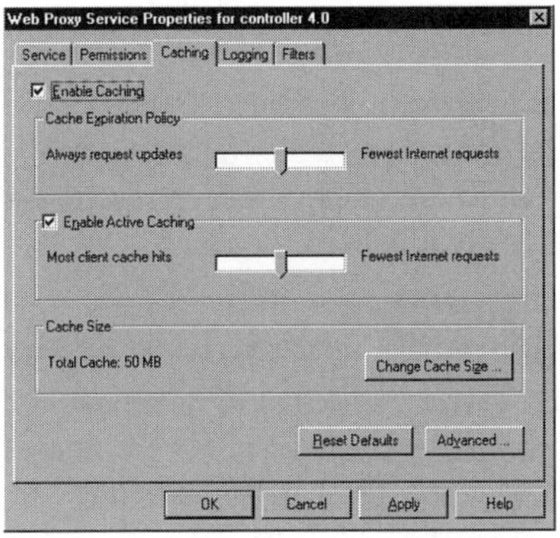

Figure 6.10.
The Caching tab.

Caching can be turned on and off through the Enable Caching check box. Turning the cache off does not mean that Microsoft Proxy Server will not serve out cached objects to clients. It means that it will not actively store any new incoming objects into the cache.

Modifying the Cache Expiration Policy

Objects held within the cache are set to expire after a certain time period. This is called an object's time to live or TTL. It is a value measured in seconds. Two things can happen to an object when it has expired:

- The object will no longer be issued out by Microsoft Proxy Server from the cache to clients, and a new version of the object will be kept when a client requests the object from the Internet.

- Or, Microsoft Proxy Server will actively update the objects on its own, if active caching is configured properly.

When the slider is to the left, Microsoft Proxy Server almost always retrieves a new copy of an object, whenever it is requested by a client. When the slider is to the right, objects will be considered fresh for longer periods. To reduce the amount of Internet traffic LAN users create, set this slider all the way to the right.

Modifying the Active Caching Policy

Active caching causes Microsoft Proxy Server to go out to the Internet and retrieve a fresh copy of an object all on its own without needing a client to prompt it to do so. This ensures that popular objects in the cache are always under their TTL and are synched with the originals of the objects on the Internet. This means that clients get HTTP objects locally and do not clutter up the Internet connection.

The Enable Active Caching check box turns Active Caching on and off. Microsoft Proxy Server does not need to be restarted for any alteration in the active caching policy to take effect.

When the slider is set to the left, Microsoft Proxy Server caches objects more actively. The active caching implementation is controlled by an advanced algorithm that factors in such elements as object popularity and Microsoft Proxy Server peak access times. When the algorithm determines it to be the correct time to update an object based on the factors, Microsoft Proxy Server will freshen the object from the Internet. When the slider is to the right, active caching occurs less frequently and the Internet connection is not crowded with Microsoft Proxy Server caching activity.

Modifying Cache Size and Directories

Microsoft Proxy Server cache should be at least 100 megs plus $\frac{1}{2}$ meg for every proxy client that will be supported. If there are many users on a LAN accessing many different sites on the Internet, the suggested size may not be enough to provide adequate caching services. Click Change Cache Size to modify where the cache directories are and how large they should be. Figure 6.11 shows this dialog box:

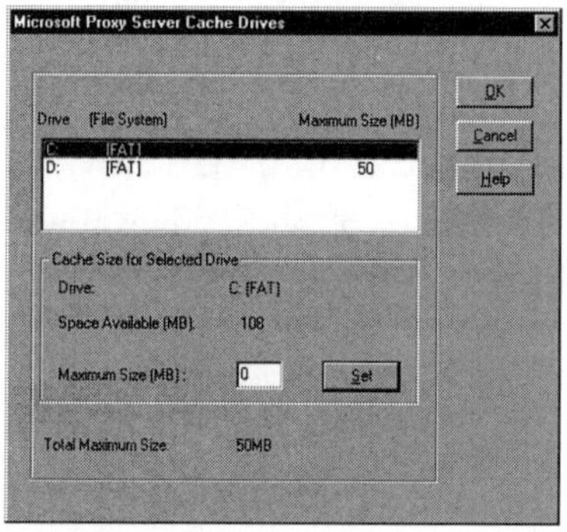

Figure 6.11.
*The Microsoft Proxy
Server Cache Drives
dialog box.*

By default, Microsoft Proxy Server sets up five directories to store cache data in. These cache directories are set up under the URLCACHE directory (they are named DIR1, DIR2, DIR3, DIR4, and DIR5). The reason Microsoft Proxy Server uses multiple cache directories is to speed up access of objects. When a single large cache directory is used, searching the directory for the right object can be time-consuming. Cache directories should always be placed on a local hard drive, not on a network drive.

Setting the cache is as easy as indicating the drive for a piece (or all) of the cache. The URLCACHE directory will be created automatically on all selected drives. Each of the subdirectories within the main URLCACHE directory will be used equally by the Web Proxy. The Set button must be clicked to set any size alterations or additions before the changes will take effect. Microsoft Proxy Server does not have to be restarted for any cache change to take effect. Chapter 12, "Controlling the Proxy Server Cache," covers the Web Proxy cache in greater detail.

Advanced Cache Settings

The Advanced button on the Proxy Service Properties dialog box allows you to control elements, such as what protocols are cached, the maximum size of objects that should be cached, and filtering sites so their objects are not cached. In Microsoft Proxy Server's current version, only WWW objects are cached so the ability to enable caching of FTP and Gopher objects is not available. Figure 6.12 shows the Advanced Cache Policy dialog box.

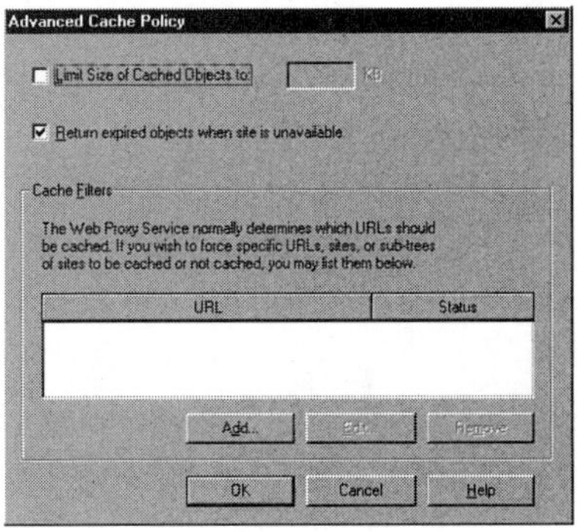

Figure 6.12.
*Advanced Cache
settings.*

The settings available on this dialog box limit the size of cached objects, return cache objects when the target site is unreachable, and set filters so specific sites are not cached. The Limit the Size of Cached Objects to check box allows you to indicate a maximum size for cache objects. Objects above the size indicated in kilobytes will not be cached by Microsoft Proxy Server and will always be retrieved from target Web sites. The default is to have all objects cached, no matter what their size.

The Return expired objects when site is unavailable check box controls whether or not Microsoft Proxy Server will return objects in the cache if the target site is currently unreachable, but the object's TTL has expired. This allows Microsoft Proxy Server to simulate a successful connection to a target site even when the objects returned are expired. This can be bad and good for the obvious reasons. It's up to you how you want to handle this setting.

The lower portion of this dialog box displays any special filter considerations you might have configured in Microsoft Proxy Server. Filters can specifically include or exclude certain sites for or from caching. Sites can be set to Always cached or Never cached. It is possible to set a general Never cache policy for a root domain, but create a special Always cache policy to cache certain sites within that domain. For example, you could set a Never cache policy for `*.microsoft.com`, but create an Always cache policy for `www.microsoft.com`. That way, only objects from `www.microsoft.com` will ever be cached from the `microsoft.com` root domain. Cache policies can be set for specific paths on a domain as well.

`www.microsoft.com` might be set as a Never cache site, but the specific path `www.microsoft.com/sitebuilders` might be set as an Always cache site. Append a site with an asterisk if you want all subpaths from the parent path to be cached as well. Without the asterisk, only the specific path will be cached.

The Add button will present a dialog box for adding a site filter to the cache configuration. This is shown in Figure 6.13.

Figure 6.13.
Adding a Site Cache filter.

Simply enter a site name in the appropriate format, as indicated in the URL field, and indicate whether the site is to be Always or Never cached. Click OK after configuring a site's caching policy.

The Edit button allows you to edit existing cache policies in the same manner as adding a new site policy.

The Logging Tab

Microsoft Proxy Server keeps a very good record of who uses the Web Proxy or WinSock Proxy services and just exactly what sites they access. By default, Microsoft Proxy Server logs data in a straight text format. Log files are stored in the `\WINNT\SYSTEM32\PROXYLOGS` directory for Web Proxy accesses and in the `\WINNT\SYSTEM32\RWSLOGS` directory for WinSock Proxy accesses. By default, both services start a new log file daily. The filenames are `iaYYMMDD.LOG` where YY is the year, MM is the month and DD is the day. Figure 6.14 shows the Logging tab.

The following is a description of each element on this tab:

- The Enable Logging check box controls whether the Web Proxy service logs information. Unchecked, the Web Proxy service will not keep track of accesses.

- The Regular logging check box controls whether or not a full range of information is stored in each log file. When unchecked, only minimal information is stored in the logs. This cuts down on the size of log files.

■ The Verbose logging check box controls whether or not each Internet access is recorded. By default, Microsoft Proxy Server Web Proxy will only keep information concerning who on the local LAN accesses the Web Proxy server. Verbose logging will force Microsoft Proxy Server to record what Internet sites were visited by each user.

Figure 6.14.
The Logging tab.

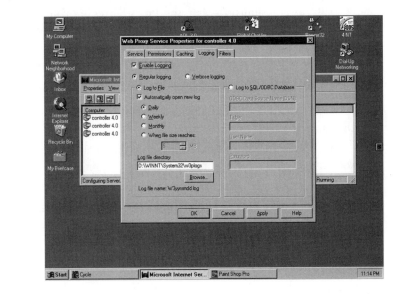

Microsoft Proxy Server can log to a text file or an SQL or ODBC (Open Database Connectivity) database, provided that such services are present on the network. Checking the Log to File check box tells Microsoft Proxy Server to log to a standard text file in the appropriate directory. The Daily, Weekly, Monthly, and When file size reaches check boxes tell Microsoft Proxy Server how often to begin a new log file. If you have little Microsoft Proxy Server activity, a longer logging period is best. The higher the activity, the shorter the turnaround time should be for opening new log files. Be very watchful of your log files. If a client has a great deal of trouble accessing Microsoft Proxy Server, it will generate an error line for each bad attempt the client makes. Some of the log files on my own network have reached 250+ megs in a single night, due to continuous automatic client reconnection attempts. It's a good idea to archive your log files or delete them on a regular basis to conserve disk space.

If you have a need to change the location where Microsoft Proxy Server stores Web Proxy logs, you can change the contents of the Log file directory field.

If the Log to SQL/ODBC Database check box is checked, Microsoft Proxy Server will attempt to connect to a database server to store its log information. This form of logging is slightly slower than writing to a straight text file, but data manipulation for reports and so on is much more powerful. Any installed ODBC drivers can be used. Microsoft Access is a common application that installs a full set of ODBC drivers for external applications such as Microsoft Proxy Server to use when attempting to save data in a database format. During installation,

Microsoft Proxy Server can install several types of current ODBC drivers. These drivers will allow Microsoft Proxy Server to interface with associated database engines for saving log information in the database engine's own format.

A SQL server is an NT databasing service that can provide database functions to client workstations. SQL Server is similar to Microsoft Proxy Server in that it is a stand-alone engine that provides a service to clients. Clients must have appropriate access to utilize the services the server has to offer. SQL Server does not have to be running on the same machine as Microsoft Proxy Server. Microsoft Proxy Server can log database information to any machine on the network.

The configuration information in this area of the Logging tab is defined as follows:

- ODBC Data Source Name (DSN): This field should contain the name of the DSN of the database engine to connect to.
- Table: This is the name of the table within the database that Microsoft Proxy Server should open to store its log information.
- Username: The username associated with the database table.
- Password: If the table is password protected, this field should contain the correct password to allow Microsoft Proxy Server to have access to the table.

Once the SQL/ODBC logging fields have been completed, Microsoft Proxy Server will immediately begin logging to the indicated database table. The service does not have to be restarted.

The Filters Tab

Setting filters for controlling which sites can or cannot be accessed is a straightforward process. By default, Microsoft Proxy Server does not filter which sites users have access to. Figure 6.15 shows the Filters tab.

Figure 6.15.
The Filters tab.

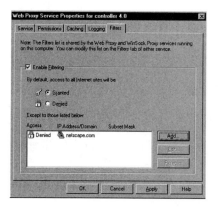

To begin the filter assignments, you must determine what approach you will need to take. If you only want to allow LAN users to access a handful of sites on the Internet, all access to all sites should be denied. If you want to deny access to certain sites, but leave the rest of the Internet accessible, all sites should be granted access by default. Click the appropriate radio button for the default permission.

Once you have determined the default permission for sites, you can begin to set the exceptions to that rule. In Figure 6.15, the default shown is to permit access to all sites. As you can see, the only exception is the domain netscape.com. Exceptions can be indicated as single computers designated by IP address, groups or computers designated by IP address, or entire domains such as netscape.com. Choose the Add or Edit buttons to add a new exception or edit an existing one. Figure 6.16 shows the Deny Access To dialog box.

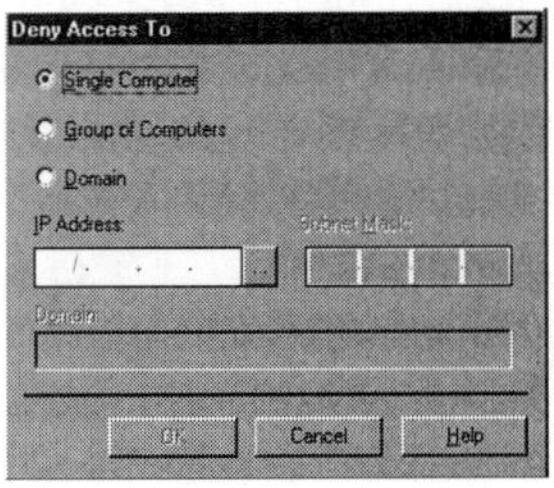

Figure 6.16.
Adding a filter
exception.

Exceptions can be indicated in the following manners:

- Single Computer: This option allows a single Internet site to be excepted from the default rule (in this case, denied access to). The IP address of the computer should be indicated in the IP Address field.

- Group of Computers: This option allows you to indicate by IP address a group of computers to except from the default rule. Enter an IP address in the IP Address field, and then enter a subnet mask. The subnet mask controls the range of addresses excepted from the default rule based on the single IP address given. For example, if an IP address of 234.176.58.5 was indicated and a subnet mask of 255.255.255.0 was indicated, any site with an address beginning with 234.176.58 would be excepted from the default rule. If a subnet mask of 255.255.0.0 was indicated, all sites with an address beginning with 234.176 would be excepted from the default rule. A subnet mask of 0.0.0.0 would nullify the entire filter process because it would contradict the default rule by excepting all addresses. Indicating a subnet mask of 255.255.255.255 would be the same as just indicating a single computer as an exception to the default rule.

- Domain: This option allows you to indicate verbosely the name of a domain to except from the rule. This will probably be the most usable option in this dialog box because this is how most people know Internet sites. Indicate the name of the domain to except from the default rule in the Domain field. An asterisk can be used to indicate multiple domains based off of one domain name. For example, *.netscape.com would except all domains such as home.netscape.com and www.netscape.com from the default rule.

Once you have set all necessary options, click OK to return to the Filters tab. The Edit button can be used to change an existing entry, and the Remove button can be used to remove an entry from the filter list.

Filtering can be very useful and is the one of the major advantages using Microsoft Proxy Server has over giving all workstations on a LAN full access to the Internet on their own. Let's face it, there are a lot of distractions on the Internet and LAN users have a tendency to be easily lured away from their jobs.

Configuring the WinSock Proxy Server

Configuration of the WinSock Proxy server is almost an identical process to configuring the Web Proxy server. The Service, Logging, and Filters tabs are identical in purpose and configuration elements. Refer back to these tab definitions in the Web Proxy server configuration section earlier in this chapter for details on the settings involved. The following differences in the three tabs apply:

- The Service tab of the WinSock Proxy configuration does not have a View Sessions button. The WinSock Proxy server cannot view a list of sessions it is currently supporting.
- The Caching tab is not present in the WinSock Proxy configuration. No caching occurs with WinSock Proxy, so this tab does not apply.
- An extra tab is present. This is the Protocols tab and is used to add support for new protocols or edit settings for support on existing protocols.

A major difference in configuration between the WinSock Proxy server and the Web Proxy server is in the Permissions tab. Like the Web Proxy server, each protocol supported by the WinSock Proxy server is assigned a different set of access permissions. Unlike with the Web Proxy server though, administrators can define support for new protocols which do not come preconfigured in the WinSock Proxy server. Remember that nearly any Internet application can communicate with the WinSock Proxy server. The WinSock Proxy client software is responsible for listening to local port requests, and then establishing a link between the client and the WinSock Proxy server. As long as a port is correctly configured in the WinSock Proxy setup, almost any Internet application can use the WinSock Proxy server as though it were directly connected to the Internet.

Protocols the WinSock Proxy Server Supports by Default

By default, the WinSock Proxy server comes preconfigured to handle all major TCP and UDP port communications. Support for Telnet, FTP (non-proxied), NNTP (Network News Transfer Protocol), SMTP (Simple Mail Transfer Protocol), POP3 (Post Office Protocol 3), Finger, RealAudio, VDO Live, and several other common Internet sockets is configured into the WinSock Proxy server. This means that unless you have special Internet applications that communicate over an uncommon port, you will probably not have to do any special configuration on the WinSock Proxy server to get all commonly used client Internet applications running correctly.

The WinSock Proxy Permissions Tab

To open the WinSock Proxy configuration, do the following:

1. Highlight the WinSock Proxy service in the service list of the IIS Service Manager.

2. Click the Properties button on the toolbar.

The WinSock Proxy Permissions tab looks considerably different than the Web Proxy Permissions tab. Figure 6.17 shows the WinSock Proxy Permissions tab.

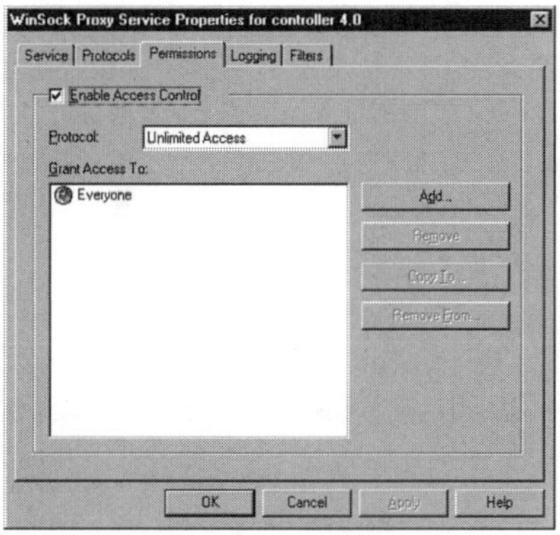

Figure 6.17.
*The WinSock Proxy
server Permissions tab.*

Assigning permissions to WinSock Proxy–supported protocols is the same process as assigning permissions to Web Proxy protocols. Select the protocol to assign permissions to in the right drop-down list, and then click the Add button. A dialog box will pop up which looks identical to the one shown in Figure 6.9. For more information concerning granting users and network groups rights to use a protocol, refer to the Web Proxy Permissions tab discussion earlier in this chapter.

The Copy To and Remove From buttons can be used to copy sets of groups and users from the currently selected protocol to groups of other protocols. For example, say a protocol had seven permission definitions in it. You could display this protocol, select five of these definitions in the traditional Windows select method (holding down the Ctrl key and clicking the desired elements) and then click Copy To. A list of all available protocols would be displayed. You could then select a protocol (or group of protocols with the multiple select method again) and then click OK. The selected groups and users would then be copied into the permission sets of the target protocols. Remove From works in the same way, but in reverse. Selected groups and users will be removed from the selected protocols rather than added to them.

The Protocols Tab

The Protocols tab allows you to modify existing protocols or create new protocols that the WinSock Proxy server will support. Figure 6.18 shows the Protocols tab.

Figure 6.18.
The Protocols tab of WinSock configuration.

You see the protocols that the WinSock Proxy server supports listed in the Protocol Definitions area. From this dialog box, existing protocols can be edited or removed, and new ones can be added. The dialog boxes produced by the Add and Edit buttons are identical.

In the following paragraphs, I give a quick overview of how to install support for an new protocol. The Internet application I use as an example is Kali for Windows 95. For those of you who are not familiar with Kali95, it's an application that allows IPX network games such as Descent, Command and Conquer, and Mech Warrior II to be played over the Internet as though the remote players were actually on the local LAN. (Yes, I am truly a geek and spend way too much time on the Internet.)

When adding support for a new protocol, the first thing you have to know in advance is on what port the client application talks to its server and what type of data packets (TCP or UDP) the application uses. Most clients will initiate communication with a server over one port, but expect a response over another port. Some clients expect the server to set the return port number, while others expect a return over a consistent port. For example, under normal circumstances, FTP clients initiate communication with an FTP server over port 21, but expect a response over port 23. However, most good FTP clients can be set for something called Passive transfer (PASV Mode), which means they will instruct the server to set up a non-standard return port.

PASV mode is a security form. It is mostly needed to pass over routers and firewalls. The purpose of a firewall is to prevent access to a network over known ports, such as the return FTP port 23. When the server sets up a non-standard return port, the communication can pass over a firewall.

You must be familiar with how a client/server pair communicates before you can correctly set up the WinSock Proxy server to connect the two. Kali95 uses UDP packets and initiates communication with Kali servers over port 2213. It expects a return channel from the server over a dynamically established port (the return port will vary). Knowing the return port is not as important as knowing the initiating port. Most of the time, the WinSock Proxy client software will be able to tell the WinSock Proxy server what port to expect a return response on from the way the actual client secures the return port on the workstation. The process happens like this:

1. Kali95 initiates communication with a Kali server over port 2213.
2. The WinSock Proxy client software intercepts this call and informs the WinSock Proxy server about it over its control port—1745.
3. The WinSock Proxy server begins to communicate with Kali95 as though it were the actual site Kali95 is trying to talk to. Understand that the WinSock Proxy server is not responding for the actual target server. It can't. It doesn't know what Kali95 wants. The WinSock Proxy server only receives the network connection as though it were the target site.
4. Kali95 initiates a listen on a dynamic UDP port for return data from the Kali server it is trying to contact.
5. The WinSock Proxy server intercepts the listen and tells the WinSock Proxy server what port Kali95 is listening to.
6. The WinSock Proxy server initiates a connection between itself and the target site over port 2213. The WinSock Proxy server at the same time begins to listen for a response over the UDP port that Kali95 is listening to.
7. When the target site responds on the dynamic return port, the WinSock Proxy server forwards the response to Kali95, as if it were the actual site itself.

The process isn't too difficult to follow. The WinSock Proxy server acts as the middleman. It pretends to be the target server when talking to Kali95, and it pretends to be Kali95 when talking to the target server. As long as it knows what port to expect an initial connection on and what type of data packets to toss around, it should be able to handle any Internet client/server combo.

To add support for a new protocol, click the Add button in the Services (protocols) dialog box. Figure 6.19 shows the dialog box that opens.

Figure 6.19.
The Protocol Definition dialog box.

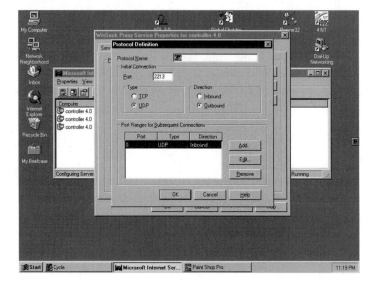

The following is a definition of each element on the Protocol Definition dialog box.

- Protocol Name: Any name you want to assign to the protocol.
- Initial Connection Port: The port the client will use when first attempting to contact a server.
- Initial Connection Type: This can be either TCP or UDP. You must know what type of packets a client uses to initiate communications with a server. If you are not sure, try TCP. TCP packets are more commonly used that UDP.
- Initial Connection Direction: This setting tells the WinSock Proxy server which direction to expect the packets on this port. Since Kali95 begins the communication, the direction is Outbound. Outbound will be the direction for 95 percent of all protocols you will want to set up.

Once you have the basics configured, next you will need to add information about how subsequent connections from the target server back to the client application will be made. With Kali95, we need to indicate that any UDP port can be used for a return connection. Clicking the Add button (or the Edit button to edit an existing return port) will produce the dialog box shown in Figure 6.20.

The return port number (or range) should be indicated in the Port or Range fields. A value of 0 indicates that any port may be used as a return port for this protocol.

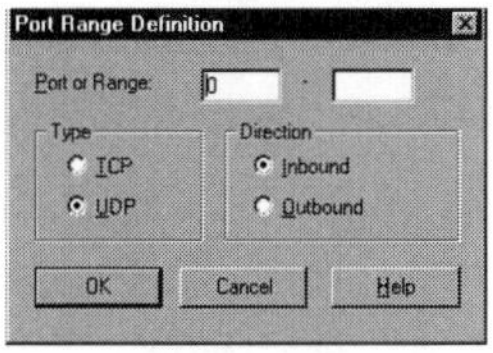

Figure 6.20.
*Adding return
connection informa-
tion.*

The Type will set the packet type that is normally the same as the outbound packet type, in
this case UDP. The Direction will be Inbound; Kali95 will not send further outbound packets
to the target server over a different port. Some protocols may need to send out packets over
multiple ports, once an initial connection to a server is made. If this is the case, you will need
to know which ports the client application will be utilizing and create multiple subsequent
connection entries, or create a range for ports.

Once you have indicated these elements, you can click OK to return to the primary Protocol
Definition dialog box. Those should be the only configuration elements you will need to set.
For most protocols you will be configuring, you can set all subsequent connections for any
valid port. I have tested Kali95 under Microsoft Proxy Server, and once I got hold of the release copy (of MPS), Kali95 worked like a charm.

Once the protocol has been completely defined, click OK to return to the Protocols tab. Don't
forget to add permissions to new protocols you configure.

Multiple Microsoft Proxy Server Gateways

More than one Microsoft Proxy Server gateway can be used on a network. The Web Proxy and
WinSock Proxy servers behave differently in a network environment where more than one
Microsoft Proxy Server is used.

Multiple Web Proxy Servers

Clients can access multiple Web Proxy servers in a cascading fashion. Web Proxy servers can
be grouped and accessed in a chain to provide the best possible performance for clients. In order
for this to be possible, some form of internal name resolution ability must be present on the
network. Either a DNS or WINS server must be available to hand out name resolution functionality.

All Web Proxy servers can be grouped into an Internet group. This group is defined as an entity by a DNS server or a WINS server. When the group is accessed, either the DNS server or
the WINS server serving out the name resolution functionality for the network will sequen-
tially choose a member from the group and resolve the group name requested as the IP of one

of the members of the group. The name server is responsible for tracking which member of the group is up for the next resolution request.

Setting up a fully functional DNS server is a pretty hefty task. Entire books have been dedicated to this topic alone. If you feel you need to use DNS over WINS (which you shouldn't need to do on a Microsoft NT–based network since WINS performs all major functions of DNS as well as some other handy functions), I suggest you grab a good UNIX book and be prepared to read it for a month or two. The NT 4.0 DNS server functions in nearly the same way as a UNIX DNS server. Much, if not all, of the information you can get from a UNIX DNS book will be directly applicable to NT DNS configuration.

Under a WINS environment, a multi-homed static database entry is created to list all of the Microsoft Proxy servers. The WINS server chooses a representative from this list in a fashion which is different from how the DNS server chooses its representative. The WINS server first matches a client's request with the client's IP. The WINS server then tries to find a Microsoft Proxy server from the list that has the same subnet as the client. Failing to do that, the WINS server then attempts to locate a Microsoft Proxy server on the same net as the client. If none of these searches finds a proper candidate, the WINS server picks a member of the group at random and resolves the request to that member's IP address.

Consult NT's online help system for more information on how to set up a DNS Internet group, or how to set up a multi-homed group under WINS. Chapter 9, "Concepts and Realities of Name Resolution with Proxy Server," also covers issues relating to name resolution in a Microsoft Proxy Server environment.

Multiple WinSock Proxy Servers

WinSock Proxy servers cannot be cascaded like Web Proxy servers can. In order to make the best use of multiple WinSock Proxy servers, network clients should be evenly distributed among all WinSock Proxy servers to make sure that no one WinSock Proxy server becomes overloaded. You need to have a good understanding of which Internet protocols demand the most out of a connection. Knowing that will allow you to separate client access correctly. Internet applications such as RealAudio and VDO Live consume huge amounts of connection bandwidth and can bring Internet applications running through the same connection by other network users to a stand still. Chapter 4, "Planning Your Installation and Configuration," covers how to best arrange your network to provide the most performance possible.

Summary

Hopefully, this chapter gave you all the configuration help you need to get your Microsoft Proxy Server(s) up and running. This chapter also gave you a clear understanding of the separation between the Web Proxy server and the WinSock Proxy server. Once Microsoft Proxy Server is initially configured, very little if any daily maintenance is needed to keep it running smoothly.

CHAPTER 7

Configuring NT Security for an Open Environment

NT security is a difficult thing for some people to grasp. Most people are familiar with logging in to Windows 3.*x* or Windows 95, but few realize what that process does as far as network security goes. This chapter details the issues involved with security on an NT-based network and how you can optimize your network arrangement when dealing with Microsoft Proxy Server.

Workgroups Versus Domains

If you're a network administrator for a company, or just for yourself, you probably already understand the difference between workgroups and domains. Much of this chapter may cover elements of NT you are already very familiar with. To be on the safe side, I'll cover security from the ground up. If you are an administrator for a medium or large NT-based network, arranging your NT security groups correctly up front can save you from redoing your security arrangement time and time again. The first element you should be clear on is the difference between workgroups and domains. The purpose of both is to group a set of users and systems into a coherent relationship for easy management and navigation. Workgroups have no central security figure while domains do.

- Workgroup logins place network validation responsibility on the workstation level. Each workstation will maintain a list of user names and associated passwords.

- Domain logins place network validation responsibility on the primary domain control, or one of the backup domain controllers of a network.

In a Windows NT-based network, you are the name and password you log in to a network workstation with. Other actions that require passwords, such as dialing in to a remote access server, allow you to enter an alternate name and password, but this information only applies to the single action, such as gaining authorization to connect. Once a RAS connection is gained with a separate user name and password, all other network authorization is done based on the Windows login name and password given when the workstation was first started.

Microsoft Proxy Server security relies directly on the internal security found in Windows NT architecture. When NT servers are used in a workgroups-based network, the user information provided on each server is separate and independent. Each server (or NT workstation system) can maintain a full database of users and groups. These user and group definitions only apply to accessing the particular server on which they are kept.

Arranging a network into a domain takes a little more effort to manage, but the benefits of less confusion and tighter security far outweigh the extra management effort. NT servers in a workgroup are like islands of independent security. The security credentials needed to access resources or services on one NT server may not be the same as those needed for a different NT server.

Login Process

Several things happen when a workstation logs on to a network. If the workstation is set to logon as a workgroup member, the workstation itself performs user authentication with its own user database of information. If the workstation is set to log on as a domain member, the workstation machine will consult the primary domain controller of the domain for user authentication. A login proceeds in this manner:

1. The domain controller must be found before the logon, when the system is started. This process is called *discovery*, and is only done when a workstation is set to log on to a domain. The actual method of discovery depends on the protocol(s) the network uses. To discover a PDC (primary domain controller), a workstation generally must perform a network broadcast, which will trigger the PDC of the network to perform

its own broadcast to indicate where the PDC can be found with a directed datagram. Once the workstation receives the broadcast response from the PDC letting the workstation know exactly where it can find the PDC with directed datagrams, the next step of logging on can proceed.

2. Once the PDC is found, the workstation attempts to establish a secure channel between itself and the PDC (or backup domain controller, if the BDC responded in place of the PDC). This secure channel consists of datagrams directed back and forth between the workstation and PDC. Both sides must prove to the other that they are who they say they are. This process is called Secure Channel Setup.

3. Once the workstation and the PDC have found each other and set up a secure channel, pass-through authentication can occur. This process is where the workstation sends the login user name and password to the PDC (or a BDC) in encrypted format. If the user information is correct, the PDC sends back an OK for the workstation to permit the login.

4. After authentication is complete, the system and user are given a security token by the controller that performed the authentication. This token is the actual network item which is passed around to network servers accessed by the client workstation. Any target server will use this token to consult a controller to find out whether it is valid and whether the associated user should be granted access to use whatever resource the user is attempting to access.

A Microsoft Proxy server is like any other resource on the network. Accessing it takes proper network validation. The Microsoft Proxy Server service is fully capable of utilizing the internal NT security process.

Domain Controllers

On an NT-based network, the central authority figures are know as controllers. There is one primary domain controller and any number of backup domain controllers. These systems are responsible for fielding all Microsoft Network Domain logins and granting or denying access to secured network resources. PDCs and BDCs will always be NT servers and will all share information. User data stored on the PDC is replicated to all BDCs across the domain. The network administrator determines which NT systems are to be BDC machines when these systems are installed. The job of BDCs is to share some of the workload of the PDC. On medium or large networks, a single authority figure might quickly become overloaded with network traffic. BDCs help to ensure that network performance is kept as high as it can be.

Administration of user data can be done from any NT machine, server, or workstation, so long as the user logged in has administrative rights. The main application for modifying user data is User Manager for Domains, which is found in the Administrative Tools folder. When systems are not members of a domain, this application will only modify user information stored in the local user database. When an NT system is a member of a domain, this application will link to an available controller and modify the domain-wide user database.

When talking about user information concerning Microsoft Proxy Server authentication, I'm talking about a domain-wide database of user information. Yes, a Microsoft Proxy server machine can be a completely isolated server, and not part of any domain. However, if a Microsoft Proxy server is running on an isolated system, the task of managing separate authorization for network users and Microsoft Proxy Server users becomes far more time-consuming and counterproductive.

Likewise, I deal exclusively with a domain-based network. If your network is a workgroup-based network, this chapter will still hold valuable information for you. However, the discussion will then pertain to managing the user database only on the NT server running Microsoft Proxy Server because workgroup machines do not share common authentication data.

The User Manager for Domains

The User Manager for Domains (UMD—don't ya just love the endless barrage of acronyms?) can be found in the Administrative Tools folder. It can also be manually started by running USRMGR.EXE. This utility will only run on an NT system. Figure 7.1 shows the User Manager for Domains.

Figure 7.1.
*The NT User
Manager for Domains.*

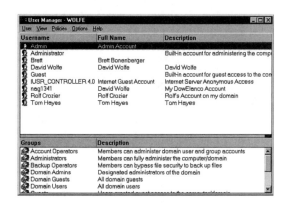

This section will not cover all aspects of the UMD. It will cover how to create security groups and perform basic user management tasks.

The top portion of the UMD shows the members of the currently selected domain (which is displayed at the very top of the UMD). The bottom portion of the UMD shows the security groups for the current domain. By default, NT comes preconfigured with a full range of security groups.

This chapter assumes that you have an understanding of the basic UMD functions, such as creating new user accounts and assigning them to local groups (the Users group or the Administrators group, for example).

NT Security Groups

NT security uses two kinds of groups, local and global. The difference between the two is difficult to grasp at times. In general, local groups define security for groups of users only on the local domain. Global groups are used to group users from one domain so that they can easily be granted access rights on another domain. Trust relationships can be established between two or more NT domains that make it simple for users of one domain to access resources found in another domain without requiring the user to get an actual login account on the other domain. Global security groups can only contain users, whereas local groups can contain users and other groups.

Another major difference between local and global groups is that by default, global groups have no permissions assigned to them. Only local groups have permissions for NT actions. Global groups are primarily used for grouping sets of users. In order to assign permissions for various NT activities, users must be assigned to a local group.

In the lower portion of the UMD, the globe and users icon denotes a global group, and the computer and users icon denotes a local group.

The best approach to NT security for Microsoft Proxy Server users is to create at least one global group for Internet users. If you need to separate out users for various Internet protocols (such as FTP, HTTP, Gopher, or any of the protocols supported by the WinSock Proxy such as NNTP, SMTP, or POP3), you can create global groups for each protocol and assign users to those groups for easy installation into the security definitions within Microsoft Proxy Server.

Creating a Global Security Group

To create a global group, follow these steps:

1. Click the File menu in the User Manager for Domains.
2. Click the New Global Group selection.
3. The New Global Group dialog box will appear, as shown in Figure 7.2.

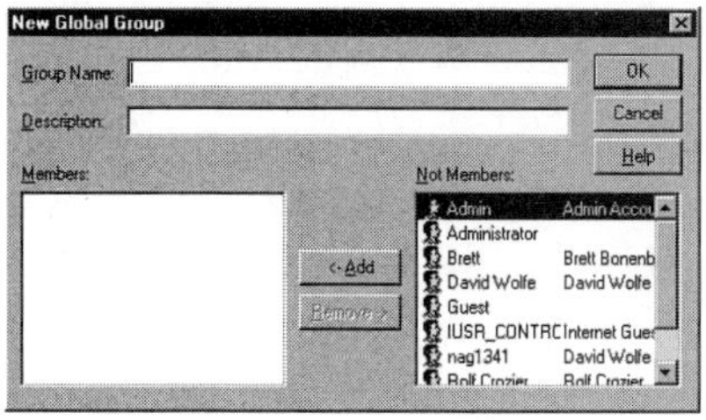

Figure 7.2.
Adding a new global group.

4. The name of the group should appear in the Group Name field. In this example it should be "Proxy Users".

5. The Description field can be any description you want to give this group.

6. Next, you will need to indicate which users should be members of this group. The Not Members list shows all users who are not currently members of this group. Because this is a new group, the Not Members list shows all NT users. Select all users who should be allowed general proxy access and then click Add.

7. Click OK, and the Proxy Users group will be created and a set of users defined.

Make sure you do not add the IUSR_servername user to the group. This account is created by the IIS installation routine and is used for anonymous access to IIS services. If this account is added to the group, anonymous users will be granted access to whatever features you assign to the Proxy Users group. This account should only be dealt with on an individual basis and never assigned to any global group.

Once the group is created, it can then be used within Microsoft Proxy Server to define access to various protocols. If this group needs to have special NT network permissions granted to it, the group can be nested within an existing local group that already has the permissions assigned to it. This approach is a simple way of cutting down some of the management time spent on security. If a group of users needs to have certain access permissions in more than one domain, two groups should be created, one local and one global. Both can have the same name. Users should then be assigned to the global group, and the global group should be nested within the local group. The local group can then be granted whatever permissions are needed, and those permissions will filter down to the global group users.

The next step is to grant this group access to a supported protocol, either in the Web Proxy or the WinSock Proxy.

Granting Proxy Permission to the New Group

Open the IIS Service Manager, and then open the properties for the Web Proxy. I will discuss how to grant permission to a group within Microsoft Proxy Server, but Chapter 8, "Configuring Proxy Server Security and Authentication," covers in greater detail the issues associated with Microsoft Proxy Server configuration. Once you have opened properties of the Web Proxy, select the Permissions tab. Figure 7.3 shows this dialog box.

By default, no permissions are configured for any protocol in Microsoft Proxy Server. Therefore, no users have access to get out to the Internet through the Web Proxy (or the WinSock Proxy). In order to grant access permission to the new Proxy Users group, do the following:

1. Select the protocol you wish to grant access to in the Protocol drop-down list. For this example, I'll select the WWW (HTTP) protocol.

2. Click the Add button. This will call up a dialog box for adding groups or users to the access list for this protocol. This dialog box is shown in Figure 7.4.

Figure 7.3.
Web Proxy Permis-
sions.

Figure 7.4.
The Add Users and
Groups dialog box.

The List Names from the drop-down list will allow you to select any domain you currently have access to. Access to foreign domains can be through a trust relationship or from having a parallel account in other domains. By default, you will be selecting users and groups from the local domain.

The default only lists both local and global groups. However, you can list users by clicking the Show Users button. This will display the users of the domain as well as the groups. Configuring individual users is OK for small networks or special cases, but can be a management nightmare for medium or large networks. You should always work with groups whenever possible.

3. Scroll down the Names list until the Proxy Users group is displayed.

4. Highlight the Proxy Users group, and click the Add button. This will add the Proxy Users group to the Add Names list.

5. You can select any additional groups or users to grant WWW access permission to if you have that need.

6. Click OK to return to the Permissions tab, and the group will show up in the Grant Access To list area as having access to use the WWW protocol.

The Members button on the Add Users and Groups dialog box will display a list of users for the currently highlighted group. This is shown in Figure 7.5.

Figure 7.5.
Displaying the members of a group.

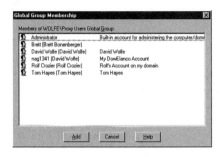

If more than one group is selected, this button will not be available. The Add button at the bottom of this dialog box will add the group to the Add Name list on the Add Users and Groups dialog box. It is not for adding additional users to the group. This function allows you to view which users are members of the group, if you can't recall from memory.

The Search button on the Add Users and Groups dialog box will let you search for users or groups on the local domain, or on domains that you have access to (either through a trust relationship, or by having a parallel account on the other domain(s)). Figure 7.6 shows this dialog box.

Figure 7.6.
Searching for a user or group.

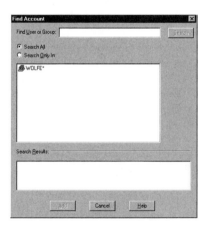

In this dialog box, you can indicate which domains to search and the name of the user or group you want to search for. You can search in the local domain or in all available domains. By default, all domains will be searched. If my network had access to other domains, the other domains would be listed as well.

Search results will be displayed in the lower area. Elements of the search result can be selected and the Add button can be clicked to add the user or group to the permissions list.

Once you have added the Proxy Users group to the permission list for the WWW protocol, the users of that group will be able to use Web browsers through Microsoft Proxy Server Web Proxy to access WWW sites on the Internet.

Complete this process for all of the protocols (WWW, FTP, Gopher, or Secure) to which you need to grant users permissions. The process for adding permissions to WinSock Protocols is very similar, but the WinSock Proxy has special universal access settings that make it easier to grant global protocol permissions for a group of users. This will be covered in greater detail in Chapter 8.

Understanding Users' Access Rights

Users' access rights are network function permissions which are assigned to local groups. User rights can grant permission to perform such actions as logging on to the PDC, and performing file backup on files owned by other users. Groups can have access rights assigned to them, and individual users can have additional specific access rights granted to them without having to be part of a group that already has the desired right. Accessing the User Rights Policy configuration dialog box is done through the User Rights option on the Policy menu in the User Manager for Domains. Figure 7.7 shows this dialog box.

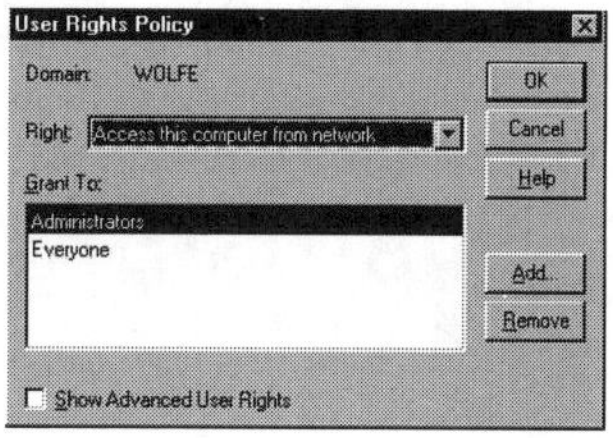

Figure 7.7.
The User Rights dialog box.

The Right drop-down list can be used to select which system right to assign to a group or a user. The Grant To list shows which groups and users already have the selected right.

The Add button can be used to assign other groups or users the selected right. The Add button will produce a dialog box which is identical to the one shown earlier in Figure 7.4. From this dialog box, you can select a group or user to whom to grant the selected right.

The Show Advanced User Rights check box will make available an expanded set of user rights to configure.

Accessing Microsoft Proxy Server requires no special user rights. Access to protocols supported by both the Web Proxy and the WinSock Proxy is controlled purely on a group or individual user basis. Some inexperienced network administrators get confused by the difference between user rights and group access. User rights are solely associated with performing pre-established network functions. To become more familiar with what user rights are part of the NT operating system, enable Show Advanced User Rights and scroll through the right drop-down list. Most of the rights are self-explanatory.

Controlling Inbound Access from the Internet

When Microsoft Proxy Server is installed, two elements of NT are altered so that security is enhanced. The first element that is altered is IP Forwarding. IP Forwarding is a setting found within the TCP/IP settings. This is turned off. It controls whether or not NT will forward IP packets between network interfaces in managers (such as a network card and a RAS connection to an Internet Provider). Under conditions wherein a dedicated full-time Internet connection is available to a network, and each workstation on the LAN is configured for its own direct Internet access, IP Forwarding must be enabled for workstations to pass their packets out to the Internet and vice versa. This in itself will halt all inbound traffic at the NT server, which is connected to the Internet.

To further restrict access to the NT server from clients connecting from the Internet, Microsoft Proxy Server disables listening on all TCP/IP ports which do not have permissions set for them. This means that any Internet server application (such as an FTP server, a Telnet server, or a POP3 server) running on the connected NT server will be unable to hear any external inbound traffic until permissions are set for the associated protocol in the WinSock Proxy. The Web Proxy only listens to port 80 for traffic. If permissions are set for any of the supported protocols in the Web Proxy, port 80 will be listened to for inbound traffic.

Isolating Microsoft Proxy Server on Its Own Domain

If you want to set your network security at a very high level for proxy access, one approach is to set up the NT server running Microsoft Proxy Server as a primary domain controller of its own domain. A one-way trust relationship can then be established between the Proxy domain and the network domain. The Proxy domain would be set to trust the network domain, but the network domain would not trust the Proxy domain. This arrangement will further limit the access that can take place between the proxy server and all other systems on the network domain.

This arrangement also works well when the network is not set as a domain, but rather as a workgroup. The NT server running Microsoft Proxy Server can be set on a primary domain controller of its own domain, which will give greater security control and allow easier expansion for future growth.

Summary

NT Security is fairly easy to understand and administer. The global nature of an NT domain makes is very simple to manage a group of users and grant them permission to access such things as Microsoft Proxy Server. How you structure your access groups depends on what level of control you need to have over your LAN users. If you have a large LAN with a wide range of users needing different types of access, setting up multiple global groups will help you maintain easy control. Setting users as members of global groups will also allow you to grant access to users from other domains to use a Microsoft Proxy Server on your domain, and vice versa.

CHAPTER 8

Configuring Proxy Server Security and Authentication

The methods with which client applications gain access to both sides of Microsoft Proxy Server (the Web Proxy and the WinSock Proxy) can be difficult to understand if you are not familiar with network security models. This chapter details how clients gain authentication when attempting to use Microsoft Proxy Server services. Both the Web Proxy server and the WinSock Proxy server are discussed independently because security is handled differently by each server.

General Client Security Overview

When any entity on a network attempts to access a secured resource, it must present the right credential to the controller of that resource before access will be permitted. This includes access to network printers, shared directories, and server services such as Microsoft Proxy Server. Presentation of credentials can be a very subtle process, completely hidden from the user requiring no user interaction, or it can be a totally interactive process where the network user must indicate a valid username, password, and (in the case of NT-based networks) the network domain to which to present the credentials. NetWare-based networks with NetWare Directory Services are similar in nature to NT-based domains in that there is an overriding authority for servers called the Tree. For the security discussion in this chapter, I focus only on NT-based networks.

The two halves of Microsoft Proxy Server can be set to follow security settings, or they can be set to ignore security settings and permit any access from any client regardless of what credentials they might try to present. In fact, when no security is used by Microsoft Proxy Server, no credentials will be demanded from clients.

When a user starts a Windows machine (Windows for Workgroups, Windows 95, or Windows NT), if the system is configured correctly, Windows will prompt the user for logon information. Logon information can be obtained through a standard Windows Logon or by a domain logon. Of the two logon methods, a domain logon is by far the most secure and useful in a complete network environment.

Windows Logon

Windows 95 workstations can be set to perform a standard Windows Logon through the Network Control Panel. By default, when a network card is present in a Windows 95 computer, all available network clients will be installed. This includes the Microsoft Network client and the default Novell NetWare client. For this chapter, the Novell NetWare client will be ignored. The Windows 95 operating system requires the installation of special network client software if the workstation will be accessing servers of that network type. A standard Windows Logon will not be sufficient to gain access to secured NT servers. The Microsoft Network client must be installed before Windows 95 will be able to present credentials to an NT server in the correct format.

Setting a Windows 95 computer to perform only a standard Windows Logon without the presence of the Microsoft Network client will only provide local machine security. Access to NT servers that are part of a domain will not be possible. Access to any Windows workgroup server won't be possible either. The Microsoft Network client controls network access to all Microsoft-based servers. Figure 8.1 shows the configuration area for controlling the logon method used by a Windows 95 machine.

However, a Windows workstation can be set to perform a standard Windows Logon and still have access to network resources when the Microsoft Network client is present. When a standard Windows Logon occurs, a network user is presented with a logon dialog box that asks for username and password. Once entered, Windows checks for the presence of a password list of the given name. If found, the password the user has given will be checked against the stored (and encrypted) password in the password list file. If the two match, Windows permits the logon and the user continues into the operating system. If the two passwords do not match,

Windows will prompt the user again for a new password (or the user can enter a new username and password). If there is no password list for the username given, Windows prompts for confirmation of the given password and a new password list is created.

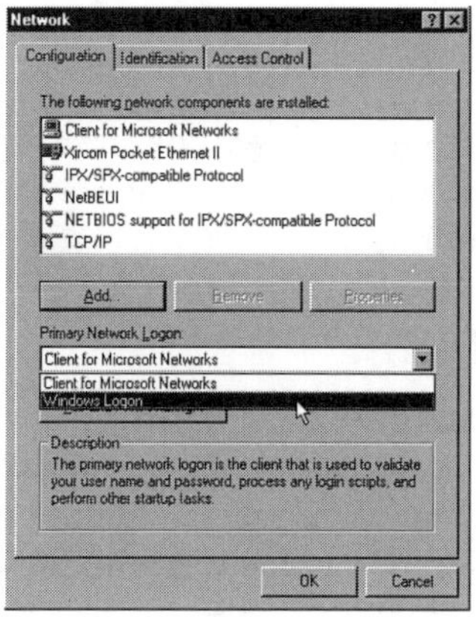

Figure 8.1.
Controlling the logon method used by Windows 95.

Note that this logon process does not involve in any way authentication by a central security agent like an NT domain controller. After a user logs in with a standard Windows Logon, the user is still unknown to the network. Only when the user attempts to access a secured network resource will the workstation be forced to present the logon credentials to the security agent requiring them. However, if the Microsoft Network client is configured to perform a domain logon, immediate network authentication will be attempted (to the default domain indicated in Microsoft Network client properties) using the username and password given at the Windows Logon dialog box. If the name and password given at the Windows Logon dialog box are not valid in the default domain, a second domain logon dialog box will be presented requiring a valid domain username and password. This means that, to Windows, a user can be known by two (or even more) identities. To Windows itself, the user is known by his or her Windows Logon. To NT servers, the user will be known by the network credentials he has presented (or the credentials that were automatically presented). If Novell NetWare servers are participating on the network, a user may be known by a *third* identity, that of his NetWare logon.

If a Windows Logon is used as the primary logon, all subsequent client logon credentials can be stored in the password list created by Windows. This means that subsequent logons will proceed without the user needing to enter a username and password for each network client installed in Windows. Changing secondary network client passwords can be done through the Password icon in Control Panel, or the password list can be deleted and the logon process can be redone (this approach is often the easiest way of changing a password for a secondary client).

If a standard Windows Logon is used, but the Microsoft Network client is set not to log on to a domain, no immediate network authentication is performed. Network authentication will be done when a network resource is accessed (for example, attempting to view a resource list of an NT server listed in the Network Neighborhood). When this is the case, the password list will be consulted for domain logon information. If none is found, the current Windows Logon name and password will be presented to a domain controller in the domain of the server being accessed. If the Windows Logon username and password are not valid in the domain being consulted, permission to access resources in that domain will not be granted and the user will not be prompted to enter new credentials.

A standard Windows Logon is very low in security because the password list files can easily be deleted or modified on the local machine. For a more advanced security model, a domain-based logon must be performed.

Domain Logon

The second type of Windows Logon that can be performed is known as a domain based logon. This type of logon is similar to a standard Windows Logon except that the credentials entered by the user will be immediately presented to an NT domain controller for authentication. The logon dialog box is nearly the same except that an additional field for indicating the logon domain is present.

In order for this type of logon to be used, the Microsoft Network client must be selected as the Primary Network Logon. Setting the Microsoft Network client as the Primary Network Logon is not the only configuration that needs to be done. Further network configuration to indicate a domain logon should be performed. Once the Primary Network Logon has been set to Microsoft Network client, the properties for the Microsoft Network client need to be altered. This is done by highlighting the Microsoft Network client entry in the components list and then clicking the Properties button. Figure 8.2 shows the Client for Microsoft Networks Properties dialog box.

Figure 8.2.
*Client for Microsoft
Networks Properties.*

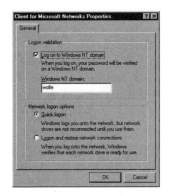

As you can see, the settings for controlling domain logon and the domain to log on to are clear. Once the Log on to Windows NT domain check box is checked and a domain name is given, all logons from that machine will be authenticated by a controller in the indicated domain. This will provide immediate network authentication. Network authentication is what Microsoft Proxy Server needs (most of the time) for it own validation purposes.

When a domain logon is performed at startup, a password list will be created for the user logging on to the system. This is done in case a domain controller cannot be found in the future. This permits a user to log on to a Windows machine based on the validation data contained in the password list, even when a domain controller cannot be found (for example, when the network is down). In this logon scenario, the Windows Logon name and password will match the domain logon name and password. When a standard Windows Logon is performed first, the logon information between the Windows Logon and the domain logon may be different.

Suggested Logon Method

"Enough of your babble," I hear you say. What does it all mean? I agree, trying to keep track of how the logon process works can get very confusing. The easiest way of setting a Windows machine to log on to a network is to set it to perform a domain logon. This will provide the highest security and immediate network authentication. This approach necessitates that a domain controller be present somewhere on the network to field all logon attempts.

If your network does not contain any domain controllers, you will need to set workstations to perform standard Windows Logons, but this necessitates that the logon information be unverifiably correct. When I say unverifiable, I mean that a user can log on with bogus credentials and will never know it until he attempts to access a network resource and gets an access denied error. However, problems other than a bad username and password can cause access denied errors, and troubleshooting this error without a central domain authority can be a real hassle.

When there is no central domain authority for a network workgroup, each NT server on the network is an island which follows its own security database. Usernames and passwords configured on NT servers that are set up as workgroup machines are not shared among other NT servers, even when those servers are members of the same workgroup. When a user attempts to access an NT workgroup server, the workstations present network credentials directly to that server. That server permits or denies access to the requested resource or service based on its own security database.

As long as the username and password are valid for a domain resource that a network user is attempting to access, permission will be granted. This means that if a user gains validation in one domain, and his credentials are valid in another domain, access to the second domain will be permitted. This process of having parallel accounts in multiple domains is difficult to manage from a network administrator's point of view, but it does overcome certain difficulties.

Another arrangement known as a trust relationship can be established between two or more domains to allow users from one domain to have access to resources in another. If your network is such that it has multiple domains, you should read up on the benefits of creating trusts between domains for the purpose of allowing users access to both domain resources.

Simply put, when deciding what the best logon method is, use a domain logon when a domain controller is present and use a standard Windows Logon when a domain controller is not present. For standard Windows Logons, be sure that the logon information used by network users is correct for the servers they will need to access. Simultaneous workgroup logons are not supported under Windows, so parallel accounts must exist on all workgroup servers that network users must access.

Web Proxy Authentication

Now that you have an understanding of how a network user is known on a network, let's proceed to discussing how the Web Proxy side of Microsoft Proxy Server grants or denies access to its services. The first element of the Web Proxy that needs to be covered is how it accepts authentication requests.

Remember that the Web Proxy is a fully CERN-compliant HTTP proxy and as such can be accessed by operating systems other than Windows. Any operating system that supports the TCP/IP protocol can run applications that can talk to the Microsoft Proxy Server Web Proxy. This being the case, the Web Proxy has to have a way of finding out who is attempting to access its services when the standard Windows network security layer is not usable.

The WWW Service is the actual security controlling mechanism used by the Web Proxy. Because the Web Proxy runs as a sub-service of the WWW Service, the security mechanisms configured in the WWW Service also apply to the Web Proxy service. The Service tab of the WWW Service Properties dialog box contains the configuration elements that control which security mechanisms are permitted. This is shown in Figure 8.3.

Figure 8.3.
The Service tab of the
WWW Service
Properties dialog box.

The Password Authentication portion of this tab contains the configuration for the permitted security mechanisms. There are three forms of security negotiation that the WWW Service (and therefore the WWW Proxy) can perform. These security methods are:

- Anonymous
- Basic (Clear Text)
- Windows NT Challenge/Response

Checking each security method enables it. The following sections discuss each security method in detail.

Anonymous

If the Anonymous security method is enabled, any client can have access to the WWW Proxy service without providing a valid username and password that can be found in the NT security database. Most practiced Internet users know what anonymous access involves. Generally, anonymous access is gained by entering a username of "anonymous" at a username prompt, and then entering an e-mail address as the password. When Anonymous security is enabled, all non-Windows clients will access the WWW Service and the Web Proxy server as anonymous clients. This will override Basic security.

When Anonymous security is enabled, clients will never see an authentication dialog box pop up in their browser or FTP client when attempting to access the Web Proxy. For Web Proxy anonymous access, no username or password will be required. This is unlike standard anonymous FTP access when a user is prompted to enter a name of "anonymous" and an e-mail address as a password.

If your goal is to allow all of your network users unlimited access to the Web Proxy, allowing only Anonymous security is not the best approach. The Anonymous security mechanism is mainly to be used with the actual WWW Service itself and not with the Web Proxy server. This is a double-edged sword that Microsoft has created. On the one hand, if your NT server runs the WWW Service along side of the Web Proxy for external Internet users, you will want to enable Anonymous security so that external Internet users are not required to enter a name and password to access your Internet site. However, enabling Anonymous security opens up the Web Proxy to any non-Windows network client wanting external Internet access. It's a bad paradox that I hope Microsoft will fix in the near future.

There are other ways of permitting any valid network user access to any protocol supported by the Web Proxy without enabling Anonymous security. These security issues will be discussed later in this chapter. It's a tough decision to make. Enable Anonymous security if you have no need to control internal access to the Web Proxy and want external Internet users to freely access your Web site. Disable Anonymous access if you want to control internal access to the Web Proxy, but require external Internet users to provide a valid username and password. For Web Proxy control, I suggest you disable Anonymous access.

Basic (Clear Text)

When this form of security is enabled, clients can pass their credentials to the Web Proxy via a low-level encryption method. This is done in a very simplistic encoding format that can be easily intercepted and decoded by devoted hackers. However, it is the only form of authentication available to non-Windows clients.

When Windows clients access the Web Proxy server with a browser such as Netscape Navigator or Microsoft Internet Explorer, and Basic security is the only security enabled, an authentication dialog box will pop up and allow you to enter a username and password. Figure 8.4 shows the proxy authentication dialog box that Internet Explorer presents.

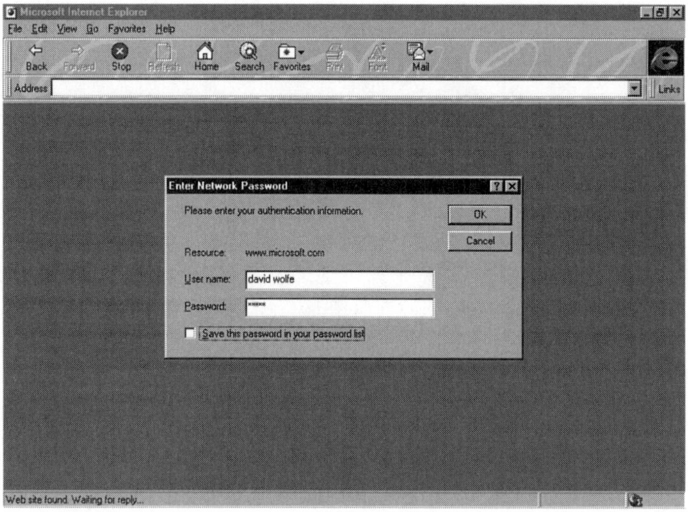

Figure 8.4.
The Internet Explorer proxy authentication dialog box.

This name and password combination will be checked against the NT user security database for authentication. Microsoft Proxy Server is the service which initiates the authentication request to the system. Once the user has been validated, the Web Proxy will consult its own security configuration to find out what protocols the user has access to. Remember that once a user has been authenticated, Microsoft Proxy Server will know what NT security groups the user has access to. This means that clients under other operating systems, such as Macintosh, will also be able to use Basic security to gain access to the Web Proxy even though they might not have a full Microsoft Network client connection to the NT server running Microsoft Proxy Server. Figure 8.5 shows the proxy authentication dialog box presented by Netscape Navigator on the Mac.

The current versions of Netscape are only capable of performing Basic proxy authentication. Credentials submitted through a Basic security connection will be checked against either the current NT user database, in the case of a stand-alone NT server, or the domain security database, in the case of a NT server participating in a domain. Users can submit credentials from another domain on the username line by entering the username as something like:

```
wolfe\"david wolfe"
```

The first part of the name is the reference to the domain to check, and the portion after the \ refers to the account name. Double quotes are needed when the account name contains a space. Referencing an account in an external domain requires a trust between the current domain and external domain. Microsoft Proxy Server does not have the ability to pass authentication requests to another domain, unless the authentication name contains a reference to where the credentials should be presented. A trust relationship must exist between the two domains in order for the client to be granted access.

Figure 8.5.
Proxy authentication
of Netscape Navigator
on the Mac.

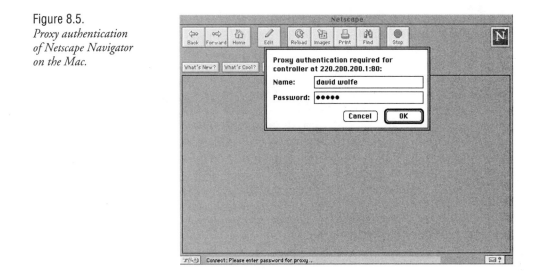

NT Challenge/Response

This is the highest form of authentication that the Web Proxy can perform. It is only available between clients that support NT Challenge/Response and the Web Proxy. This is a proprietary Microsoft form of authentication and is used by standard Windows workstations and NT servers. The only current client that supports NT Challenge/Response is Internet Explorer. Understand that all authentication discussed in this chapter is negotiated between Internet client and Microsoft Proxy Server. At no time is the operating system itself performing any negotiation with Microsoft Proxy Server. An Internet client may be able to draw on existing logon information, but the client itself is passing the information to Microsoft Proxy Server and receiving its responses. It is for this reason that the client application must support NT Challenge/Response in order to utilize its advanced security. The current versions of Netscape Navigator (as of the writing of this book) do not support NT Challenge/Response in any way.

This form of authentication utilizes the existing user logon information for validation to the Web Proxy. When a client attempts to access the Web Proxy, it sends an authentication demand back. If NT Challenge/Response is enabled, this is the first authentication form that is demanded. If the client supports NT Challenge/Response, it will automatically respond with the current domain logon information that the user presented when he first logged in to the Windows operating system. The username and password given during a standard Windows Logon will be used if there has not yet been a domain logon.

Clients running on other operating systems can use NT Challenge/Response. It is not a feature that is necessarily embedded in the operating system itself. Obviously, clients running on other operating systems may not yet have any default user information they can automatically send to the Web Proxy. In these cases, the user will be presented with a dialog box for entering username, password, and logon domain. For example, Internet Explorer 2.1 for the Mac attempts to respond with an NT-formatted response when it attempts to access the Web Proxy and NT Challenge/Response is enabled. This is shown in Figure 8.6.

Figure 8.6.
The NT Challenge/
Response dialog box in
IE 2.1 for the Mac.

The dialog box is fairly clear. The user is prompted to give a username and password as well as indicate to which domain to present the credentials. If the domain is a domain other than the one the Web Proxy is running on, a trust must exist between the other domain and the Web Proxy domain or access will be denied even if the credentials are valid on the other domain. Unfortunately, Internet Explorer 2.1 for the Mac does not fully support NT Challenge/Response. Attempting to access the Web Proxy with Internet Explorer 2.1 through NT Challenge/Response will produce the dialog box shown in Figure 8.7.

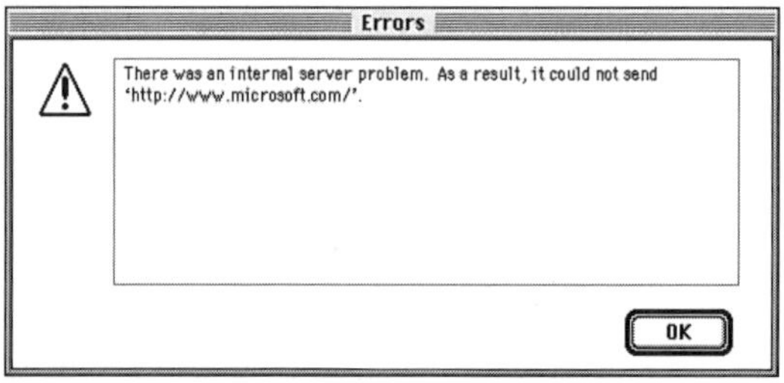

Figure 8.7.
IE 2.1 does not fully
support NT Challenge/
Response.

At present, Internet Explorer 3.0 for the Mac is available in beta form, but would not run on the test Mac I had available. Internet Explorer 3.0 for the Mac is supposed to fully support NT Challenge/Response authentication just as the Windows version of IE does. I assume the dialog box demanding credentials is nearly identical to the one shown in Figure 8.6, but I can't be certain of that.

When a network client authenticates to the Web Proxy with NT Challenge/Response, a much higher level of username and password encryption is used. This greatly decreases the chance that an intermediate hacker might steal vital information. Another aspect of NT Challenge/Response is party verification. When the negotiating process is begun during NT Challenge/Response, each side will attempt to prove to the other that he is who he says he is. A client that supports NT Challenge/Response will attempt to ensure that the target party requesting logon credentials is a valid server.

Anonymous Security with Basic Security

If Anonymous and Basic security are enabled, but NT Challenge/Response is disabled, some clients will be permitted anonymous access while others will be required to perform Basic logon to the Web Proxy. Some clients support password-less proxy access. This means that they can talk to a CERN-compliant proxy, but do not recognize the authentication demand the proxy may respond with. In these cases, where the client does not initially respond with an acknowledgment of an authentication demand, the Web Proxy will permit the client to continue as an anonymous access. If, however, the client acknowledges the demand response, the client will be required to provide valid logon credentials.

Anonymous Security with NT Challenge/Response

When Anonymous and NT Challenge/Response security are enabled, but Basic security is disabled, any client that is not capable of performing NT Challenge/Response authentication will be granted anonymous access to the Web Proxy. Those clients that do support NT Challenge/Response will be required to provide valid logon credentials through NT Challenge/Response.

If you establish an Internet Explorer 3.0-only policy in your company, you can force network users to adhere to the security configuration you create under the Web Proxy. Simply because you enable anonymous logon does not mean that anonymous logons have any rights in the Web Proxy. In order to fully utilize anonymous logons, the permissions for the Web Proxy protocols must be set for anonymous access. This will be covered shortly.

By severely limiting anonymous access to the Web Proxy, you can steer network users to Internet Explorer 3.0 because this browser will be the only one that can give them full proxy access. It will make Netscape Navigator useless to network users if Basic security is disabled and anonymous access is severely limited.

Basic Security with NT Challenge/Response Security

When Anonymous security is disabled, but Basic and NT Challenge/Response security are enabled, no anonymous access will be permitted to either the WWW Service or the Web Proxy. Clients will have to provide some form of authentication before they will be granted access to the Web Proxy. Obviously, this also passes through to the WWW Service, which in most cases is bad. Most network administrators want their Web site to be accessible to everyone on the

Internet. If you have the luxury of running your Web server from a different machine than the one running Microsoft Proxy Server, this problem is not a factor.

Using the Anonymous Account

When Internet Information Server (IIS) is first installed, a user account called IUSR_*servername* is created on the domain or in the local NT user database, if the NT server is a stand-alone server. Servername refers to the name of the NT server itself. For example, the account created on my network's primary domain controller was IUSR_controller 4.0. This user account is the account that controls the level of access given to anonymous logons for all Microsoft Internet server applications.

You'll note that in Figure 8.3, there is a field for entering the password for the anonymous account. Remember that the WWW server and the Web Proxy server actually present authentication requests to the NT security layer as they would any normal user logon. If you have a password assigned to the anonymous account, be sure to indicate that password in this field, or the WWW server and the Web Proxy server will be unable to gain anonymous authentication when necessary. Normally, the anonymous account can have no password assigned to it because it doesn't have rights to normal network resources.

By default, the presence of this account will grant anonymous users access to the WWW service without any further configuration needed. However, this is not true with the Web Proxy and WinSock Proxy services. In order to grant anonymous access to the protocols supported by the Web Proxy or the WinSock Proxy, protocol permissions must be granted to the IUSR_*servername* account just as permissions for any other network user is granted. This will be covered later in this chapter.

WinSock Proxy Security

In the current version of Microsoft Proxy Server, only NT Challenge/Response is used between the WinSock client software and the WinSock Proxy server. Because the WinSock client software runs under a Windows-based system, the underlying architecture is present for only NT Challenge/Response security negotiation.

In order for WinSock clients to access the WinSock Proxy, special client software must be installed. Client software is available for all flavors of Windows, but no other operating systems are supported yet. NT Challenge/Response authentication is built into the WinSock client software. The WinSock client software will automatically grab the current username and password from the system logon information and pass it correctly through to the WinSock Proxy when a WinSock client attempts to make external Internet contact.

Two new security DLL files are added to the \WINDOWS and \WINDOWS\SYSTEM directories when the WinSock client software is installed. These files are SECURITY.DLL (\WINDOWS) and SECUR32.DLL (\WINDOWS\SYSTEM). These libraries control WinSock client authentication to the WinSock Proxy server. Without these files, WinSock clients will be unable to access the WinSock Proxy.

IPX

One of the best security features of WinSock Proxy is its ability to utilize IPX as the transport protocol from WinSock Proxy to network client. Only the NT server running the WinSock Proxy needs to have the TCP/IP protocol installed (for communicating with the actual Internet). The WinSock Proxy can use the IPX protocol for communicating with actual network clients. This will make absolutely certain that any intrusion attempts into your network stop at the NT server running the WinSock Proxy because the TCP/IP protocol does not extend beyond the server itself.

Enabling and Disabling Access Control

All of this discussion about how security is handled goes out the window unless Access Control is enabled. On the Permissions tab for both the Web Proxy and the WinSock Proxy, you'll note a check box entitled Enable Access Control. When this check box is checked, the permission structure you set for either of the servers will be followed. If this check box is cleared, any user will be granted access to any protocol supported by the respective server.

This does not mean that anyone can log in to the services. The logon security methods defined for the Web Proxy must still be met before access to the actual service itself will be permitted. However, once a successful logon has been performed, no further access restrictions will be applied to the user accessing the service. Obviously, for WinSock Proxy accesses, clients must still meet the NT Challenge/Response logon requirements before being allowed to proceed.

Step-by-Step Breakdown of Each Logon Process

The following sections will give you a step-by-step definition of how a logon to the Web Proxy server proceeds. This will hopefully give you a better idea of how all of these pieces fit together.

An Anonymous Logon

This example of an anonymous logon assumes Netscape Navigator 3.0 will be used to access the outside Internet through the Web Proxy and that anonymous security is the only security method that can be used.

1. The browser attempts to contact an Internet site through the Web Proxy. If Basic security is disabled, the browser will have to rely on Anonymous security because it cannot perform NT Challenge/Response security.
2. The Web Proxy receives the Internet request.
3. The Web Proxy sends an NT Challenge/Response authentication demand to the browser.

4. The browser receives the authentication demand, but does not respond to it because it does not understand it.

5. Upon receiving no response to its authentication demand, the Web Proxy permits the browser to have anonymous level access to its services.

6. If the target site is an HTTP site and the HTTP protocol in the Web Proxy does not permit anonymous access, the Web Proxy will respond with an access denied message. If anonymous access is configured in the HTTP protocol under the Web Proxy, the Web Proxy will retrieve Internet data from the target site.

7. The Web Proxy begins acting as an intermediary between the browser and the target Internet site.

A Basic Logon

The following example assumes that Netscape Navigator is used and that Basic security is enabled. In this example, all three forms of security can be enabled and because Netscape supports Basic security, it will respond to any Basic authentication demand. The operating system for this example does not matter.

1. The browser attempts to access an Internet site through the Web Proxy.

2. The Web Proxy receives the access request and issues an NT Challenge/Response authentication demand from the browser. The browser will not respond to this initial authentication demand because it does not understand it.

3. The Web Proxy will then send a Basic authentication demand that will be received and responded to by the browser.

4. The browser will display an authentication request dialog box for the user to fill out. This dialog box will ask for username and password.

5. After completing the necessary data and selecting OK, the browser will forward the authentication data to the Web Proxy.

6. The Web Proxy presents the logon credentials to the NT security layer for verification.

7. NT will check the credentials against the NT user database. If there is a match, the logon can proceed. If there is not a match, or if the user does not exist in the user database, the Web Proxy will receive an invalid logon response from the NT security layer and will then prompt the browser to attempt the logon again.

8. Once a valid set of credentials have been presented by the browser, the Web Proxy then examines its own permissions database to see whether the authenticated user has permission to access the protocol he is requesting.

9. If the user does not have access to the requested protocol, the Web Proxy will respond with an access denied message and the logon process will be halted.

10. If the user does have permission to use the requested protocol, the Web Proxy will begin acting as an intermediary between browser and target Internet site.

As you can see, there are many services involved with a Basic authentication. The NT user database is referenced and then the internal permissions settings of the Web Proxy are applied.

An NT Challenge/Response Logon

If a client supports NT Challenge/Response authentication, this form of authentication will be used above all others because it is attempted first. In this example, it is assumed that the browser is the Windows 95 version of Internet Explorer 3.0.

1. The browser attempts to access an Internet site through the Web Proxy server.

2. The Web Proxy server issues an NT Challenge/Response authentication demand to the browser.

3. The browser receives the authentication demand and acknowledges it.

4. The browser references the existing logon information given at the time of system startup and passes the username and password to the Web Proxy. The browser also sends information about which domain to present the credentials to.

5. The Web Proxy receives the data and passes it to the necessary domain for validation. If it is the local domain, no trust relation is required. If it is an external domain, the external domain must be trusted by the local domain.

6. The NT security layer of the target domain processes the logon request and gives a thumbs up or a thumbs down, depending on username and password combination.

7. If the logon is permitted, the Web Proxy begins to act as the intermediary between the browser and the target Internet site.

If the authentication attempt is originating from a non-Windows operating system, the user will need to provide on-the-fly logon information (username, password, and logon domain) when the browser demands credentials.

This process also applies to WinSock clients accessing the Internet through the WinSock Proxy, because the WinSock client software supports NT Challenge/Response authentication.

The Difference Between a Basic and an NT Challenge/Response Logon

You can actually see the difference between a Basic logon and an NT Challenge/Response logon by viewing the current sessions through the General tab of the Web Proxy configuration. Figure 8.8 shows the Current Sessions dialog box through the Web Proxy configuration.

The first session listed is a session between a Mac and the Web Proxy server. The client being used is Netscape Navigator 3.0 for the Mac. As you can see, the client passed along the logon credentials to the Web Proxy as david wolfe. Because this name does appear in the NT domain user database, access was granted.

Figure 8.8.
*Current Web Proxy
sessions.*

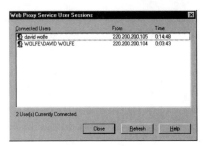

The second session listed is a session that started using Internet Explorer 3.0 from a Windows 95 workstation. The workstation was set to perform a domain logon to the WOLFE domain, and as such the user logged onto that workstation is known to the network as WOLFE\DAVID WOLFE. When Internet Explorer 3.0 was started on this machine, no authentication information was requested because IE was able to draw it from the operating system itself. The information was then passed along to the Web Proxy in the form you see listed in Figure 8.8, and validation was provided by the WOLFE domain controller.

Viewing current sessions doesn't give you a whole lot of detail about what's going on with the Web Proxy, but it is nice to see who is actually using the service. It would be much nicer if the session viewer showed exactly what Internet sites were being accessed and what data was being transferred. This would increase the network administrator's ability to police the Web Proxy and control access to the Internet. Perhaps this will be an added feature to later releases of Microsoft Proxy Server. Currently the network administrator has to go to the log files created by the Web Proxy to find out this type of data.

Setting Protocol Permissions

Once primary authentication has been gained, the user accessing either the Web Proxy or the WinSock Proxy must still have permission to use the requested protocol. The Permissions tabs of both the Web Proxy and the WinSock Proxy are utilized in the exact same manner. Each proxy controls a certain set of protocols. Users or groups of users will be granted permission to use these protocols. Unless permissions are configured for the necessary protocols, access will still be denied even if the user trying to gain access presents valid network credentials. Figure 8.9 shows the Permissions tab of the WinSock Proxy.

The supported protocols are listed in the Protocol drop-down list. The Figure shows that the NNTP (Network Newsgroup Transport Protocol) is selected. The Add button will allow you to select a user or group of users to whom you will grant permission to access this protocol. Chapter 6, "Configuring Proxy Server," covers the actual process of adding users and groups to the protocol permission list.

Figure 8.9.
The WinSock Proxy
Permissions tab.

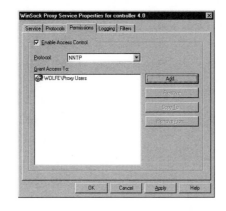

There is a special Protocol setting you can configure in the WinSock Proxy Permissions tab that is not present in the Web Proxy. This protocol is the Unlimited Access protocol. Any group assigned to this protocol will be granted access to use all other protocols under the WinSock Proxy. If you do not want to worry about which network users are accessing which protocols, you can add the Everyone group to the Unlimited Access option. This can be dangerous, however, because it opens the WinSock Proxy to nearly any request generated by an external Internet client. It might be a good idea to follow the instructions given in Chapter 7, "Configuring NT Security for an Open Environment," for setting up an NT security group for users who need some form of proxy access. That group can then be added to the Unlimited Access option.

Once you have set the necessary protocol permissions, network users will have the ability to use the two proxy servers to access the outside Internet from their desktops. The last configuration element that needs to be addressed is site filtering.

Site Filtering

Site filtering is a process whereby the Web and WinSock Proxy servers permit or prohibit access to the Internet based on a list of permissible sites. By default, neither the Web Proxy nor the WinSock Proxy will prohibit access to any site on the Internet. This means network users will have free reign to browse where they want. To some companies with small Internet connections, this can pose a substantial problem. The Filters tab on both the Web Proxy and the WinSock Proxy configuration interfaces allows the network administrator to indicate to which sites users are permitted or denied access.

A general permit or deny filter policy must first be established. If you want to allow access only to a handful of sites on the Internet, it will be easiest to set a general deny filter and then list exceptions to this rule. However, if your users need access to most of the Internet, but you want to make sure they stay off a certain site, you can set a general permit policy and then list exceptions to that rule. Figure 8.10 shows the Filters tab of the WinSock Proxy.

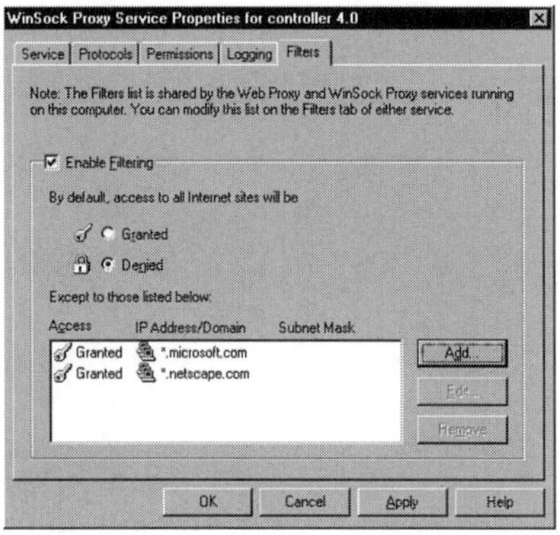

Figure 8.10.
The Filters tab of the
WinSock Proxy.

The figure shows that a general deny policy has been set and that users will only be granted access to sites within the `netscape.com` and `microsoft.com` domains. Chapter 6 covers the details of how to establish the actual filter settings.

Unfortunately, the current version of Microsoft Proxy Server does not have the ability to perform site filtering for individual users. If you have only a few problem users, you cannot as of yet filter their access. The filter settings made on the Filters tab in the Web Proxy and the WinSock Proxy apply to all proxy users.

Summary

To most medium or large companies using Microsoft Proxy Server, the most important feature of the service will be the security and control element. Understanding how this service deals with user authentication and access is essential to maintaining a well-run proxy server. Hopefully, this chapter gave you the information you need to correctly manage all security elements of Microsoft Proxy Server.

PART IV

Use

Concepts and Realities of Name Resolution with Proxy Server

Name resolution is an element of a network that can make a network administrator's job ten times easier. If you are familiar with the Internet or TCP/IP concepts, you should already know what name resolution means. But, to be certain, this chapter covers this topic from the basics on up so forgive me if I cover topics that are already well known to you.

Name resolution is the action of translating a written, alpha-type Internet address (like pandy.com) into the actual TCP/IP numeric address (like 198.144.70.211). Of the two, the numeric address is the more important, though humans tend to have a problem remembering only numbers. The written form of an Internet address is only a convenience address.

A network can operate via the TCP/IP protocol completely without name resolution or it can have some service available that performs the act of translating an alpha name to an actual IP address. On a Windows NT 4.0–based network, two main methods of name resolution can be implemented to take care of this need. These two methods are WINS (Windows Internet Name Service) and DNS (Domain Name Service). Either of these services may be present on an NT network, or both can run parallel to each other to handle a wide range of needs a network might have.

This chapter will not cover how to completely set up a WINS and/or DNS server, but it will cover the two topics sufficiently to allow you to set them up to handle basic network client name resolution needs.

The Benefits of Name Resolution

Imagine this scenario. You are the network administrator of a 100+ workstation network. For your Internet needs, you are using Microsoft Proxy Server so that network users can have external access to your ISDN link to the Internet. Figure 9.1 diagrams this example.

Figure 9.1.
A sample network.

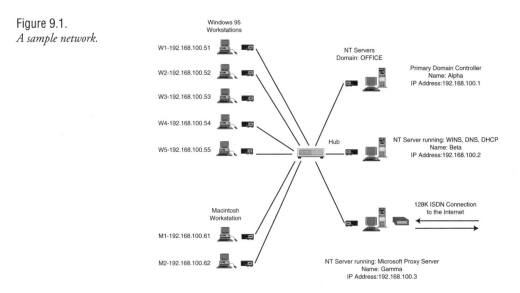

The following elements are in play:

- The NT domain is named OFFICE.
- The network protocol being used is TCP/IP.
- The IP subnet used for this network is 192.168.100.*. This subnet is one reserved by the InterNIC for use by private networks.
- This network has both Windows 95 and Macintosh workstations.

- The WINS, DNS, and DHCP (Dynamic Host Configuration Protocol) services are all running on the NT server named Beta.
- Microsoft Proxy Server is running on the NT server named Gamma.

Any other network information is unnecessary for this example. Make sure you have a good grasp of Figure 9.1. This figure shows only seven workstations, though I'll refer to the network as having more than 100 workstations.

Without any name resolution service available on this network, the network administrator must hard code the IP address location of Microsoft Proxy Server into each workstation. This could include several configurations on each workstation, depending on what Internet applications the workstations have installed. For example, Netscape Navigator does not follow any of the Internet settings made through the Internet control applet found in the Control Panel of Windows 95. Netscape Navigator utilizes its own internal configuration for addressing a proxy server. All Microsoft Internet applications, however, will follow the settings in the Internet section of Control Panel. If users use both Internet Explorer and Netscape Navigator, that means at least two separate configurations have to be dealt with.

Should the IP address location of Microsoft Proxy Server change on this network, the network administrator has a two- or three-day project altering all workstations on the network to see the new IP address. What is much more convenient is to let the name of the Microsoft Proxy Server machine control the location. The name used for resolution purposes can be the actual name of the Microsoft Proxy Server machine (which is not advised), or it can be a name created on the name resolution servers to stand for Microsoft Proxy Server.

Let's take, for example, the name "Proxy_Server." An entry of "Proxy_Server" in the name resolution service can be used to reference the IP address 192.168.100.3—the IP location of Microsoft Proxy Server. The name "Proxy_Server" can be added to the WINS or DNS databases as a static name. Which name resolution service workstations will use depends on what form of name resolution workstations can perform. When workstations resolve the name "Proxy_Server," they'll find out from the name server what IP to access for proxy access. In order to make network-wide changes to the proxy server location, all the network administrator has to do is alter the name server database entry for "Proxy_Server," and all network clients will begin to access the proxy server at the new IP address without having to do any reconfiguring.

Keep in mind that WINS name resolution is only supported in Windows environments. Macintosh, UNIX, and OS/2 operating systems do not support WINS name resolution of any kind. DNS, on the other hand, is universally accepted by all operating systems as a basic component of the TCP/IP protocol. Windows NT 4.0 can run both a WINS server and a DNS server in tandem, both working together to resolve any and all name resolution requests that come from any client. Many third-party DNS servers are now available for NT. However, only the built-in DNS server that comes with NT 4.0 has the ability to reference a WINS server if it gets a name resolution request it cannot handle.

Herein is the real beauty of NT 4.0 name resolution. To be quite honest, configuring a DNS server is a real pain unless you are a long-time UNIX guru and understand all the non-intuitive terms involved with DNS. With NT 4.0, you can use WINS for nearly all your name resolution needs and simply tell your DNS server to reference the WINS server for all requests it cannot handle. This way, you will only need to manage one database of names through the WINS Manager which, in my opinion, is a much, much easier task.

The Differences Between WINS and DNS

I've already mentioned a few differences between WINS and DNS. They both perform the same basic function—translating a name into an IP address for client requests. WINS, however, was designed as a flat database and DNS is a hierarchical database. For most networks, this is a minor difference, because most network administrators will only need to worry about a few static names and IP address combinations. When I say flat database, I mean that the database records of a WINS server are all "equal." If I want to reference two names in a WINS database, ftp.pandy.com and www.pandy.com, I simply create two records for these names. If, on the other hand, I want to add these two addresses to a DNS database, I add the names ftp and www to the pandy.com zone and associate the necessary IP addresses with them. The major benefit of DNS is that all DNS servers on the Internet work together to resolve names.

If a client attempts to resolve ftp.microsoft.com through the DNS server of his own ISP, the DNS of the ISP looks on the Internet for the Start of Authority (SOA) for the microsoft.com domain. Once found, the ISP's DNS server passes the request to the DNS server for the microsoft.com domain. Once the DNS server of the microsoft.com domain has the request, it simply looks in its database for the server "ftp" and sends the name resolution back to the client.

The major benefit of WINS is that it works in tandem with the NT DHCP server. Remember that on a network, a DHCP server is the application responsible for assigning dynamic IP addresses to workstations when they start up. Now the problem dynamic addresses cause on a network is that a workstation may never have the same IP twice. Therefore, it's difficult to find workstations by their IP addresses. For example, one of my Win95 workstations on my network is named "pentium." When this workstation starts up, it receives a new IP address from my NT server through DHCP. If any other workstation needs to address the "pentium" workstation through TCP/IP, they'll have to know the IP address of "pentium." Because the IP of "pentium" varies, there is no way of being certain what its address is at any given time. WINS allows network workstations to address the machine names of other workstations and their IP addresses will be doled out automatically. WINS tracks all IP addresses handed out by the DHCP server and maintains a dynamic database of workstation names to dynamic IP address associations. DNS does not have this ability.

However, because the NT 4.0 DNS server has the ability to reference a WINS server when its own database fails to resolve a name, it can now also resolve dynamic IP addresses through WINS for non-Microsoft clients. This plays very heavily when dealing with Microsoft Proxy Server, if the NT server that Microsoft Proxy Server is running on also gets its address dynamically like any other workstation. WINS can be used to track the IP location of the proxy server, and workstations can continue to reference the proxy server through one name even though the IP address of the proxy server may change periodically.

Using WINS

By default, the WINS server is not installed when NT Server 4.0 is installed. You can install it as a network service during installation if you choose. If you have not already installed WINS, follow these steps to install it:

1. Open the Network Control Panel (the easiest way is to right-click on Network Neighborhood and then click Properties).

2. Select the Services tab.

3. Click the Add button. NT will generate a list of known services. Scroll down until you see Windows Internet Name Service (see Figure 9.2). Click that.

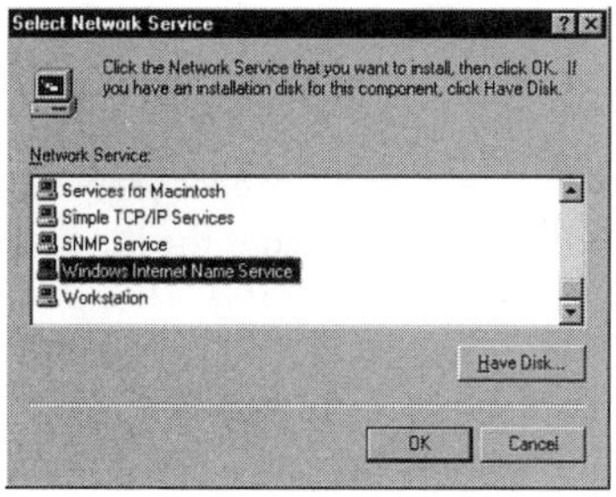

Figure 9.2.
The lists of known NT services.

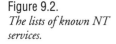

4. Click OK. NT will ask you for the location of the NT installation CD-ROM. Enter the location (typically e:\i386 for Intel-based systems) and click OK.

5. WINS will be installed and the system will need to be rebooted before it will become active.

Once installed and rebooted, you will find a new application in the Administrative Tools folder called WINS Manager. The WINS Manager is the main interface for modifying the WINS database. Figure 9.3 shows the WINS Manager.

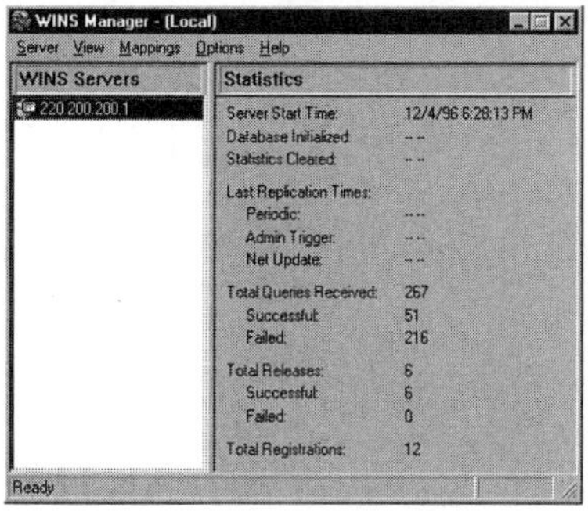

Figure 9.3.
The WINS Manager.

When the WINS Manager starts, it displays some stats for the local WINS services. Like nearly all NT service managers, the WINS Manager can be used to control WINS servers running on other NT servers on the network or even WINS Managers running on a machine across the Internet.

On my network, the WINS service is running on my primary NT server located at 220.200.200.1. This WINS server tracks all dynamic IP address assignments to all machines that obtain their IP addresses from the DHCP server (which is also running on the same NT server). To view the database of names, select Show Database from the Mappings menu. This database (shown in Figure 9.4) will display all mappings, both recent and current.

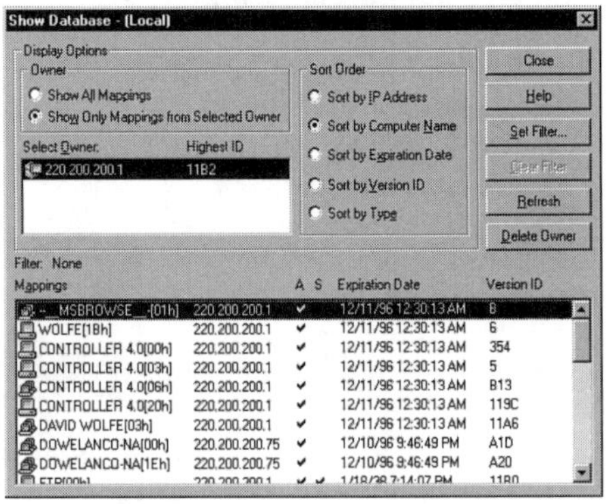

Figure 9.4.
The WINS database.

Figure 9.4 also shows both static (manually entered IP mappings) and standard (dynamically assigned) IP addresses. Viewing the WINS database is a good way of seeing when an IP address is set to expire. When an IP address is received from a DHCP server, it has a lease term assigned to it. Once that lease term is up, the client must renew the IP address from the DHCP or obtain a new IP. For our need right now, there is no functionality on this dialog box that needs to be covered. Feel free to experiment with viewing the database. It's a very informative experience that will give you some insight on how TCP/IP works.

The main functionality that I deal with in the WINS Manager is the ability to create static mappings. For example, on my own network, my FTP server and my WWW server both run on my NT server, located at 220.200.200.1. The actual machine name of the server is "Controller 4.0." The Internet domain I have created for my own network is pandy.com. Without creating a static entry for my FTP server, users on my network would have to address the FTP server as "Controller 4.0" rather than the more commonly accepted name of ftp.pandy.com. Keep in mind that all the discussion of this chapter is focused toward a network that does not have a valid, full-time connection to the Internet. All the information given here is focused toward setting up WINS and DNS to support a local network only. Connecting your network to the Internet and providing full DNS support to external clients is not covered here.

I can create an entry in the WINS database for ftp.pandy.com (associated with the IP 220.200.200.1, which is the IP of the server it is running on); and thereafter all network workstations will be able to access my FTP server through the name ftp.pandy.com.

The Static Mappings option on the Mappings menu is the gateway to adding and controlling static mappings. Select this option and the dialog box shown in Figure 9.5 will be displayed.

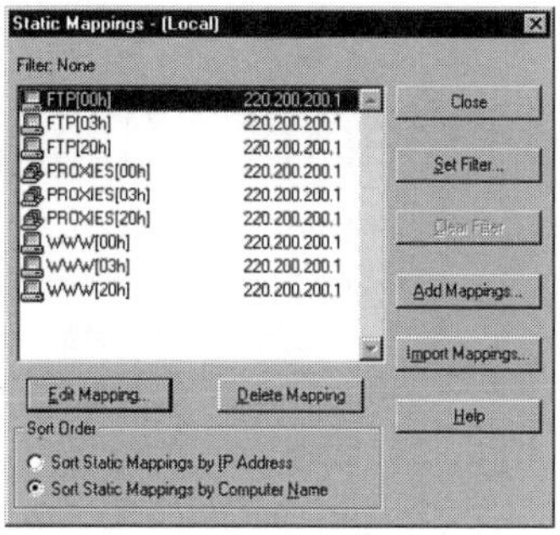

Figure 9.5.
Modifying static mappings in the WINS Manager.

As you can see, I've already created a few mappings for FTP, WWW, and PROXIES. Don't worry about this for right now. Their main purpose is for the DNS cascade to WINS. Right now, let's create an entry for ftp.pandy.com so workstations can use this name for accessing the FTP server in question.

1. Click the Add Mappings button. A dialog box will be displayed (shown in Figure 9.6).

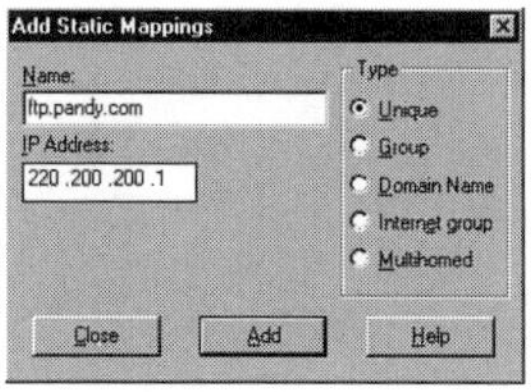

Figure 9.6.
Adding a static mapping to the WINS database.

2. Enter the name ftp.pandy.com in the Name field.

3. Enter the IP address 220.200.200.1 in the IP Address field.

4. By default, the Unique Type radio button is selected. This is the type of entry ftp.pandy.com is, so leave it unchanged.

5. Click Add and the WINS database entry for ftp.pandy.com at 220.200.200.1 will be created.

6. Click the Close button to return to the Static Mappings dialog box.

Several different types of WINS entry types can be created; however, for our needs, only unique and multi-homed entries matter. The definition for each type of entry is as follows:

■ Unique defines a singular entity on the network. Three separate references for a unique entry will be created. However, these are all part of a single entry.

■ A multi-homed entry is an entry that defines a group of servers associated with a single name. Later in this chapter I'll show you how to create a multi-homed entry to reference a group of proxy servers.

Once a static entry has been created, it is immediately available for client resolutions. The WINS server does not need to be stopped and restarted for the addition to be in effect. You can add static entries into the WINS database to reference any number of elements on your network that would not normally have an entry in the WINS database.

Creating Multi-homed Groups

Multi-homed groups are very simple to create under WINS. They can be created under DNS, but this is a harder process. It's far easier to create a multi-homed group under WINS and let the DNS server reference the WINS server when resolution requests for the group are received. Creating a multi-homed group is necessary to daisy chain (also known as a round-robin group) a set of independent proxy servers so that clients can access them as a single unit.

The real purpose of a multi-homed group is to provide support for systems which are members of two or more domains. For our purposes, we'll use it for grouping proxy servers.

When the Multihomed radio button is selected when adding a static mapping (Figure 9.6), the dialog box will change into one which looks like Figure 9.7.

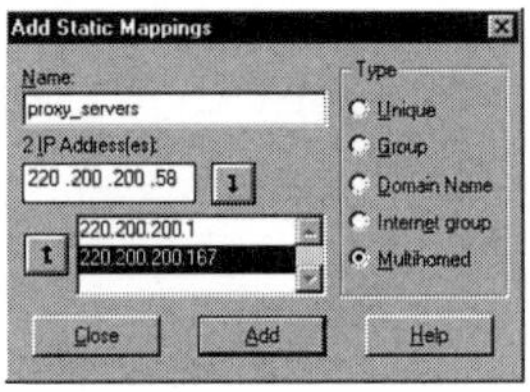

Figure 9.7.
Adding a multi-homed
static mapping.

To complete a multi-homed entry, do the following:

1. Enter a name for this group. In this example, I'll use the name proxy_servers.
2. Enter the IP address of the first proxy server. In this example, I'll use the address 220.200.200.1.
3. Click the down pointing arrow to the right of the IP address field. This will add the address to the list box.
4. Add any additional addresses to this group in the same manner. I'll add the IP addresses 220.200.200.167 and 220.200.200.58.
5. Click Add to add the entry to the WINS database.
6. Click Close to return to the Static Mappings dialog box.

Now, any client referencing the name "proxy_servers" will receive IP resolution for any one of the members of the group. Under WINS, which member of a multi-homed group that has its IP resolved for the group name depends on several factors, such as the requester's own subnet and so on. Considering these factors helps to ensure that the proxy server closest to the requester is the one that will have its IP address resolved for the name request. However, when no one member of the group stands out as the best choice, the WINS server will choose a member of the group randomly to have its name resolved for the request.

You can test this multi-homed group by using the PING command. Try pinging the group several times from a workstation on the same subnet (so the WINS server will randomize the selection of member resolution). You should find that the IP addresses listed in the group get randomly pinged. It may take a few attempts, but you will eventually see the ping target change.

Keep in mind that for this version of Microsoft Proxy Server, separate proxy servers do not work in concert. Meaning, they do not share cache data, security settings, log files, and filter settings. Each operates independently. Setting up a group of Web Proxy servers in a multi-homed group under WINS helps to automatically distribute the work load between all servers when it doesn't matter which server fields a client request for Internet access. If you want to control which clients access which proxy server when there is more than one proxy server for a network, you will have to reference each proxy server independently.

Hopefully, later versions of Microsoft Proxy Server will have the ability to truly cascade proxy servers without having to go through WINS to do it.

Setting Up DNS

Oh boy, setting up DNS… I have never claimed to be an expert on DNS; however, in the same breath, I can claim to have successfully set up my own DNS server to meet the needs of my own network. I will try to impart to you my experience in hope that you can do the same. If you are familiar with DNS, please don't be offended if my methods seem crude or poorly done. All I can say is, "It gets the job done!"

The focus of this section will be to show you how to set up your DNS server to do one thing: reference the WINS server for nearly all DNS name resolution requests. I personally prefer to use WINS as my primary name resolution database, though admittedly my needs are pretty minor in the grand scheme of Internet addressing. If you have a desire to use DNS as your primary name resolver, I suggest you run out and grab one of the multitude of books totally dedicated to covering how to set up a DNS server. This might be a little tricky though, because most of these books are customized to setting up DNS on a UNIX machine. Look around, I'm certain someone has written a DNS book on the NT 4.0 DNS Server.

The first thing to do is install the DNS server, if it is not already installed. Complete the following steps to install the DNS server:

1. Open the Network Control Panel (the easiest way is to right-click the Network Neighborhood and select Properties).
2. Select the Services tab.
3. Click the Add button. A list of known NT services will be displayed (see Figure 9.8). Select Microsoft DNS Server and click OK.

Figure 9.8.
*Adding the DNS
server software to NT.*

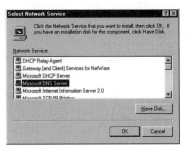

4. Enter the location of the NT installation CD when asked (typically e:\i386) and
   click OK.

5. The DNS server software will be installed. You will need to reboot your machine
   before the DNS server becomes active.

Once the DNS server is installed, you will find a new application in the Administrative Tools
folder called DNS Manager. Like the WINS Manager, the DNS Manager is the graphical interface for controlling the DNS server. Figure 9.9 shows the DNS Manager interface when
first started.

Figure 9.9.
The DNS Manager.

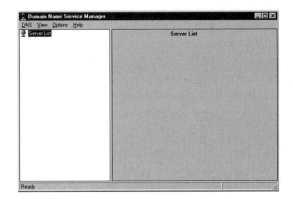

When first installed, the DNS server will be pretty much non-functional. It won't have any
database to serve, and it won't be linked to any IP address. The first step to take is to add a
DNS server to the DNS Manager for control. This is done through the DNS menu with the
Add Server option. Figure 9.10 shows the process of adding a DNS server to the DNS Manager.

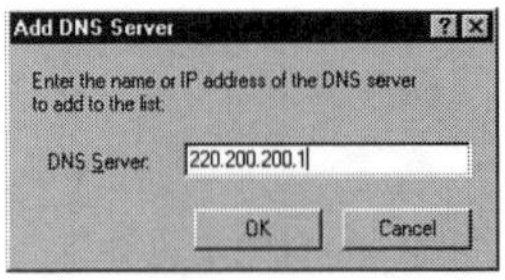

Figure 9.10.
*Adding a DNS server
to the DNS Manager.*

Simply enter the IP address of the DNS server you wish to add. In Figure 9.10, I am adding the server at 220.200.200.1. The IP address 220.200.200.1 is the address of the network card connecting my NT machine to the rest of my network. You can also use the universal local IP address of 127.0.0.1 for the server running on the local machine. This is often the better choice because the address of the network card may change, but the local address will always be 127.0.0.1.

Once you have added a server to the DNS Manager, you will see it listed in the Server List area with several branches underneath. These branches are necessary Internet data and must be present. In a situation where a network is authentically linked to the Internet with a full-time connection, these branches tell the DNS server where to locate the primary root servers of the Internet. For internal DNS needs, no data on these branches needs to be modified (thank God). If you do not see these branches, make sure the Show Automatically Created Zones option is checked in the DNS Manager Preferences (Options menu, Preferences option).

The Server Statistics part of the display is showing some DNS hit information. Your display should show all zeroes. My DNS server has been running for a while and has taken some request hits.

The next thing to do is create a zone for your network. The zone will be named whatever you have decided as your Internet-style domain name. Mine happens to be pandy.com and will be used in this example. If you do not have a domain name assigned to your network from the InterNIC, you can select one that fits your needs.

Creating a zone is a little confusing. Let's go over some points:

- For every zone you create for your DNS server to manage, you must provide a DNS file. This is a standard text file containing the DNS database information for the zone. This must exist prior to creating the zone with the DNS Manager or the DNS Manager will give you a really odd message stating the "Zone Already Exists." This makes no sense, but you just have to roll with it. Luckily, some sample files exist for you to use as your own. Using these files will be covered shortly.

- The default data directory for the DNS server is c:\winnt\system32\dns. From this directory you will find two subdirectories: BACKUP and SAMPLES. The samples directory contains the sample DNS text files you can copy into the c:\winnt\system32\dns as your own zone file and then use the DNS Manager to modify for your own needs.

- A primary zone is any zone which is primarily responsible for the DNS services of an Internet domain. A secondary zone contains a copy of the primary zone's data and is used as a backup in case the primary goes down.

- For our purposes, we'll just be creating one primary zone; however, a DNS server can be responsible for managing the DNS services of any number of zones (Internet domains and sub-domains).

Alrighty, now that we have those points cleared up, let's create our zone. Follow these steps to create a zone:

1. In the `c:\winnt\system32\dns\samples` directory, copy the sample file `PLACE.DNS` back into the `c:\winnt\system32\dns` directory as the file `PANDY.DNS` (or whatever you will be naming your own zone). This sample file contains a lot of junk that we'll need to clean out with the DNS Manager.

2. In the DNS Manager, highlight the server entry for your DNS server (`220.200.200.1` in this example) and from the DNS menu select the New Zone option (see Figure 9.11).

Figure 9.11.

Highlight the DNS server on which you want to create a new zone.

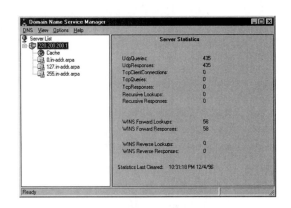

3. A dialog box will appear prompting you to indicate whether this zone is a primary or secondary zone. Highlight the Primary radio button and click Next. A new dialog box will appear (see Figure 9.12).

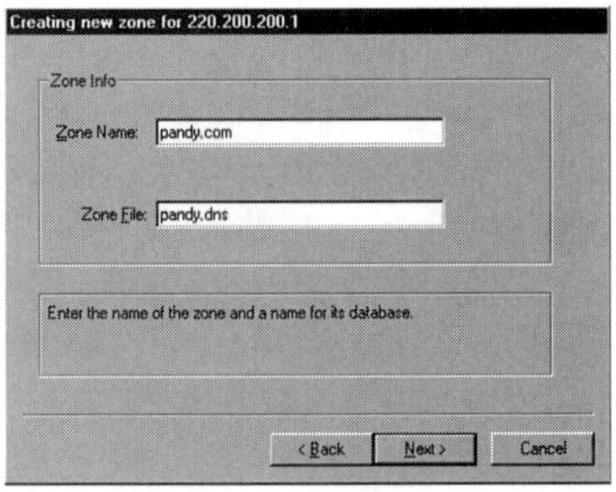

Figure 9.12.

Creating a new zone and indicating a new zone file.

4. A second dialog box will appear asking you for the name of the zone and the zone's dns file. I'll enter `pandy.com` as the zone and `pandy.dns` as the zone dns file. Remember that `pandy.dns` must exist in the `c:\winnt\system32\dns` directory prior to this point, or the zone creation will fail.

5. Click Next, then Finish. The zone will be created and will appear at the end of the branch list for the DNS server. You'll note that the sample data file contains a sub zone off the primary zone called NT. We'll delete this in a second. Figure 9.13 shows the DNS Manager after adding the zone.

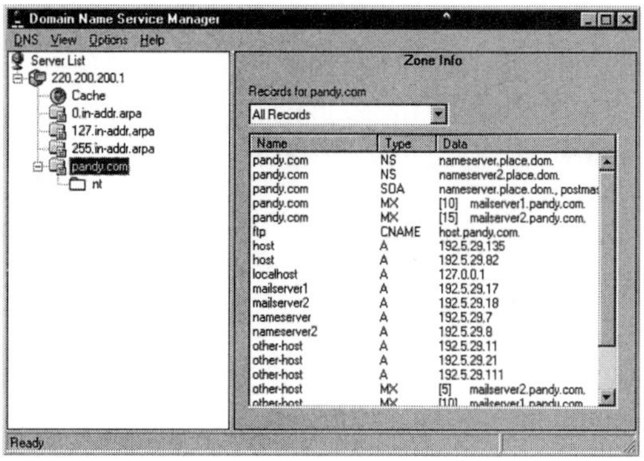

Figure 9.13.
The DNS Manager with the sample zone data loaded.

6. Highlight the new zone if it's not already highlighted. Whooaa, look at all the stuff in the zone information panel. We need to delete every record there except the SOA (Start of Authority) record. Just highlight each record and hit Del. Confirm the deletion. Do this for every record except the SOA record. While you're at it, delete the NT branch off of the pandy.com branch in the same manner.

7. Once you have cleaned out all the records we don't need, double-click the SOA record. We need to edit it to suit our needs. Figure 9.14 shows the edit record dialog box.

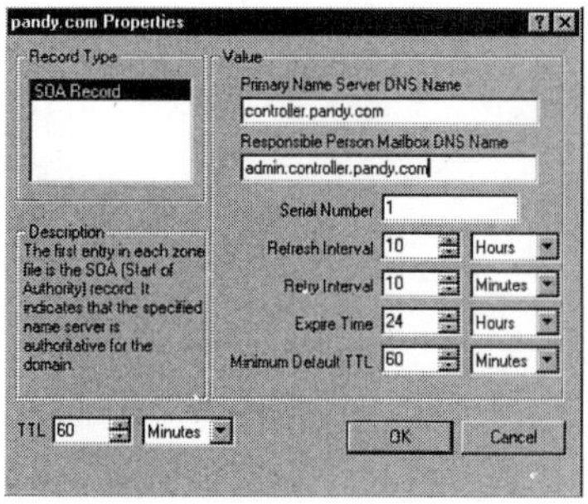

Figure 9.14.
Editing the SOA record.

8. The Primary Name Server DNS Name needs to be changed to controller.pandy.com. This will correspond to the settings of your DNS server's TCP/IP configurations. In the TCP/IP configuration, there is a tab called DNS. DNS must be enabled on this tab. Controller is the host name for the DNS machine and pandy.com is the domain setting of the DNS machine. This will be covered shortly.

9. The Responsible Person Mailbox DNS Name should be changed to your contact location. My NT server runs a POP3 mail server and my administration account is ADMIN. The complete string for this field should be admin.controller.pandy.com (name, host, domain). This is not really important on an isolated network, but normally tells outside users who is responsible for the DNS server on your domain.

This can point anywhere. I could have pointed it to an account I have on an ISP here in town (`dwolfe.pop.iquest.net`).

10. The rest of the settings can be left as default; they control such things as refresh time and time to live. These settings are not important on an isolated network.

11. Click OK and you'll return to the DNS Manager. The SOA record is adjusted, and the next step is to modify the zone properties. Highlight the zone in the Server List (`pandy.com`) and select Zone Properties from the DNS menu (see Figure 9.15).

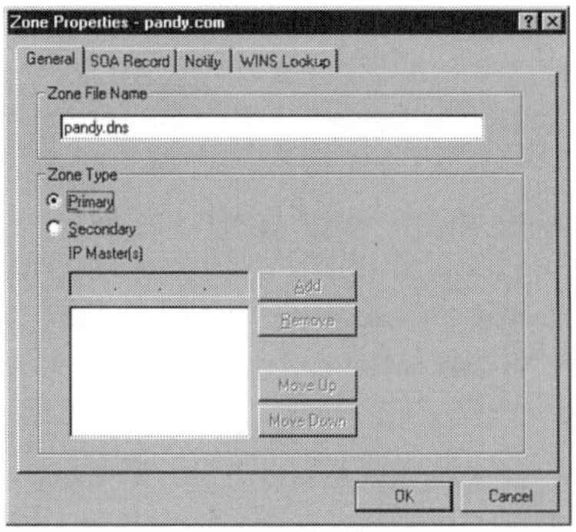

Figure 9.15.
Modifying Zone
Properties.

12. Select the WINS Lookup tab (see Figure 9.16). This is the most important setting we will set. This next step links the DNS server to the WINS server.

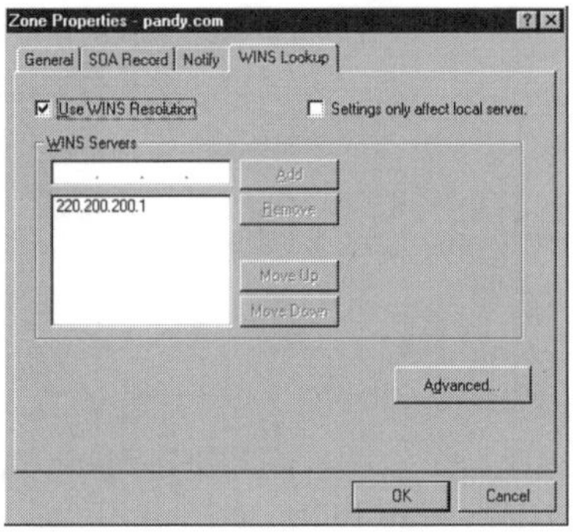

Figure 9.16.
The WINS Lookup
tab of Zone Properties.

13. Check the Use WINS Resolution check box. Enter the location of your WINS server. My WINS server is on `220.200.200.1`, the same machine. The WINS server can be located anywhere, not just on the local machine. It doesn't even have to be in the same subnet as your DNS server. Click the Add button after you enter the IP address of the WINS server.

14. Enter any more WINS servers you want to be checked. If a DNS request is passed to a WINS server and the first WINS server cannot locate the address, the next WINS server will be checked until one finds the address or all available WINS servers fail.

15. Click OK in Zone Properties and you'll be returned to the DNS Manager. All resolution requests that come into the DNS server now that can't be resolved by the DNS database (which none will be because pandy.dns is clean) will be passed along to the WINS server.

16. Next, we need to create a DNS record for indicating the name of the DNS server. Some applications may need the DNS server to tell them its name. Make sure the pandy.com zone is highlighted. Then, from the DNS menu, select New Record (see Figure 9.17).

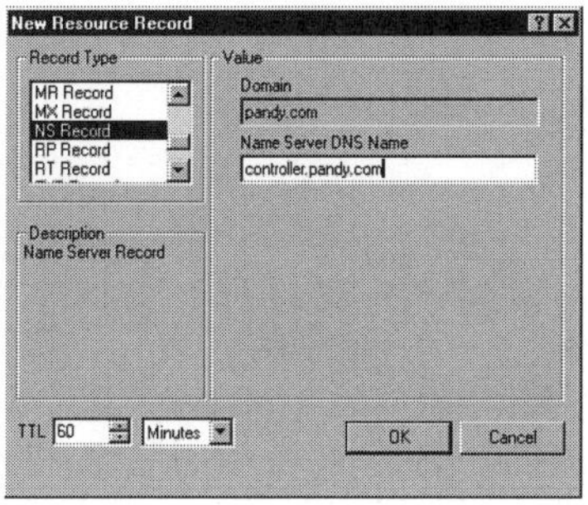

Figure 9.17.
Creating the Name Server record for the zone.

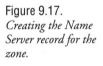

17. In the Record Type list, select NS. An NS record indicates the name server data. Only one NS record should exist for each zone. The Name Server DNS Name field should be filled in with the complete DNS name of the DNS server (controller.pandy.com = host name + domain name). Again, this is gathered from the TCP/IP settings of the DNS server machine.

18. Click OK and you'll return to the DNS Manager.

19. And finally, just for good measure, let's create a record for the localhost. The localhost is a DNS term which is always used to refer to the local machine. The IP of the localhost is always 127.0.0.1. If a workstation enters a command to "ping localhost" that means to see whether the workstation itself is going to respond to a ping request. Under Windows 95, if TCP/IP is running correctly, a workstation should always respond to a localhost ping.

20. From the DNS menu, select New Host. Figure 9.18 shows this dialog box.

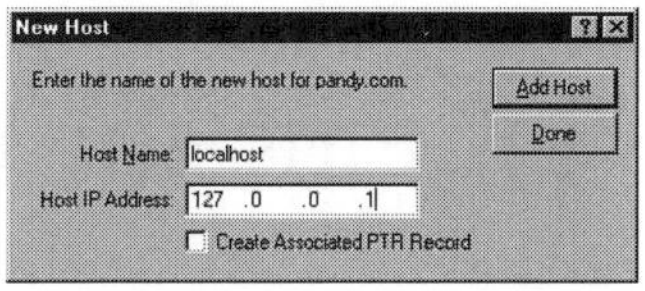

Figure 9.18.
Creating the localhost record.

21. Enter the Host Name of localhost and an IP address of 127.0.0.1. Actually, this record existed in the original sample file, so if you didn't delete it in the beginning, you will not need to recreate it. Click OK to return to the DNS Manager.

That's it! Your DNS server should work like a charm now. If you want to use the DNS server to resolve name requests on its own rather than forwarding the requests to the WINS server, you can just create new host records as we just did with the localhost entry. Keep in mind though, when you create a host, it is a sub-set of the zone it is created in. For example, to create a DNS record for `ftp.pandy.com`, you would create a host record for just "ftp" within the `pandy.com` zone. When a DNS resolution request for `ftp.pandy.com` is received by the DNS server, this "ftp" record is the one that will determine the IP resolution for the request. You cannot create any host record with a name that contains a ".".

Once you have made all of the above changes, make sure you use the Update Server Data Files from the DNS menu in order to commit your changes back to the DNS file (`pandy.dns`). It's also a very good idea to keep a copy of your DNS file in a safe place in case you need to restore it.

Using WINS and DNS Together

When you set a DNS server to consult a WINS server for name resolution, you have to understand how things work. When the DNS server receives a request for a resolution on `ftp.pandy.com`, it will pass to the WINS server only the left-most portion of the name, "ftp." Because the resolution request falls within the `pandy.com` zone, the DNS server only wants to resolve the left portion of the request through the WINS server that is the fallback for the `pandy.com` zone. If you'll remember back earlier in this chapter, you will recall that my static mappings in my WINS database contained entries for "ftp" and "www." Now you should see why this is. These are the only portions of a request to `ftp.pandy.com` and `www.pandy.com` that the WINS server will receive. Since this is the case, static entries should exist which will correspond to these requests.

Remember also that we set up a group of proxy servers in a multi-homed group, called `proxy_servers`. To configure clients to access the group, you can set clients to address just `proxy_servers` or `proxy_servers.pandy.com`. If clients address `proxy_servers`, the WINS server will handle the request on its own. If clients use the name `proxy_servers.pandy.com`, the DNS server will first receive the request and forward it on to the WINS server as just `proxy_servers`. You will have to configure non-WINS-aware clients (for example, Mac clients and other operating systems that do not utilize WINS) to access `proxy_servers.pandy.com` in order for them to correctly get name resolution on the group by the DNS server.

TCP/IP Settings for Windows 95

Setting up workstations to have access to a WINS or DNS server is a fairly simple and straightforward process. It is done through the Network Control Panel. To access this control panel, right-click on the Network Neighborhood and select Properties. Figure 9.19 shows this dialog box.

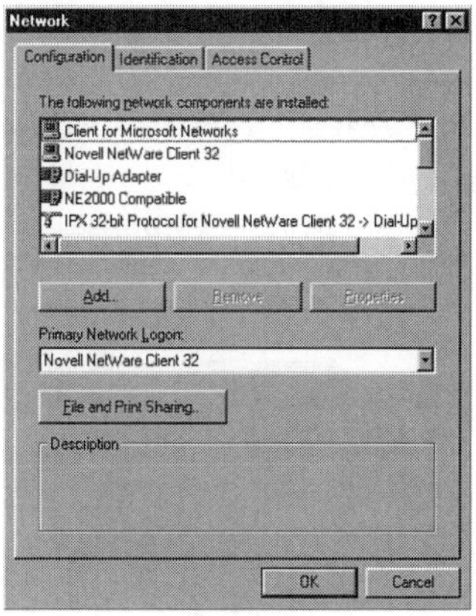

Figure 9.19.
*The Windows 95
Network Control
Panel.*

Scroll down the components list until you find the TCP/IP protocol entry (assuming it's loaded). Highlight the TCP/IP entry for the installed network card, not the Dial-Up Adapter. Click the Properties button. A TCP/IP settings dialog box will appear, as shown in Figure 9.20. Select the WINS Configuration tab.

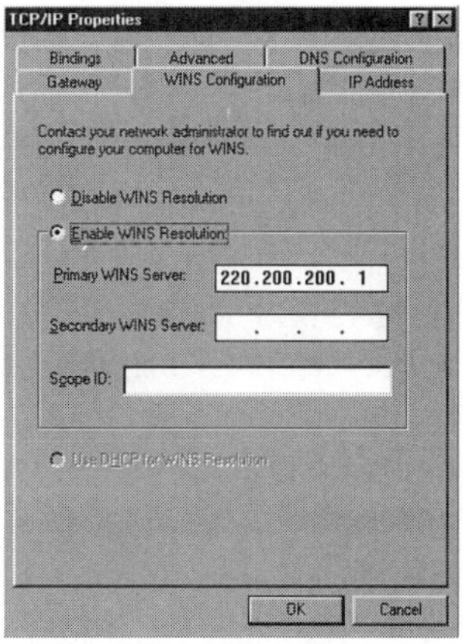

Figure 9.20.
*The WINS Configura-
tion tab of TCP/IP
settings.*

Simply click the Enable WINS Resolution radio button and enter the IP address of the WINS server in the Primary WINS Server field. If you have more than one WINS server on your network, you can enter the location of a second one in the Secondary WINS Server field. Next, select the DNS Configuration tab. Figure 9.21 shows this tab.

Click the Enable DNS radio button to turn on DNS resolution for this workstation. The Host field and the Domain field should be filled in with the host name you are going to assign to this workstation and the Internet (style) domain name this workstation is a member of. Each workstation on a network should have a unique DNS host name. Keep in mind that the NT domain and the Internet domain are two different units. These two names together constitute the complete host name for the workstation (or server in the case of NT servers): pentium.pandy.com. Just because a host name is assigned to a workstation in this manner, don't think that it will be available for other workstations to access via commands like PING and so on. Unless the host name is listed in the WINS database, or within the pandy.com zone in the DNS server, any name requests to pentium.pandy.com will go unresolved even though pentium.pandy.com does have an IP address.

Figure 9.21.
The DNS Configuration tab of TCP/IP settings.

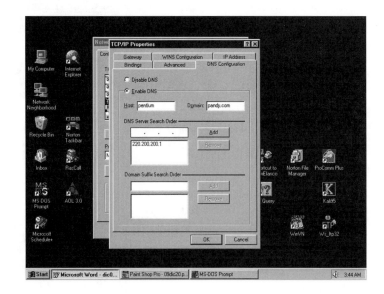

If it happens that the NetBIOS name (machine name set in Identification tab of the Network Control Panel) matches the host name set in the DNS configuration, then the WINS server should automatically know the IP address given to the workstation and other workstations should be able to resolve name resolution requests to the workstation (pentium.pandy.com). This discussion applies to the TCP/IP settings of NT as well, although the tab arrangement is visually different.

Once the host name and domain name have been set, you can next enter the DNS server IPs this workstation will reference for DNS requests. The TCP/IP settings can list up to three DNS servers which will be searched in sequence if necessary to resolve a DNS request. Enter the DNS IPs and then click the Add button to add it to the list of possible DNS servers.

There is a possibility that after you get a local DNS server up and running on your network, you may find dial-up links made by local network workstations to the Internet are not working correctly. This is most likely because Windows is trying to use your local DNS server to handle the name resolution requests of clients attempting to access the Internet. If this is the case, you will need to add the IP address of the ISP's name server to your DNS configuration in the TCP/IP settings. Any external DNS servers should be listed *before* any local DNS servers so they will be tried first. When not connected to the Internet, these addresses will still be tried, though the DNS servers will not be found. Windows will then go on to attempt to access any additional DNS servers listed. This means a slight pause for name resolution when not connected to the Internet, but it will ensure that workstations can resolve Internet names when directly connected with a dialup connection.

This is a pain because Dial-Up Networking entries have their own sections for indicating the name server address(es) for an ISP. You would think that when connected to the Internet, the addresses listed for the name servers used by the Dial-Up connection would automatically be tried before any locally listed DNS server. This does not seem to be the case and may be a bug in Dial-Up Networking. If this is the case for your workstations, simply enter the ISP's DNS address in your TCP/IP settings before your own network's DNS server IP.

Once the WINS and DNS configuration tabs have been completed, you can click OK to return to the Network Control Panel. Clicking OK again will close the Network Control Panel and you will be prompted to restart the workstation. From this point on, the workstation should be able to use both DNS and WINS to resolve names.

DNS is always checked before WINS. If the DNS and WINS servers have matching records for a network host, the DNS server's address will be the one resolved for the request.

Local Machine Name Resolution

If there are no name resolution servers on a network, a Windows 95 workstation can still perform simple name resolution on its own. This is sometimes more effort-intensive for the network administrator than just using direct IP addresses to reference the proxy server location(s).

In the c:\windows directory there can be a configuration file called simply hosts. In fact, there is a sample file, hosts.sam, in the c:\windows directory that you can look over. All this file contains is simple name-to-IP associations. The format of the file is very basic. One record per line, IP address listed first (starting at the very beginning of the line, no indentation), and then the name associated with this IP. The name must be separated from the IP address by at least one space. That's all there is to it.

If Windows fails to resolve a name request from a client application by all other means available, the hosts file will be consulted as a last resort. If you do not want to use a WINS or DNS server, it may be easier for you as network administrator to create a host file to copy to all network workstations. Of course, this still means some leg work to update all workstations if addresses change, but it is often easier to copy over one file than to reconfigure three or four Internet client applications per workstation.

Name Resolution After Connection

Don't get confused by having a local name resolution server and resolving names from an outside source. Once a client has made a connection to Microsoft Proxy Server, the proxy server itself will perform name resolution for clients thereafter until the connection is broken. Obviously, if you run an isolated network, your name server is not going to know all the addresses of the outside Internet. When you create a connection to the Internet from the proxy machine, the connection method will have its own name resolution settings. For example, if you connect to the Internet through RAS, the Dial-Up Networking application will allow you to indicate the name servers to be used with each ISP you call. Microsoft Proxy Server will contact the external name server(s) indicated to resolve Internet name requests for clients. Setting up a local DNS or WINS server is primarily to make it easier for clients to connect to Microsoft Proxy Server, not to enhance their ability to externally browse the network.

This was very flakey in the beta versions of Microsoft Proxy Server (known as Catapult) and didn't always work. However, the full release version of Microsoft Proxy Server is very solid at resolving names via an external name server.

Summary

When setting up proxy clients, you can choose to have them access Microsoft Proxy Server by IP or by a name. If clients access by IP, your proxy flexibility is severely limited and in a large network environment it's almost unmanageable. In order to eliminate that problem, a good combination of DNS and WINS server ability will go a long way toward giving you as network administrator the tools you need. Hopefully this chapter showed you at least the basics, and possibly more, about how to set up both a WINS server and a DNS server to take care of all local name resolution needs.

CHAPTER 10

Proxy Server Performance Issues

The entire premise behind the use of Microsoft Proxy Server is an entire network of local users accessing the Internet through one nexus point (also known as the gateway computer on which Microsoft Proxy Server is running). Depending on how large your network of users is and how often they access the Internet, the stress on Microsoft Proxy Server may require you to optimize it for the job of gatewaying data from 10, 100, or perhaps even more connections.

The majority of LANs in use by everyday people and businesses are 10-Mbps (megabits per second) networks. By comparison, a T1 line (the most common line used by businesses to bring in Internet access to an office LAN) is only a 1.54-Mbps channel. Though this speed is very fast by Internet standards (compared to a standard dial-up connection at 28.8 Kbps or 0.0288 Mbps), a 10 Mbps network can quickly overload a T1 line. With the onset of newer 100-Mbps networks, a T1 line seems almost puny by comparison.

It's important that the Microsoft Proxy server on a LAN be set up as efficiently as possible to handle outbound and inbound Internet traffic. There will be inevitable hiccups in Internet-related traffic if the outside channel is overloaded, but it is your job as the network administrator to see to it that there are no network hiccups due to server inefficiency.

NT Network Priority

Even though Windows NT Server is designed as a network-oriented system, user applications can still be executed on it while background network services are being performed. Novell servers do not permit any execution of normal applications on the server itself. This is one of the major differences between NT servers and Novell servers. People have opinions on both sides of the fence on this issue.

By default, NT gives quite a bit of CPU attention to any task that may be executing in the foreground on the server. If no user tasks are being executed, the priority NT gives to foreground execution is not an issue. However, if Microsoft Proxy Server will also be used as a network workstation, the application performance boost time should be lowered in order to ensure that Microsoft Proxy Server traffic is not slowed down.

To alter the boost time NT gives to foreground applications, complete the following steps:

1. Open the Control Panel.
2. Within the Control Panel, select the System icon. The System applet will execute and the System Properties dialog box will open.
3. Select the Performance tab (see Figure 10.1). From this point, you can adjust the Boost slider as needed.

   By default, the Boost slider is set to the maximum value. This gives a great deal of extra CPU time to any foreground application. Moving this slider to the left decreases the boost time.
4. Moving the slider all the way to the left (None) forces NT to handle background and foreground tasks equally. The best value here should be "None."

Once the Boost slider has been adjusted, simply select OK. The NT server must be restarted in order for the new settings to become effective.

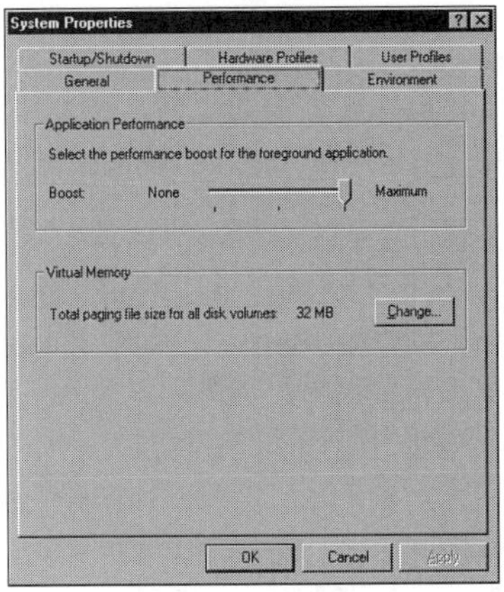

Figure 10.1.
The Performance tab of System Properties.

Screen Savers

While screen savers may look nice and can also increase server security, the high-end screen savers of NT 4.0 can be real CPU hogs. The Open GL screen savers, while very impressive, can be real drains on server performance. It is suggested that no high-end screen saver be used on any NT server that is responsible for any significant amount of network traffic. If a password-protected screen saver is being used on an NT server to prevent unauthorized access to the server, simply logging off of the server will accomplish the same thing without placing any additional overhead on the duties the server must perform. In fact, NT servers perform better when no one is logged on to them (resources consumed by the Explorer shell are freed up when no one is logged on).

Unbinding Unneeded Services from the Internet Gateway

When new NICs (Network Interface Cards) are set up under NT, NT automatically binds all appropriate installed services to the cards. These services range from actual protocols to services such as WINS (Windows Internet Name Service). NT assumes that all NICs are destined to be full network interfaces. Because the purpose of Microsoft Proxy Server is to establish Internet connections to the outside world for LAN workstations, certain protocols and services can be unbound from the NIC that Microsoft Proxy Server will use to channel Internet-destined data from the network. This will improve network performance over the Internet channel.

> **Caution:** Unbinding base elements from a NIC may cause higher-level services to fail. When a base element (such as protocol) is unbound from a NIC, make certain that no dependent services are still bound to that NIC.

If a base-level service is unbound and some network services do not start on the next boot, rebind the service/NIC in question to remedy the situation. Unbinding network services should not prevent NT from being able to start. Such actions might simply stop the NT server from seeing or being seen on the network.

If RAS (Remote Access Services) is the primary Internet channel, special care must be taken to ensure that RAS is not adversely affected because of unbinding elements. The primary NIC that connects the Microsoft Proxy Server machine to the rest of the LAN should also not be touched. Only alter the bindings of the NIC that gives Microsoft Proxy Server its Internet connection.

Alteration of network bindings is done through the Control Panel via the Network icon. To access the bindings dialog box, complete the following steps:

1. Open Control Panel.
2. Select the Network icon.
3. Select the Bindings tab (see Figure 10.2).

Figure 10.2.
Network bindings
for all services.

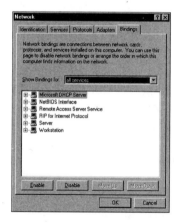

The Show Bindings for drop-down list can be used to change how the bindings are displayed. Bindings can be displayed from the top down (to see which NICs are bound to what services), or from the bottom up (to see which services are bound to which NICs). Depending on how the bindings need to be altered, the view of the bindings can be adjusted. To alter the way bindings need to be changed now, it is best to view the protocol bindings. This will display a list of the protocols and to which base elements they are bound.

In the Show Bindings for drop-down list, select all protocols. The protocol bindings are shown in Figure 10.3.

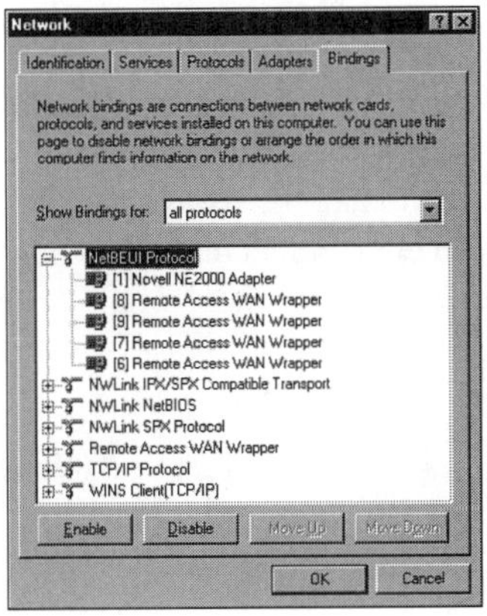

Figure 10.3.
Network Bindings
for all protocols.

All bindings on the Internet NIC that are not related to the TCP/IP protocol can be disabled (unbound). Your arrangement of protocol bindings may be different than the one shown in Figure 10.3. On my system, I do not have a dedicated Internet channel and have to use RAS to connect my LAN to the Internet.

RAS channels can be treated like regular NICs for binding purposes. If RAS is used for dial-in access to a LAN, make certain that inbound callers can get by with just the TCP/IP protocol. If RAS callers will need other protocols and services on the RAS channel, the bindings can still be adjusted to move the bindings to the TCP/IP protocol high in the priority chain.

Because the binding list of your network may appear different from the one shown in Figure 10.3, the NetBEUI binding will be used as an example. To unbind the NetBEUI protocol from the RAS channel (or from a dedicated NIC), complete the following steps:

1. Select the + sign to the left of the NetBEUI protocol. This will expand the binding details of the NetBEUI protocol. The details for the NetBEUI protocol are already shown as expanded in Figure 10.3.

2. Lower elements (network NICs and RAS Wrappers) that are bound to the NetBEUI protocol are displayed. Highlight the first reference to the Remote Access WAN Wrapper.

3. Select Disable.

All channels that have their bindings disabled from a protocol are denoted as such by a universal No sign (red circle with a slash through it).

Complete this procedure for all references to the specific NIC card or RAS channel that is to be streamlined for the TCP/IP protocol. In order to ensure network stability, unbind only the Internet NIC from the NetBEUI and IPX/SPX protocols. All other bindings should remain intact unless you are very familiar with altering binding. Services such as WINS and DHCP are related specifically to the TCP/IP protocol and should not be altered.

Changing the NIC Hierarchy in Bindings

If the hierarchy of network interfaces needs to be adjusted to give the Internet NIC the highest priority when dealing with TCP/IP data, this can be easily done. Rather than selecting the Disable button to unbind a NIC from a protocol, the Move Up button can be used to raise up the selected NIC or RAS channel in the binding hierarchy. If all bindings must be kept intact, but the performance of the Internet NIC still needs to be improved, moving the Internet NIC up in the binding hierarchy will do just that.

Removing Unneeded Network Services

Another way of streamlining an NT server for Internet gatewaying is to remove all nonessential services or move the services to another NT server on the network. Many NT administrators make the mistake of overloading an NT machine with all network services simply for the ease of having all services in one centralized location that is easier to manage. An efficient network is one that has network services such as WINS, DHCP, gatewaying, DNS, WWW Servers, and RAS spread out over as many NT servers as possible.

Converting to NTFS

NT 4.0 supports two types of hard disk formats: traditional FAT and NTFS (NT File System). Because, hopefully, a large amount of Internet information will be stored in Microsoft Proxy Server's disk cache, it is a good idea to convert all hard disks on any NT server to the NTFS format. NTFS format has several major advantages over FAT:

- True 32-bit file system
- Advanced, network-oriented security options for files and directories
- Quicker access time
- Less wasted space

The major drawback to NTFS is that it is not supported by MS-DOS. NT servers can be multiboot systems, allowing an administrator to reboot the machine to another operating system, such as MS-DOS. When a hard disk is converted to NTFS, only NT Server and NT Workstation operating systems can read these volumes. If the boot disk of a system is converted to NTFS, the system can be booted only to an NT operating system.

Initial setup of NT allows the administrator to select which disk format the NT installation target disk should be. NT does have the ability to convert FAT hard disks to NTFS hard disks, while still maintaining data integrity of the disk. FAT hard disks can also be converted to NTFS at any time, not just during installation of NT. This can be done safely and without much effort or system downtime.

To convert a disk from FAT to NTFS, simply run the program CONVERT.EXE with a parameter indicating which disk is to be converted. The following is an example:

CONVERT.EXE E:

If the boot disk is being converted, the NT server must be restarted. Conversion of a boot disk to NTFS must be done prior to the full operating system being started and must therefore be done during the boot process.

Bandwidth Equals How Many Users?

The majority of people who will be needing Microsoft Proxy Server will be those who have a periodic network connection, such as a dial-up connection to an ISP (Internet Service Provider), and would like to offer the rest of the users of a LAN the ability to connect to the Internet without having to have their own dial-up accounts.

By far, the most bandwidth-consuming Internet activity is downloading files from FTP servers. Microsoft Proxy Server allows a great deal of flexibility when it comes to limiting which types of outside connections are permitted. If a LAN has only a small 28.8- or 33.6-Kbps connection to the Internet, it might be wise to prohibit the use of FTP in order to prevent serious outside connection bog downs. One FTP user can quickly drag down the normal performance of three or four WWW users. Chapter 8, "Configuring Proxy Server Security and Authentication," covers Microsoft Proxy Server security issues and how to limit types of connections Microsoft Proxy Server will allow.

Another drawback to FTP users on a network is that Microsoft Proxy Server does not cache FTP files. In other words, if a user downloads a file via FTP, and then later must download it again, the file must be completely downloaded again from the Internet. Microsoft Proxy server does cache WWW objects such as graphics and sound bytes so that if those objects are referenced again, the Microsoft Proxy server can issue them to the requesting client without having to pull them in from the Internet. This greatly speeds up performance and allows more users to access the Microsoft Proxy Server channel without performance problems.

The numbers given below are my own estimations based on my experience with Internet traffic and NT Server. The following table shows on average how many WWW clients should be able to use various bandwidth Internet connections through Microsoft Proxy Server:

Table 10.1. WWW clients to bandwidth speeds.

Bandwidth Speed	Number of WWW Users
28.8 or 33.6 Kbps	2–3
64 Kbps	5–7
128 Kbps	12–14
1.54 Mbps	50–75

Obviously, these numbers take into account some cached data as well as non-concurrent accessing of large amounts of data, such as graphics or sound bytes.

Under normal network conditions, Microsoft Proxy Server's performance will allow LAN clients to experience no appreciable network lags. In other words, network clients should see the same performance from Microsoft Proxy Server as they would if they were actually dialed into an ISP on their local machine. Similar proxy servers, such as WinGate, while very good in their own right, cannot claim such an accomplishment. Microsoft Proxy Server's performance level is very impressive even when serving out data to multiple LAN clients.

Making certain that Microsoft Proxy Server has a large cache for WWW objects will also help ensure that connections to the Internet seem to be as fast as possible. Microsoft Proxy Server should be configured for 100 megabytes plus ½ meg per Microsoft Proxy Server user of disk space for its cache. If you have many LAN clients accessing many different places in the outside world, it might be a good idea to increase Microsoft Proxy Server's cache so that it can maintain local copies of most outside objects. Chapter 12, "Controlling the Proxy Server Cache," deals with controlling Microsoft Proxy Server's cache and how to effectively use it to ensure the highest level of Internet access performance.

Packet Latency

When the Microsoft Proxy Server connection to the Internet becomes heavily used or overloaded, clients may begin to see errors like `Unable to Resolve Host Name` or `Connection Timed Out`. These all stem from packets being delayed in transit—so much so that the client believes the connection to have been broken.

If these errors are cropping up on a network and the Microsoft Proxy Server connection is not overloaded by LAN clients, the ISP itself may be overloaded. I have tried many ISPs and know for a fact that just because they claim to be the biggest and the fastest does not always mean they are the least overloaded. The late afternoon and early evening are normally when ISPs experience their highest volume of users. During these times, you may find the most problems with outside connections. Most of the time, attempting a connection again will prove successful after a while. However, there are just some times when an ISP is too overloaded to be of any use. That's when a dedicated channel is nice to have.

Multiple Microsoft Proxy Server Gateways

If the only connections to the Internet are modem-based dialup connections, it might be wise to look at installing multiple Microsoft Proxy servers. When communicating with the Internet through RAS, Microsoft Proxy Server will use only the latest connection. Installing two or three modems on a single server and connecting all of them to an ISP will not yield any higher data throughput than connecting just one.

When connecting an NT server to another NT machine, multiple modems *can* be used to gain a larger channel. This is called multi-link and is an RAS option which allows multiple connections to server as a single connection. Since (sad to say) NT is not yet the preferred choice of ISPs for their dial-in service systems, multi-link will not be an option for Internet connections. The nature of routing under TCP/IP is such that when NT finds the first available gateway to the outside world, it will use that. This means that only the latest RAS connection will ever be used for outbound Internet traffic from the LAN. If RAS is used to offer separate inbound traffic a connection method, then yes, two or more connections may be used. Figure 10.4 shows my own personal scenario and use of Microsoft Proxy Server.

Figure 10.4.
Multiple RAS links.

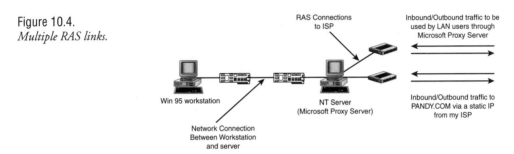

The diagram in Figure 10.4 also shows two RAS connections to the ISP, one being used for Microsoft Proxy Server traffic from LAN users and the other for the domain connection to the Internet that allows outside Internet users to access any Internet servers (WWW and FTP for example) running on the NT Server. Obviously, two dial-in accounts must be available on the ISP for use in this manner. Obtaining a domain name and a static IP is a special arrangement that must be made with the ISP. I have personally had my domain established for some time, and when connected to my ISP through that domain account, outside users can connect to my NT server and browse my WWW server or FTP server.

In order for similar situations to work correctly, the Microsoft Proxy Server connection must be made last. Remember that Microsoft Proxy Server will always use the last connection made to the Internet. In order to leave the domain connection to itself, it must be connected to first. In this arrangement, the modem connected to the ISP that is maintaining the domain connection is not overloaded with incoming Internet traffic as well as outbound traffic from LAN users.

If the last connection is broken, Microsoft Proxy Server will automatically use any other connections to the Internet . This can be used as a form of redundancy to ensure that the Internet connection is not severed should one of the modems accidentally hang up.

Many ISPs have inactivity time-out periods for dial-in connections. This means that if there is no activity on a dial-in connection for a certain amount of time (usually around 15 minutes) the ISP will disconnect the connection. There are many nice shareware applications available that are designed to keep a dial-in connection open by pinging a server at preset times. The one I use is called Ponger, and can be downloaded from windows95.com.

Of course, the Auto Dial feature of Microsoft Proxy Server can always be used to make an Internet connection if the connection is down. However, making a connection can sometimes take as long as a full minute. Some client applications will time-out with an error before Microsoft Proxy Server can establish a RAS connection to the Internet. That's why I like to simply leave my NT server connected to my ISP via RAS. Many ISPs now offer "unlimited" access. I usually put that claim to the test. ISPs hate to see me coming.

Splitting Up LAN Users Between Multiple Microsoft Proxy Servers

If one Microsoft Proxy server is not enough to service the needs of the users on a LAN, multiple Microsoft Proxy servers can be set up on different computers. Different permissions can be granted to different LAN groups, giving only certain groups permission to use certain Microsoft Proxy servers. This gives the network administrator the ability to evenly spread out the load which LAN users will place on Microsoft Proxy servers.

Because each network workstation must be told which proxy address to communicate with, any number of proxy servers can be on a LAN. Microsoft Proxy Server also has the ability to deny access to certain sites on the Internet. If LAN users are misusing the Microsoft Proxy Server connection, it is possible to indicate which IPs are allowed to be connected to a specific site. Administrators can filter out sites like www.playboy.com and prevent users from connecting to these sites.

If the network resources are available to dedicate multiple machines to outside connections, it's a good idea to have a plan of action for Microsoft Proxy Server's organization. It is possible to dedicate one Microsoft Proxy Server to WWW connections and another to FTP connections. However, it might make more sense to arrange separate groups of users who are authorized to connect to certain Microsoft Proxy servers. Chapter 8 covers security issues and describes how to set up Microsoft Proxy Server to allow or deny access to particular LAN users or Internet servers.

Using the Performance Monitor

This section will briefly describe how to use the NT Performance Monitor to examine such things as CPU usage, RAS port usage, and other important bits of information that may help to track down bottlenecks on a Microsoft Proxy server. This section does not attempt to cover all the possibilities of the Performance Monitor, but rather to give a general overview of how it can be used correctly.

Performance Monitor can be located in the Administrative Tools folder on the Start menu. When started, no counters are shown, so it appears that the Performance Monitor is displaying nothing. Figure 10.5 shows the Performance Monitor when it is initially started.

Figure 10.5.
The NT Performance Monitor.

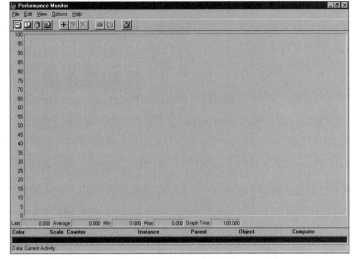

Like most Windows applications, Performance Monitor has a top toolbar of command buttons. The middle area of the display will show performance information when counters have been added to the display. Information is displayed in a percentage of usage line chart. The display area ranges from zero-percent usage, when chart lines are at the bottom of the display, and near 100-percent usage, when chart lines reach the top of the display. The bottom of the display area shows which counters are being displayed in the display area. Each new counter added will be represented by a different color and/or line thickness.

To add a counter to the display, select the + icon on the toolbar. A dialog box will open that will allow a specific counter to be added. Figure 10.6 shows the Add to Chart dialog box.

Figure 10.6.
The Add to Chart dialog box in Performance Monitor.

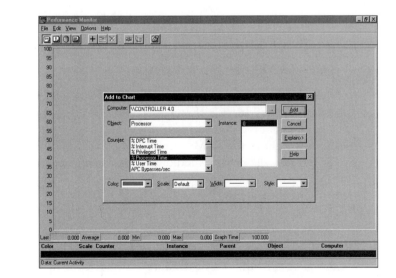

A wide range of counters can be added to the display. Once the IIS servers and Microsoft Proxy Server have been added to an NT server, a specific set of counters can be used to display pertinent data concerning these applications. The following is a description of each of the major elements of the Add to Chart dialog box:

- Computer: Indicates the computer to show performance data. Any NT computer across the network can be monitor, not just the local machine.

- Object: Indicates the class of counters that can be selected from the Counter list box. For example, the processor is an object that can be monitored in various ways. Running applications like the WWW server are also considered objects.

- Counter: This list box lists the various counters for the currently selected object that can be added to the monitor display.

- Instance: If a counter can be shown in more than one instance, this list box will show the instances available. For example, some counters display data concerning disk usage. When such counters are selected, the Instance list box will show available disks on which the counter can display data.

- Color: The color of the chart line for the select counter.

- Scale: The scale used for the counter selected. Depending on how in-depth the counter needs to be, the scale can be adjusted up or down from its default to see greater detail in the chart line.

- Width: The width of the chart line for the selected counter.

- Style: The line style of the selected counter. This can be a solid line, a dashed line, a dotted line, and so on.

The Add button will add the selected counter to the display. The Explain button will expand the Add to Chart dialog box with a Counter Definition area and show a description of the selected counter. This is very handy because the relevance of some of the counters is difficult to visualize.

The following is a small list of some of the counters that are useful when tracking the performance of Microsoft Proxy Server:

- Object: Processor, Counter: percent Processor Time—This counter is among the most useful of counters. It tracks the amount of busy time experienced by the CPU. If this counter is indicating a constantly high CPU load of 70 percent or higher, this may indicate that the computer Microsoft Proxy Server is running on is not strong enough to do the job well. Or it may indicate that too many other services are being run on the NT machine, and some services should be removed and/or moved to other NT servers on the network.

- Object: Processor, Counter: percent Interrupt Time—This counter tracks the amount of CPU time devoted to services hardware interrupts (IRQs). If this counter is showing a constantly high chart line (above 70 percent), this may indicate that an actual piece of hardware is demanding too much CPU time. Serial ports may cause performance problems if their DTE speed (data terminal equipment—also know as port speed) is not high enough to handle the actual connect speed of the modems that are attached to them. A 28.8-Kbps modem should have a port speed of at least 57.6 Kbps. If the hardware supports it, a 115.2-Kbps port speed should be used. If the port speed is too low, the serial port is constantly having to interrupt the CPU to offload incoming data from the modem. Improving a serial port to a 16550 UART, or if possible, the newest 16650 UART will also help relieve interrupt problems.

■ Object: HTTP Service, Counter: Bytes Total/sec—This counter tracks the total in and out bytes of data the HTTP server is handling. Because Microsoft Proxy Server uses the HTTP server for most proxied WWW, FTP, and Gopher data, this counter is a good indication of the workload of the Microsoft Proxy server. However, it also tracks HTTP requests to the local WWW server. If the total bytes per second counter is showing a constant near maximum number (2900 to 3200 for a 28.8-Kbps modem) for the speed of the Microsoft Proxy Server connection to the Internet, the connection is being overused and should be upgraded if possible. Another option is to cut back traffic in some way.

■ Object: Inet Proxy Service, Counter: Inet Bytes Total/sec—This counter is nearly identical to the above counter except that it shows just the amount of data being passed to and from the Internet by the proxy server.

■ Object: Inet Proxy Service, Counter: Maximum Users—This counter indicates the number of users that are or have been connected to the proxy server over the displayed time period.

■ Object: RAS Port, Counter: *—The counters of the RAS Port object are extremely useful in tracking the performance of RAS connections. Many of the counters for this object deal with connection errors and port overruns. These types of counters can help find physical problems with a connection. If error counters run high, the problem may be in the quality of the connection line, or the port hardware itself. Other counters of this object can show the exact amount of data being passed through a RAS port. The Instance list box of the Add to Chart dialog box allows each RAS port to be shown as an independent counter.

■ Object: LogicalDisk, Counter: *—The counters of this object allow for tracking information concerning disk performance to be displayed for logical disks. Don't get confused with another similar object, PhysicalDisk. The LogicalDisk object allows counters to be displayed for logical drive letters, such as C:, D:, and E:. PhysicalDisk counter displays information on actual hard disks only. More than one logical disk can be held on one physical disk. The percent Disk Time counter is very useful in tracking how busy the selected disk (in the Instance list box) is. A busy disk is better than a busy connection to the Internet. A busy disk indicates Microsoft Proxy Server is pulling a large percentage of its data from its cache and not having to go outside to the Internet to get it. Though a very high percentage of disk usage might mean far too many Microsoft Proxy Server users for Microsoft Proxy Server to handle. It is possible that the NT server on which Microsoft Proxy Server is running is also serving out shared resources, such as hard drive space. A high percent Disk Time counter may mean that the NT machine is very busy serving out shared resource data. Disk accessing is the single most common process that will cause Microsoft Proxy Server to hiccup when transferring data. All other processor tasks are paused until data from a disk is read or written.

Once the desired counters have been added to the display, selecting Close will close the Add to Chart dialog box and the display area of the performance monitor will begin to show the added counters.

By default, the display area shows data for the past 100 seconds of system activity. The tracking bar jumps at one second intervals, though this can be increased if more than 100 seconds of data must be displayed. The Options icon on the toolbar (the last one on the right) can be used to alter some of the chart settings, such as interval time and grid line options. Figure 10.7 shows the Chart Options dialog box.

By default, the chart is periodically updated each second. This can be changed to a manual update if desired. A manual update is handy to use if random, user-initiated snapshots of system activity are desired. The periodic interval can be adjusted to any interval desired. The display chart is broken down into 100 segments so the overall time displayed in the chart will be 100 times whatever interval is selected in this dialog box. If the interval is five seconds, the overall chart time will be 500 seconds.

Figure 10.7.
The Chart Options dialog box.

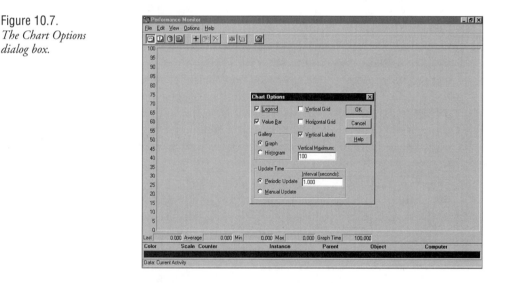

The vertical scale can also be adjusted. If lowered, more detail will be shown for counters with smaller scales, but it may show other counters as constantly maxed out. If raised too high, the display may not show enough detail to be of any use. Trial and error is the best way to find the right vertical scale for a system.

Charts can be saved and later reloaded. From the File menu, the Save Workspace command will save the chart in its current view. Chart settings can also be saved by using the Save Chart Settings command from the File menu.

The Performance Monitor is the best tool to use for finding out where there might be a problem with a system. The wide range of data the Performance Monitor can display will keep you, as system administrator, informed of how well Microsoft Proxy Server is operating, and which parts of the system are overly taxed. Become familiar with Performance Monitor and use it frequently. If nothing else, it'll let you look smart in office meetings when you can tell the boss things such as, "Yep, Microsoft Proxy Server usage went up 37 percent last month. We need a larger budget for our Internet connection!"

Figure 10.8 shows what the Performance Monitor looks like with several counters displayed.

This view of the Performance Monitor shows three counters: percent Processor Time, RAS Port COM3 Bytes Transmitted/Sec, and RAS Port COM3 Bytes Received/Sec. Note that the counters for the RAS Port information max out for short periods. This is because these counters are not percentage counters, and their data goes beyond 100. To fix this, the scale of these counters should be decreased to a value that will allow the counter data to fit within the display area. RAS Port COM3 is a 28.8-Kbps modem and its bytes per second in either direction (transmitting or receiving) could rise as high at 3,200 bytes per second. Setting the scale for these counters to 0.01 (or 1/100th scale view) will allow the data to fit nicely within the display. At a 0.01 scale, this RAS data will range from 0 to roughly 32 for a normal maximum value.

Figure 10.8.
An active view of Performance Monitor.

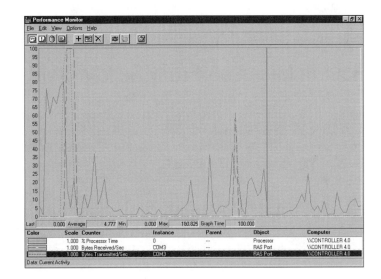

Specific Microsoft Proxy Server Objects and Counters

Several new objects and counters are available to the Performance Monitor once Microsoft Proxy Server is installed. These objects and counters are specifically intended to show vital information on how well Microsoft Proxy Server is servicing the needs of LAN users for outside Internet access. The following objects deal specifically with Microsoft Proxy Server:

- Web Proxy Server Cache—This object has counters for tracking the status of the Web proxy cache. Such things as how full the cache is, how often it is accessed, and the number of URLs cached can all be tracked with counters in this object.

- Web Proxy Server—This is probably one of the most important objects that deals with Microsoft Proxy Server. The counters of this object track many things, including the traffic that passes through the Web Proxy, the number of each type of request (HTTP, FTP, or Gopher), the number of users denied access, and the number of sites granted access. All of these counters deal only with Web Proxy. The WinSock Proxy server has its own object.

- WinSock Proxy Server Service—This object has counters that track data similar to the way the Web Proxy Server Service object tracks data, but for the WinSock Proxy instead. Because each service is independent, each has its own Performance Monitor object.

You can use the counters from these objects to design performance monitoring charts to track all activity on Microsoft Proxy Server. However, Microsoft has created a basic chart and included it with Microsoft Proxy Server.

Built-in Microsoft Proxy Server Chart

In the Microsoft Proxy Server folder, you'll find a pre-made chart which will detail the basic performance counters that pertain to Microsoft Proxy Server's operation. This chart can be loaded by clicking the Monitor Microsoft Proxy Server Performance link found in the Microsoft Proxy Server folder. This link runs the Performance Monitor and automatically loads the chart, MSP.PMC. This chart should be found in the C:\MSP directory with the other Microsoft Proxy Server files.

The following counters are part of this chart:

- HTTP Server/Connections per Second—This counter tracks the number of HTTP connections per second that are made to the HTTP server. Because Microsoft Proxy Server runs as a subservice of the main HTTP server, this counter is useful in seeing the stress load of the HTTP server in general.

- Processor/percent Processor Time: INETSRV—This counter tracks the percentage of processor time devoted to the INETSRV process. The INETSRV process is the general process that drives the HTTP server.

- Processor/percent Processor Time: WSPSRV—This counter tracks the percentage of processor time devoted to the WinSock Proxy Service process.

- WinSock Proxy Server/Active Sessions—This counter tracks the number of active connections maintained by the WinSock Proxy server over the tracking period.

- Web Proxy Server Service/Cache Hits Ratio percent—This counter tracks the percentage of cache hits to extra data retrieval. The more data that comes from the cache, the higher the counter percentage.

- Memory/Available bytes—This counter tracks the amount of memory used by the system. The lower the available memory, the lower the performance of the system as a whole.

These counters will provide all the necessary tracking elements to see the basic performance of Microsoft Proxy Server, as well as how the entire system is performing. Feel free to add to or subtract from this included chart to track counters that you consider equally or more important.

Summary

NT offers a wide range of services to network users. It's easy to overload an NT server with many tasks. Having a clear plan for network layout and arrangement can be the best defense against problems that might pop up later that are difficult to get around. Make sure to spread out network services among as many NT servers as possible, and all services will run at their highest efficiency. This chapter gave important information you can use to better arrange your network services and ensure that Microsoft Proxy Server runs as best it can.

CHAPTER 11

Proxy Server and Client Applications

Because Microsoft Proxy Server is actually two separate servers, it's important that you understand what it takes for clients to connect to each server. A client application is any Internet application, such as an FTP client like WS_FTP, a Web browser such as Netscape or Internet Explorer, or a newsgroup reader such as WINVN. These clients would normally use a direct Internet connection obtained through such connectors as the Win95 Network Dialer, or Trumpet WinSock in the case of Windows for Workgroups environments. Obviously when in a proxy environment, these clients will connect to Microsoft Proxy Server, and Microsoft Proxy Server will in turn connect to the outside world for these clients. This chapter covers how to correctly configure clients to talk to Microsoft Proxy Server.

The majority of this chapter deals with the Windows 95 environment, although Microsoft Proxy Server can be accessed by other environments such as Windows for Workgroups, UNIX, or even Macintosh systems. From a user's standpoint, Windows NT 4.0 Workstation is nearly identical to Windows 95. Any client that adheres to CERN-compliant proxy standards, no matter what platform it runs on, can access the Web Proxy side of Microsoft Proxy Server over a TCP/IP network. The WinSock Proxy server side of Microsoft Proxy Server does require special client software to be installed on each workstation before clients requiring WinSock Proxy access will function correctly.

Client Proxy Support

As with many configuration elements, Web Proxy configuration is globally handled by Windows 95. True Windows 95 applications will draw from global settings set within Control Panel for their own operation. For example, true Windows 95 communication programs, such as Qmodem Pro for Windows 95, will use the internal telephony settings set within Control Panel for its own configuration. Qmodem Pro will use modem configuration, dialing configuration, and port configuration information set by Windows 95 for its own operation. True Windows 95 Internet clients will likewise draw from Internet settings set through Control Panel for their settings.

The Internet icon in Control Panel is the gateway to configuring most internal Windows 95 Internet settings. Don't have the Internet icon in your Control Panel, you say? Well, you won't unless you have installed some version of Internet Explorer. Installing Internet Explorer 3.0 will add the Internet control applet to the system. Internet Explorer is Microsoft's core Internet application, and any updates to the Windows 95 Internet control applet will be released with new versions of Internet Explorer. Even if you choose to use another browser such as Netscape as your default browser, you should always obtain the latest version of Internet Explorer to ensure that you have the most recent core Internet features available to Windows 95.

Other applications that do not get any of their Internet configuration from the internal settings of Windows 95 will have to be configured separately. This chapter covers how to set up Netscape Navigator for Web Proxy communication.

The Internet Control Applet

Once Internet Explorer has been installed into a Windows 95 or Windows for Workgroups system, the Internet icon will be available in the Control Panel. Settings made through this control applet will be held in the Windows 95 Registry and can be manually edited if you happen to be any good at dealing with the Registry (ah, for the bygone days of text-based INI files…). This section will detail how to correctly configure the internal Internet setting of Windows 95 through the Internet control applet. Figure 11.1 shows this applet.

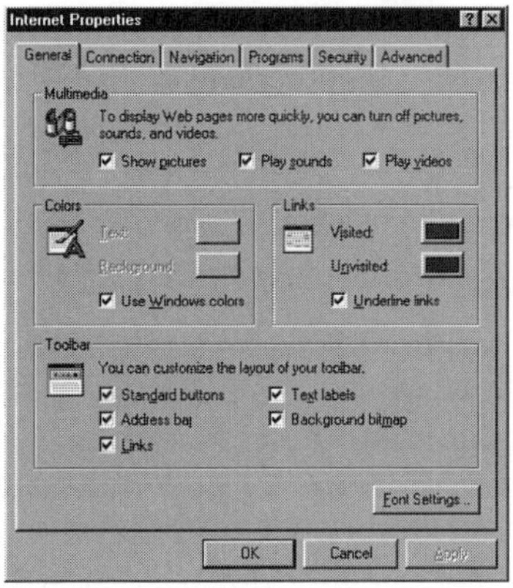

Figure 11.1.
The Internet control applet.

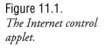

This chapter will not detail all the settings that can be configured through the Internet control applet, just the ones that deal with setting up Web Proxy communication. Many of the settings in this control applet are designed specifically for Internet Explorer, and others are used by different Internet applications, such as Microsoft's e-mail and newsgroup clients. The Connection tab will be covered here.

Keep in mind that configuring these Web Proxy settings only affects those applications that can communicate via a CERN-compliant proxy. This is a specialized form of communication and must be a built-in feature of each Internet client application you use to be of any value. Figure 11.2 shows the Connection tab of the Internet control applet.

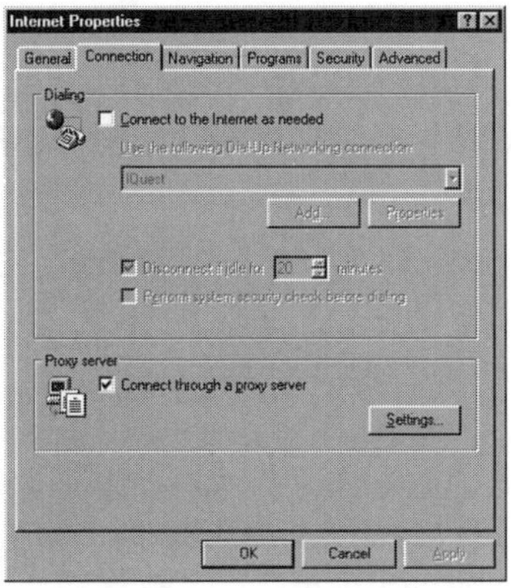

Figure 11.2.
The Connection tab of the Internet control applet.

The Connection tab controls how clients will gain access to the Internet. On this tab is the Connect to the Internet as needed check box. This is also known as Auto Dial, and when checked, and an existing Network Dialing entry is indicated, Windows 95 will automatically initiate a dial out to the indicated provider whenever an Internet client attempts to contact a server that is not within the local TCP/IP subnet. When a workstation will be connecting to the Internet through a proxy, this check box should not be checked. If it is, Windows 95 will always prompt the user with the Dial-Up Networking dialog box whenever a client attempts to contact an outside server. This happens even when the workstation is configured to connect through a proxy. Kinda strange, I know. You'd think the proxy configuration would take precedence over the demand dial, but that's not the case.

When the Connect through a proxy server check box is checked, the Settings…button will become available. This is the check box that enables Web Proxy communication. If you have installed the WinSock Proxy client software, this may have automatically been checked and correctly configured. This will be covered shortly.

Clicking the Settings…button will produce the dialog box shown in Figure 11.3.

Figure 11.3.
The Settings portion of
proxy configuration.

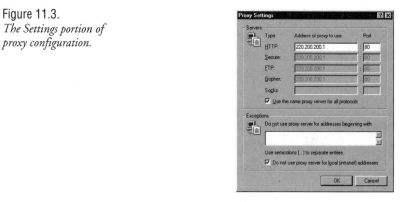

This is the most important configuration dialog box for controlling Web Proxy communication. As you can see in Figure 11.3, a Web Proxy server at 220.200.200.1 is indicated and all protocols are set to communicate with the same proxy server through port 80.

The address of available Web Proxy servers can be indicated either by Internet name, such as mydomain.com, or by direct IP address, such as 220.200.200.1. There are benefits and drawbacks to both forms of addressing.

If a verbose Internet name is used to indicate proxy location, there should be some form of name resolution capability on the internal network. Microsoft NT networks can use WINS (Windows Internet Name Service) and/or DNS (Domain Name System, Server, or Service, depending on who you talk to) to resolve names to addresses. When verbose names are used, changing actual locations of proxy servers is simple, as far as reconfiguring client workstations goes. All that needs to be done is to alter the address associated with the proxy server name in either the WINS or DNS database. Workstations will automatically resolve the name to a new address once the name server has been updated.

Using verbose names also allows WINS or DNS servers to automatically cascade client access to a group of proxy servers. The nature of name resolution under WINS or DNS makes it possible to associate a group of servers with a single name, such as proxies.com. When clients access proxies.com as a single entity, the name server will rotate which member of the group has its IP address resolved for the group name. In this manner, a name server can spread out the proxy load evenly among a group of servers. Chapter 9, "Concepts and Realities of Name Resolution with Proxy Server," deals with name resolution issues in greater detail.

A name server is not absolutely required for verbose naming of proxy servers to work correctly. If no internal name resolution server can be found by a workstation, it will rely on an internal configuration file called HOSTS as a last resort for name-to-IP pairing. The format of this file is very simple. It is a standard text file found in the \WINDOWS directory. Its format is such that each line of the file indicates a single name-to-IP pairing. The IP address is indicated first and the name is indicated second. At least one space must separate the two bits of information. A sample of this file can be found in the \WINDOWS directory under the name HOSTS.SAM. Consult this file for more details on using local name resolution.

Local name resolution will add more work than it saves. If proxy locations ever change on a LAN, the network administrator will need to manually edit the HOSTS file of all workstations requiring notification of new proxy locations. Local name resolution will also not provide cascading of a group of proxy servers as an actual name server will.

If proxy locations are indicated as actual IP addresses, no name resolution needs to be present on the network, but it does mean that each workstation will need to be manually altered if proxy locations change. Using IP addresses also ensures consistent performance should the LAN name server go down for any reason.

The Use the same proxy server for all protocols check box allows you to indicate that a single proxy server should be used for all protocols (such as HTTP, FTP, or Gopher). You can leave this check box unchecked and manually indicate different proxy servers for each protocol. It's up to you as network administrator to properly arrange multiple proxy servers in the most efficient manner. Keep in mind that the FTP protocol is the most bandwidth-demanding protocol because it normally deals with transferring large files. If you want to ensure that Web clients have smooth Internet access, it might be a good idea to set a proxy server to handle all FTP requests, leaving other proxy servers to handle HTTP (Web) requests.

The SOCKS protocol is slightly different. A SOCKS host is a network host which controls outside Internet access when clients must pass through a network firewall. Normally, communications with a SOCKS host happens on port 1080.

Under default circumstances, all communication with a proxy server will take place over port 80. Unless you have a server application on a workstation which is also listening to port 80, you should not have to change the port that clients use to communicate with the proxy server. If you happen to have an Internet-type server application running, such as a personal Web server or the like, you will need to make sure there is no port conflict. The Microsoft Proxy server can be configured to listen to a port other than 80, but this causes more confusion than it solves and must be done through the Windows NT Registry. There is no simple way of altering which port the Microsoft Proxy server listens to. It's far easier to alter any personal servers that might be running on a few workstations on the LAN to listen to another port.

As you can see in Figure 11.3, clients on this workstation will be communicating with the Internet through a single proxy located at `220.200.200.1`. Again, the address is meaningless and just happens to be the address I chose for the NT server on my LAN. I would have been better off had I chosen one of the reserved IP subnets that the InterNIC has set aside for private TCP/IP LANs. Consult Chapter 6, "Configuring Proxy Server," for more information on which subnets have been set aside for private LAN use.

The bottom part of the Proxy Settings dialog box allows you to set local exception to proxy use. You can indicate which types of addresses will not be passed to the proxy server. The names can be indicated as IP addresses or verbose Internet names. Asterisks can be used to set ranges. Some examples are: `*.netscape.com`, `*.netscape.*`, `www.*`, `209.*`, `209.176.*`, and `www.microsoft.com/sitebuilders`. Any address matching an indicated value will only be attempted as a local contact and not passed to the proxy server. Separate entries with a semicolon (;).

The last check box, Do not use proxy server for local (intranet) addresses, should be checked by default. It controls whether or not clients should go through the proxy server even when attempting to contact an Internet-type server on the LAN. When checked, the proxy server will not be contacted for local attempts. When not checked, the proxy server will handle both local and remote contacts. The proxy server can be used to control the flow of intranet traffic as well as Internet traffic.

Once all settings have been configured, click OK until you have returned to the Control Panel. Close the Control Panel. Proxy clients which rely on Windows 95 to issue Internet configuration information should now be able to contact any proxy server(s) on your network.

Configuring Netscape for Proxy Communication

Netscape can be easily configured to communicate with the Internet over the Microsoft Proxy server. This section covers how to set up Netscape 3.0 for proxy communication, although the same principles apply to configuring previous versions of Netscape as well. To start, you should have the latest version of Netscape Navigator installed. Once installed, you should start the Navigator. By default, Netscape Navigator will try to contact `home.netscape.com` when it starts. If you have checked the Connect to the Internet as needed check box in the Internet control panel, Dial-Up Networking may start to make the Internet connection for you. Make sure you cancel the connection attempt.

To get to the proxy configuration area of the Netscape options, follow these steps:

1. Click the Options menu.
2. Click the Network Preferences option. The Network Preferences dialog box will appear.
3. Click the Proxies tab. Figure 11.4 shows this dialog box.

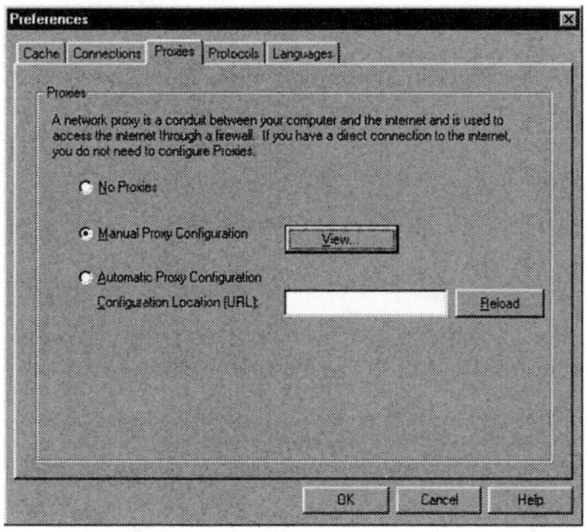

Figure 11.4.
The Proxies tab of Netscape's Network Preferences.

There are three main options on the Proxies tab of Network Preferences. The definition of each option is as follows:

■ No Proxies—When this option is selected, Netscape will attempt to communicate with the Internet directly and not use a proxy server.

■ Manual Proxy Configuration—When this option is selected, you will have the ability to manually indicate the address(es) of all proxies Netscape should be configured to talk to.

■ Automatic Proxy Configuration—When this final option is selected and a full URL (site name, directory, and target file) is indicated, Netscape can download a proxy configuration file and set itself up dynamically. The current version of Microsoft Proxy Server does not support dynamic client configurations, so this option should not be used.

The Manual Proxy Configuration option should be selected. Once it is selected, you can click the View button on this tab to further configure proxy locations in the same manner you configure the global Windows 95 proxy settings. Figure 11.5 shows the Manual Proxy Configuration dialog box.

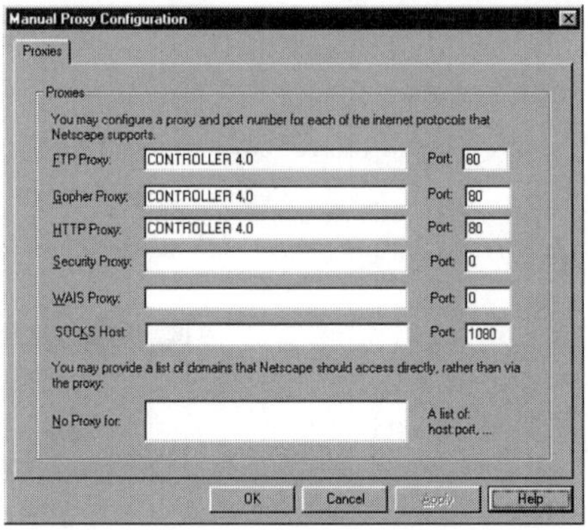

Figure 11.5.
The Manual Proxy
Configuration
dialog box.

You can see in Figure 11.5 that I am using the verbose name of the NT machine running Microsoft Proxy Server. I use WINS on my internal network and so can use the names of servers and workstations on my network for address configuration.

Just as with the global Windows 95 proxy configuration, all proxies should be set to communicate over port 80 unless there is an important reason to alter this port. If you have multiple proxy servers on your network, you can set each protocol to talk to a different proxy server. In Figure 11.5 you can see that all protocols are set to communicate with the proxy server running on "Controller 4.0." Microsoft Proxy Server does not provide SOCKS protocol proxying at this time. It may in future releases of the software.

You can also configure a list of domains that Netscape should not use the proxy to contact. These are entered in a similar manner to the way exclusions are entered in the global Windows 95 proxy configuration; however, Netscape is slightly more limited. You can only enter full domain names such as www.micrsoft.com to exclude from proxy contact. No wildcards can be used to configure partial domain names as they can in global Windows 95 proxy configuration.

Once you have configured all necessary settings on the Proxies tab, click OK and Netscape should now correctly communicate with the Internet through your proxy server.

There has been a nagging bug in the beta version of Microsoft Proxy Server that is supposed to have been fixed for release. This bug is one that causes Netscape to display FTP downloaded files as plain text in the display area. This is caused by Netscape assuming all information it receives to be HTTP documents. A supposed workaround for this is to hold the Shift key down while clicking an FTP file link. This will force Netscape to save the link as a file. This workaround only partially worked for me, saving only the first few bytes of files and then aborting the transfer. I mention it here in case you might have better luck than I with this bug, should it still be present in the release version of Microsoft Proxy Server in some form.

Installing the WinSock Proxy Client Software

Unlike proxy support, which must be internally supported by clients, the WinSock Proxy server side of Microsoft Proxy Server will allow most standard non-proxy Internet client applications to access the Internet through Microsoft Proxy Server. In order for this to happen, though, special WinSock Proxy client software must be installed on workstations before non-proxy Internet clients will be able to see the outside Internet.

It is for this reason that currently, only Windows NT, Windows 95, and Windows for Workgroups environments are supported. This means that network workstations of other operating systems, such as UNIX or Macintosh, will only be able to use the Microsoft Proxy Server Web Proxy for outside communications. Internet clients on these other types of operating systems must support CERN-compliant proxy communication to contact the outside Internet.

When Microsoft Proxy Server is installed, a shared resource is created on the server called MSPCLNT (Microsoft Proxy Client). This shared resource will contain the WinSock Proxy client setup files for all flavors of Windows NT (Alpha, Intel, for example), Windows 95, and Windows for Workgroups. Client workstations can connect to this shared resource and run the SETUP.EXE program and install WinSock Proxy support. Figure 11.6 shows this shared resource in the Network Neighborhood.

Figure 11.6.
The MSPCLNT *found in the Network Neighborhood.*

The SETUP.EXE found in the root of the MSPCLNT share can be executed for all platforms. The specific operating system will automatically be detected and the correct sub-installation routine started. On the Microsoft Proxy Server machine, the directory for the MSPCLNT share is \MSP\CLIENTS.

Another minor bug I have found in Microsoft Proxy Server that I am not certain has been fixed before final release is a bug dealing with installation. Most Windows 95 installation routines can be executed directly through the Network Neighborhood without the need of actually mapping a drive letter to a particular shared resource. With the Microsoft Proxy Server WinSock Proxy client installation, you might find that the installation routine fails about 50 percent of the time if you run it directly from the Network Neighborhood. I have had nearly 100-percent installation success from mapping the MSPCLNT to a drive letter, then running SETUP.EXE from that drive letter via the Windows 95 Explorer or from a command prompt. If you can't get the WinSock Proxy client installation routine to work through Network Neighborhood, try mapping the MSPCLNT to a drive letter and executing it from that network connection.

When Microsoft Proxy Server is installed, it examines the local network and creates some configuration files that are then used by network workstations. The important files to understand are MSPCLNT.INI and MSPLAT.TXT. If your Microsoft Proxy Server configuration changes slightly, you can manually modify these two files and save yourself from having to run through the Microsoft Proxy Server installation routine just to change a few settings. Making changes to the MSPLAT.INI file can be done manually through the internal LAT editor that is accessed through the configuration interface for the WinSock Proxy.

The MSPCLNT.INI file looks like this:

```
[Internal]
scp=9
Build=1.0.193.3

[RAPLAYER]
RemoteBindUdpPorts=6970-7170

[Master Config]Path1=\\CONTROLLER 4.0\mspclnt\

[Servers Ip Addresses]
Addr1=220.200.200.1

[Servers Ipx Addresses]
Addr1=02020202-00400526bfe8

[Common]
Port=1745
Configuration Refresh Time (Hours)=6
Set Browsers to use Proxy=1
Re-check Inaccessible Server Time (Minutes)=10
Inaccessible Servers Give Up Time (Minutes)=2
WebProxyPort=80
WWW-Proxy="CONTROLLER 4.0"
```

The definition of the important INI lines are as follows:

■ Path1—This INI element indicates the path (UNC) to the MSP Client files. It should always point to the MSPCLNT share. If you decide to move your WinSock Proxy client share to another location, make sure you change this element to reflect the new location.

■ Addr1—The address of the Microsoft Proxy Server WinSock Proxy for which this set of installation files is intended. When the WinSock Proxy client software is installed, it will configure the client workstation to talk to a specific WinSock Proxy server. Addr1 indicates the address of this server. This is found in two locations, one for the IP location of the WinSock Proxy server or the IPX location. If you have configured the WinSock Proxy to be addressed via a name, the Addr1 settings will be replaced with Name= configuration lines.

■ Port—This element indicates the control channel port the WinSock Proxy client software should use when contacting the WinSock Proxy server. By default, this is 1745 and should not be changed unless there is a very good reason to do so. If this is changed, the WinSock Proxy server itself must be changed to listen to another control channel port in the NT Registry. There is no simple user configuration area which allows you to control which control channel port the WinSock Proxy server listens to. The MSPCLNT.INI file, found in the \MSP\CLIENTS directory on the NT server running the WinSock Proxy server, controls which port the WinSock Proxy server listens to. Editing the Port= setting under the [Common] section will adjust which port the WinSock Proxy server listens to. When this setting is changed, the WinSock Proxy server must be stopped and restarted before the change will take effect.

■ Configuration Refresh Time (Hours)—This configuration element controls how often WinSock Proxy clients will contact the WinSock Proxy server to get updated connection information.

■ Set Browsers to use Proxy—If this element is set to 1, when the WinSock Proxy client software is installed, it will also modify the global Windows 95 Internet proxy settings for proxy use. This means that the Internet control applet will automatically be set for proxy communication when the WinSock Proxy client software is installed. If you do not want the WinSock Proxy client installation routine to automatically set the proxy settings for clients, set this element to equal 0.

■ WWW-Proxy—This element indicates the proxy address that the WinSock Proxy client installation routine will set clients to access. This can be either an IP address or a server name. If the server name contains a space, it should be enclosed in quotes or the WinSock Proxy client installation routine may only use the part of the name after the last space. For example, my Microsoft Proxy Server is located on the machine "Controller 4.0." If "Controller 4.0" is indicated for this element without quote marks, the WinSock Proxy client installation routine will only configure proxy clients to address a server called "4.0." This is a minor installation bug and may be fixed before full release of Microsoft Proxy Server.

If your Microsoft Proxy Server configuration changes slightly, you can edit the MSPCLNT.INI file manually and then rerun the WinSock Proxy client installation routine on client workstations to update them. Or, this INI file is also found on local workstations in the \MSPCLNT directory (default directory). The simplest way of making minor changes is to edit the INI file on the server, then copy it down to workstations in their \MSPCLNT directories.

The second file that can be manually edited is the MSPLAT.TXT file. This file contains the local address table. The local address table is a table of IP address ranges that indicate which IP addresses are local to the private LAN. The MSPLAT.TXT file looks like this:

```
10.0.0.0 10.255.255.255
172.16.0.0 172.31.255.255
192.168.0.0 192.168.255.255
220.200.200.0 220.200.200.255
127.0.0.0 127.255.255.255
224.0.0.0 255.255.255.254
```

Each line of this file indicates a range of IP addresses that can be reached on the local network segment. Any address outside of these ranges will be considered an outside Internet address and when accessed by an Internet client, the request will be remoted to the WinSock Proxy server. If you need to indicate an address of a single machine, use the machine's address as the starting and ending address, as can be seen on the second line of the above example. These address ranges are normally set up automatically when Microsoft Proxy Server is installed and the administrator selects to load the LAT from the internal NT routing table. However, if you need to add a range after installation, simply edit this file and copy it to client workstations in the \MSPCLNT directory.

Keep in mind that the local WinSock Proxy client software itself determines whether or not an Internet request is a local or remote request. Once it determines that, it will either keep the request local by passing it off to the original WinSock DLL of the system, or remoting the request to the WinSock Proxy server through the control channel port. The MSPLAT.TXT file is periodically updated by the WinSock Proxy client software on the time frame set in the MSPCLNT.INI file via the Configuraion Refresh Time (Hours) element.

If you are using a dedicated Internet connection, the address of the NIC providing this access should be indicated in the MSPLAT.TXT file as a local address.

The Physical Installation Routine

The following section details the installation process for the WinSock Proxy client software. To begin installation, execute SETUP.EXE found in the root of the MSPCLNT share from either the Network Neighborhood or from a mapped drive letter to that share. After clicking Continue at the license dialog box, the first setup dialog box appears. Figure 11.7 shows the initial setup dialog box.

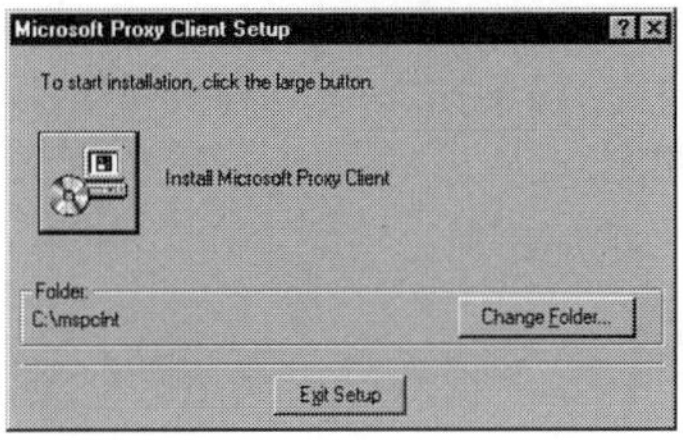

Figure 11.7.
*The initial WinSock
Proxy client setup
dialog box.*

By default, the WinSock Proxy client software will be installed into C:\MSPCLNT. This can be changed by clicking the Change Folder button and then selecting a new target directory. Once you have selected the correct target directory or accepted the default directory, click the Start button to begin the installation.

There are no other steps to the installation. Once the Start button has been selected, the WinSock Proxy client will be installed, and the original DLLs will be replaced with the WinSock Proxy DLLs. The system will need to be restarted after the WinSock Proxy client has been installed before WinSock Proxy clients can access the WinSock Proxy server.

Modifying the WinSock Proxy Client After Installation

As already mentioned, the WinSock Proxy client software draws configuration information from data files stored in the \MSPCLNT directory on each workstation. These files can be manually edited if Microsoft Proxy Server's location changes, or the network is expanded to include a wider range of addresses. The easiest way to reconfigure the WinSock Proxy client for novice users is for the network administrator to simply make the appropriate changes to the WinSock Proxy server (by reinstalling it or using the internal LAT editor) and then users can reinstall their client from the MSPCLNT share on the server. Figure 11.8 shows the setup dialog box when the WinSock Proxy installation is rerun on a system with the WinSock Proxy client already installed.

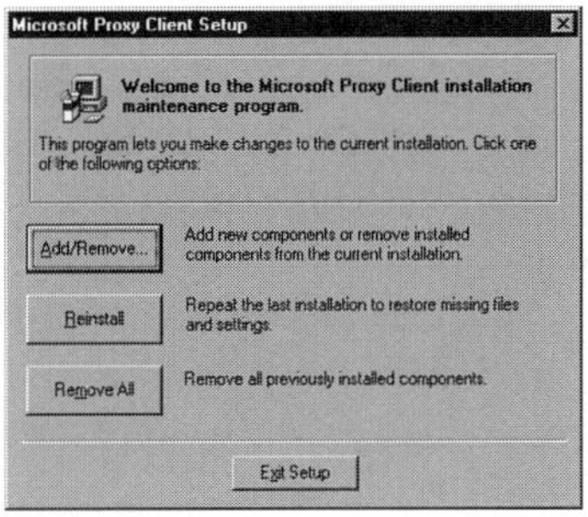

Figure 11.8.
*WinSock Proxy client
reinstallation/removal.*

The first two selections, Add/Remove and Reinstall, are nearly identical. I have no idea why Microsoft has chosen to have two options that do the same thing. The only difference is that Add/Remove will allow you to rerun the installation and choose a different target directory and Reinstall will rerun the installation using the existing target directory.

The Remove All button will remove the WinSock Proxy client completely from the system. Keep in mind that proxy configuration is separate from the WinSock Proxy client, and removing the WinSock Proxy client in no way affects the settings for proxy communication. Once the WinSock Proxy client has been removed, the system has to be restarted.

What Happens When the WinSock Proxy Client Software Is Installed

In order for the WinSock Proxy client software to do its magic, it must supersede the internal WinSock DLLs of an operating system. When the WinSock Proxy client is installed, the existing `winsock.dll` (for 16-bit clients) and `wsock32.dll` (for 32-bit clients) files are renamed and the WinSock Proxy client DLLs are copied over in their place. In this manner, the WinSock Proxy client will always receive any Internet-type requests. If the request is for a machine that can be found on the local network, the replacement WinSock Proxy WinSocks will simply forward the request to the original WinSock DLLs for normal handling. If the request is found to be a remote request, the WinSock Proxy WinSocks will contact the WinSock Proxy server through the control channel port, and a socket will be established between WinSock Proxy client and WinSock Proxy server as though the Internet client were talking to the actual Internet target server directly.

In original configurations, the `winsock.dll` file is found in the \WINDOWS directory and the `wsock32.dll` file is found in the \WINDOWS\SYSTEM directory. When the WinSock Proxy client software is installed, the original `winsock.dll` is renamed `_msrws16.dll` and the original `wsock32.dll` file is renamed `_msrws32.dll`. The directory locations stay the same. You can manually uninstall the WinSock Proxy client by deleting the replacement DLLs and renaming the original DLLs back to their original names. Be very careful not to delete the original DLLs.

One of the major drawbacks to the WinSock Proxy client software is that it is difficult to de-activate for short periods of time if you want to access the Internet directly from a dial-up connection from a local workstation. If the WinSock Proxy client can contact the WinSock Proxy server, it will always use that connection over a locally established connection. There are some Internet clients that simply do not take kindly to having their packets forwarded, so they have to have a locally established connection. The workaround for this is to do a little copying of DLL files back and forth when needed. Unfortunately, the `winsock.dll` and `wsock32.dll` files will be locked open if they have been used and cannot be overwritten, so you will need to boot to DOS in order to copy over them.

If the WinSock Proxy client software cannot connect to the WinSock Proxy server, it will allow a local Internet connection to function normally, but there will be a nagging delay between request and contact. The WinSock Proxy client will always try to contact the WinSock Proxy server on all Internet requests, so the delay in response may be too annoying to accept.

Disabling the WinSock Proxy Client Without Copying Files

Microsoft seems to be vacillating back and forth on which programs store configuration data in the registry and which still use the old-fashioned INI files. The WinSock Proxy client relies exclusively on INI files to store configuration data. As already mentioned, the MSPCLNT.INI file found in the \MSPCLNT directory is the primary configuration file, but some WinSock Proxy settings are held in the SYSTEM.INI file found in the \WINDOWS directory. The following entries are added to the SYSTEM.INI file upon WinSock Proxy client installation.

```
[Microsoft Proxy Service]
Ini File Path=C:\mspclnt\mspclnt.ini
Configuration Location=C:\mspclnt\
Security32=secur32.dll
Security16=security.dll
Disable=0
```

The Ini File Path entry indicates where the WinSock Proxy client can find MSPCLNT.INI. The Configuration Location entry indicates where the WinSock Proxy client can find the MSPLAT.TXT file for determining which requests are to be kept local and which requests are to be forwarded to the WinSock Proxy server. The Security16 and Security32 entries point to the security DLL files the WinSock Proxy client should call on when attempting to get authorization from the WinSock Proxy server for a user to access a given protocol. The WinSock Proxy server can be configured to limit access to any protocol based on standard NT username and password. Without the security DLL files, the WinSock Proxy client will be denied access to the WinSock Proxy server.

An additional INI directive can be added. This directive is

```
Disabled=1
```

When present, this is supposed to turn off the WinSock Proxy client and return the TCP/IP operation of the system to normal. The system will have to be restarted before the changes will take effect.

Controlling the WinSock Proxy Client Software Through the WinSock Proxy Control Applet

After the WinSock Proxy client software is installed, a new control applet will be present in the Control Panel of all Windows systems (WFWG, Win95, and WinNT Workstation 3.51/4.0). This control applet is called WSP Client and can be used to quickly turn on and off the WinSock Proxy client software redirector. Figure 11.9 shows this control applet.

Figure 11.9.
*The WinSock Proxy
client control applet
found in the Control
Panel.*

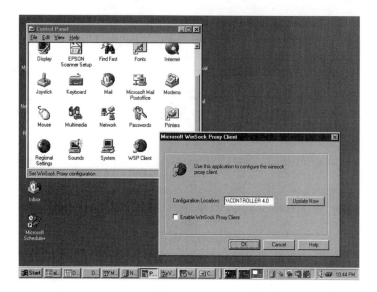

To enable or disable the WinSock Proxy client, simply check or uncheck the Enable WinSock Proxy Client check box. The system will need to be restarted after the client software status has been changed.

The WinSock Proxy server that the workstation communicates with can be quickly changed as well by indicating a different machine name in the Configuration Location field. The machine name listed here must be a NetBIOS machine name and not a DNS host name. Once a new machine has been indicated, the Update Now button will force the workstation to contact the new WinSock Proxy server and download a fresh set of configuration files from it. The workstation should not need to be restarted after changing the WinSock Proxy server that it communicates with, but it's always a good idea to restart after any significant configuration change has been made.

Installing the WinSock Proxy Client Software Under Windows 3.11

Installing the WinSock Proxy client under Windows 3.11 (and Workgroups) is done in a similar fashion to setting up the WinSock Proxy client under Windows 95. The same SETUP.EXE can be run from the MSPCLNT share on the server, and the installed file arrangement is the same. Once the appropriate files have been installed, the installation routine will present the dialog box shown in Figure 11.10.

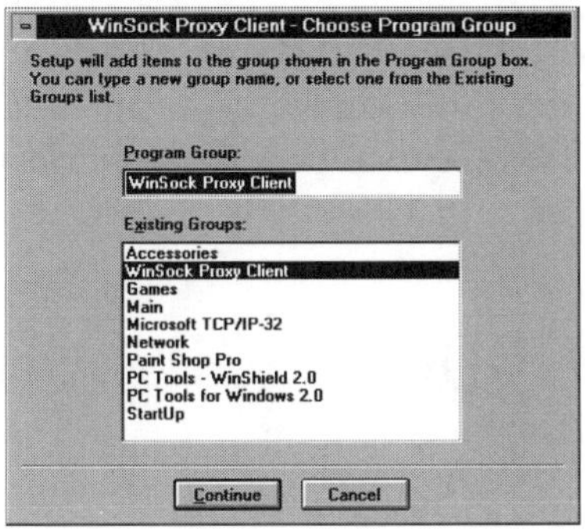

Figure 11.10.
*Creating a Microsoft
Proxy Server Client
group under
Windows 3.11.*

At this stage, you can indicate the name of the group to add to the system for the Microsoft Proxy Server client. The installation routine only adds one file, SETUP1.EXE, to this group. If you prefer, you can simply add this entry to the Main group or to the Accessories group.

You do not need to have TCP/IP for Windows 3.11 installed in order for the WinSock Proxy client to work. The WinSock Proxy client can operate over an IPX connection on Windows 3.11 workstations with some limited functionality. For complete functionality, you should obtain TCP/IP for Windows 3.11. Support for the TCP/IP protocol under Windows 3.11 can be downloaded from ftp.microsoft.com in the \softlib\mslfiles directory as TCP32B.EXE. At present, this archive contains the latest TCP/IP support files for Windows 3.11.

Reinstallation of the WinSock Proxy client is similar to reinstalling the client under Windows 95, except the Add/Remove option is not available. Figure 11.11 shows the setup dialog box when running SETUP.EXE from the MSPCLNT share when the WinSock Proxy client is already installed.

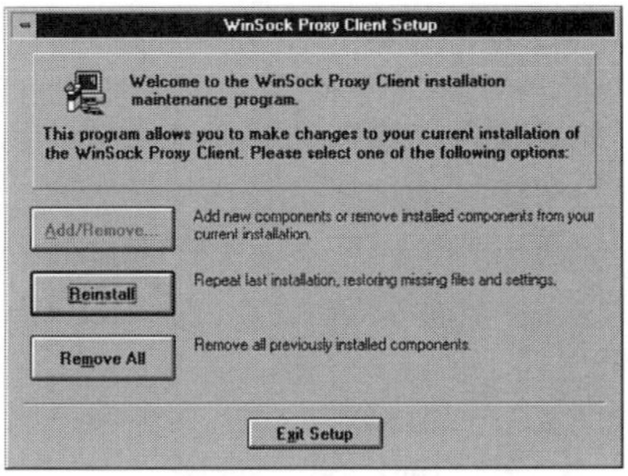

Figure 11.11.
*Reinstalling the
WinSock Proxy client
under Windows 3.11.*

The Reinstall option will reinstall the client in the default, directly using the settings found from the server. The Remove All option will remove the WinSock Proxy client from the system. The system will need to be rebooted after the client is removed.

Proxy Configuration Under Windows 3.11

Unlike proxy settings in Windows 95, Windows 3.11 does not have a global control panel for controlling proxy communication. Each individual client (such as Netscape Navigator and Internet Explorer 2.0) will need to be configured independently for proxy communication.

Client Application Setup

Very little, if any, extra configuration should need to be done to Internet clients that will use the WinSock Proxy server. These applications will operate without any problems. They will assume they are talking directly to a server on the Internet, when in reality they are talking to the WinSock Proxy server that is talking to the target Internet server for them. The WinSock Proxy server will simulate the operation of the remote server in every way, and the client application will never know the difference.

The only exception to this comes with FTP clients. Normally, FTP clients send out requests over port 21 and receive information back from a target server over port 23. In order to operate correctly with the WinSock Proxy server, FTP clients must be able to do something called PASV mode, which is sometimes called Passive Transfers. PASV mode is an alteration to normal FTP communication where the client tells the server which port to respond back on. This allows FTP clients to correctly communicate over such things as firewalls. A firewall is designed to prevent unauthorized inbound connections over known ports, such as FTP port 23. By having the client tell a remote server which port to respond on, the firewall will allow the return connection. The following is a short connection log made by WS_FTP32, a very popular FTP client. This log shows how PASV mode is established.

```
WINSOCK.DLL: Microsoft Windows Sockets Version 1.1.
WS_FTP32 951229, Copyright _ 1994-1995 John A. Junod. All rights reserved.
- -
connecting to 205.199.96.2 ...
Connected to 205.199.96.2 port 21
220 slc.axxis.com FTP server (Version wu-2.4(4) Fri Mar 10 12:53:25 MST 1995)
➥ready.
USER anonymous
331 Guest login ok, send your complete e-mail address as password.
PASS xxxxxx
230 Guest login ok, access restrictions apply.
PWD
257 "/" is current directory.
SYST
215 UNIX Type: L8 Version: BSD-199306
Host type (2): UNIX (standard)
PASV
227 Entering Passive Mode (205,199,96,2,8,164)
connecting to 205.199.96.2:2212
- -
connecting to 205.199.96.2 ...
Connected to 205.199.96.2 port 2212
LIST
150 Opening ASCII mode data connection for /bin/ls.
Received 375 bytes in 0.5 secs, (8241.76 bps), transfer succeeded
226 Transfer complete.
```

You can see that once the client has logged in to the server, it sends the PASV command to the server. The server then lets the client indicate which port further communication should take place over, in this case, port 2212. Once the handshake is complete, the FTP client and FTP server begin normal operation.

Without enabling PASV mode, FTP clients can still connect to FTP servers, but full data transfers will abort with odd errors as the WinSock Proxy server steps over the data flowing back from the FTP server.

Enabling PASV mode is a simple task with WS_FTP32. This is done by altering the Advanced Settings for any given Session Profile. Figure 11.12 shows an average WS_FTP32 Session Profile with the advanced settings opened.

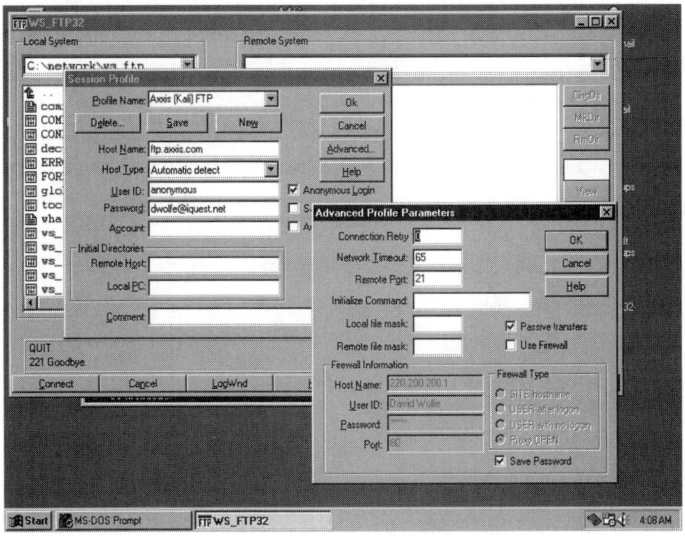

Figure 11.12.
A WS_FTP32 Session Profile with the Advanced settings open.

Sessions under WS_FTP32 can be set up normally, as though the workstation would be directly connected to the Internet. The only difference is that the Passive transfers check box must be checked. Make sure you don't alter the default outbound port (Remote Port setting). If this is changed, the WinSock Proxy server will not correctly see the connection attempt and/or deny access permission based on the security settings for another protocol.

All other major Internet applications, such as SMTP and POP3 (e-mail) clients and NNTP (newsgroup readers) clients, should not need any extra configuration. Simply configure them as though the workstation would be directly connected to the Internet, and they will operate as normal through the WinSock Proxy server.

Web Browser WinSock Proxy Access

Web browsers such as Netscape Navigator and Internet Explorer can use the WinSock Proxy server also. They are not confined to using the Web Proxy server for their access. The major benefit in letting Web browsers use the Web Proxy server over the WinSock Proxy server is that the Proxy server provides caching features that help increase performance. The WinSock Web Proxy server provides no caching services for any protocol it supports.

In order to force a Web browser to use the WinSock Proxy server, simply turn off proxy communication support for the browser. The WinSock Proxy client will then receive the browser's traffic and handle it accordingly. The WinSock Proxy server comes preconfigured to handle HTTP requests over port 80.

Wait a minute though, if the Web Proxy server listens to port 80 requests, and the WinSock Proxy server also listens to port 80 requests, how does Microsoft Proxy Server determine which server is being called upon? It's a simple enough answer. When a proxy client attempts to contact the proxy server, it does so by directing its request specifically to the IP address of the proxy server over port 80. In this request is a standardized data format containing information about which Internet server the proxy server is supposed to contact and exactly what the proxy server is supposed to retrieve. When a non-proxy browser requests data over port 80, it is doing so by directing the request to an IP beyond the WinSock Proxy server. The data format of such a request is different than the data format used under proxy communications. This is how the two servers maintain separate operation while still listening to the same port.

Summary

Setting up Web Proxy and WinSock Proxy clients is a relatively simple process, once you understand the principles of what's going on. The flexibility Microsoft Proxy Server offers to small and medium businesses is amazing. Until now, Windows users had very few options when it came to accessing the Internet. They either had to have a local dial-out connection, or have a permanent connection to their machine. Some smaller companies have produced applications which provide similar functionality to Microsoft Proxy Server, but at a poorer performance and with a lesser degree of flexibility. Microsoft Proxy Server allows network administrators to set up client workstations in about five minutes with very little configuration needed for individual applications.

CHAPTER 12

Controlling the Proxy Server Cache

The Web Proxy server side of Microsoft Proxy Server can perform data caching of any and all objects that pass through it. The WinSock Proxy server side of Microsoft Proxy Server performs no caching. That is one of the main advantages the Web Proxy server has over the WinSock Proxy server. Rumor has it that Microsoft will develop a caching feature for the WinSock Proxy server in future releases of Microsoft Proxy Server. In the current release of Microsoft Proxy Server (1.0), only the Web Proxy server performs caching.

Caching is the process of storing objects such as graphics, sound bites, and document text on a local hard drive. If a client requests information from the Internet that has already been cached by Microsoft Proxy Server, Microsoft Proxy Server will pass the cached information to the client rather than going out to the Internet site and retrieving the information. Caching enhances Microsoft Proxy Server's performance in the following ways:

- The ability to support more clients with a smaller connection.
- A much faster response time for clients when cached information is present.
- The ability to service clients with Internet information when the target Internet site is unreachable.

Without caching, Microsoft Proxy Server has to retrieve all requests directly from the Internet. This creates a great deal of traffic even when clients are requesting the same information over and over again. Web browsers perform their own caching of data, but this is generally done on a small scale. Cache sizes for client browsers are usually set to around five megabytes. There is no default cache size for the Microsoft Proxy Server; however, the suggested amount is 100 megs plus ½ meg for each proxy client that will be supported. If your network has 25 proxy clients, the minimum cache size that should be set is 113 megs. Because Microsoft Proxy Server will be forwarding requests from many clients on a network, individual clients may benefit from the activity of other Microsoft Proxy Server users. Microsoft Proxy Server also has some advanced caching features that allow it to ensure the objects in the cache are always current. Client browser caches are only able to check how current an object is when the object is directly requested.

When the Microsoft Proxy Server starts, it performs integrity checks on the data contained within the cache. If the cache is very large and spread out over many drives, it may take a while for the integrity check to be completed. You will be unable to alter the cache settings in any way until the check is complete. If you jump in to configuring the cache immediately after the NT machine starts, you may get a message stating that you cannot configure the cache. You should be allowed to reconfigure the cache settings after waiting a few minutes and retrying the action.

The Cache

In a default installation, Microsoft Proxy Server stores its cache in five subdirectories from the primary directory C:\URLCACHE. These subdirectories are DIR1 through DIR5. Microsoft Proxy Server breaks up the cache content between multiple smaller subdirectories to increase search speed. Searching a single huge directory can take longer than searching multiple smaller subdirectories.

Each subdirectory will be used equally by the Web Proxy server. All cached objects will be stored equally among these five subdirectories. For example, if the default cache size for a drive is 50 megs, each cache subdirectory will contain about 10 megs of data when the cache is full.

The objects stored in the cache are not stored under their original names. They are renamed to a coded format that ensures that conflicts between objects of identical names do not overwrite each other. The cross reference data of coded name to actual name is stored in data files also held in the cache subdirectories. These data files are the elements which are searched when clients request Internet objects that might be found in the cache. This increases performance, but does run the risk of wasting the entire contents of a cache directory should the data files themselves become corrupt. Another benefit of using data files to reference cache objects is the ability to set time to live (TTL) values for objects. Once an object's TTL has expired, Microsoft Proxy Server will no longer pass it out to clients. Microsoft Proxy Server will retrieve a more recent copy from the Internet and update the object in the cache.

Microsoft Proxy Server cache subdirectories can be on any local hard drive. They should be located on the quickest drives and if possible should be held on drives with the NTFS format. The NTFS format is a faster and more reliable disk architecture than FAT and also provides greater security features for a network environment. The primary drawback to NTFS is that it is inaccessible to DOS systems. If you dual boot your computer between NT server and a DOS system, changing a disk to NTFS will render that disk unreadable to DOS.

Modifying the Cache Size

The cache location and size can be modified from the Caching tab of the Web Proxy properties dialog box. The Change Cache Size button allows you to manually alter or add to the cache structure and size. Figure 12.1 shows this dialog box.

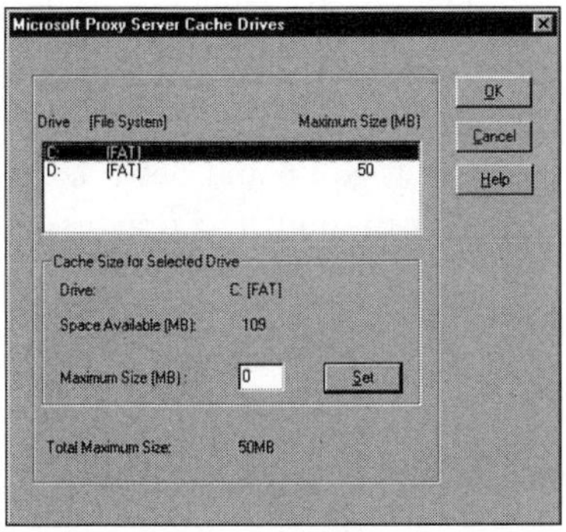

Figure 12.1.
The Web Proxy cache size and location.

Setting the cache size and location is as straightforward as highlighting the desired drive for a piece of the cache and entering the maximum size for the cache that drive should hold. Once a size has been indicated, clicking the Set button will set the indicated cache size for the selected drive. The total cache size between drives should meet or exceed the suggested total size of 100 megs plus ½ meg for each Web Proxy client that will be supported.

Modifying Maximum Object Size and Filters

If clients are constantly requesting pages containing large graphics and sound bytes, the performance of the cache will be poor because it will contain few overall objects, just a few larger ones. If you would like to set a maximum size for cache objects, the Advanced button on the Caching tab of proxy properties will allow you to do this. Figure 12.2 shows this section of Web Proxy properties.

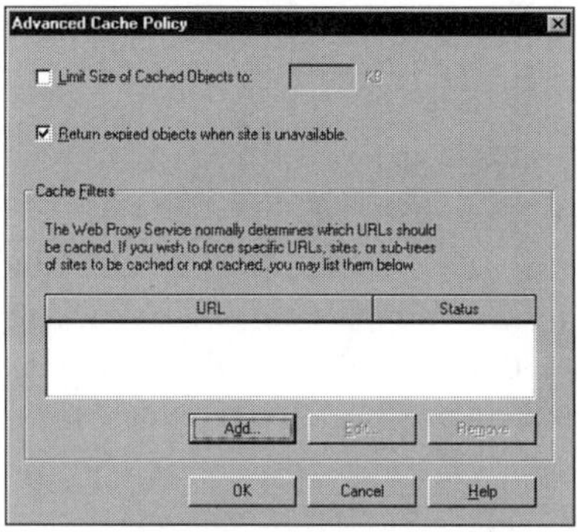

Figure 12.2.
Microsoft Proxy Server's Advanced Cache Policy settings.

If you wish to limit the size of cached objects, check the Limit Size of Cached Objects to check box and indicate an object size. I do suggest limiting the size to about 100 KB. If any single object exceeds 100 KB, it is unlikely that it will be requested time and time again by clients. It is more likely a large graphic that will only need to be seen once.

The Return expired objects when site is unavailable check box controls whether the Web Proxy will send an expired cache object to a client when the Web Proxy server cannot contact the target site. Many sites will go up and down constantly. Another beneficial responsibility of Microsoft Proxy Server is to simulate a response from down sites.

The lower portion of the Advanced Cache Policy settings dialog box allows you to configure the cache filtering of specific Internet sites.

Some Internet sites have data that changes daily. The normal document header should contain page expiration information that will allow Microsoft Proxy Server to automatically expire these types of pages almost immediately and not cache them. However, not all sites include page expiration information and therefore should be manually excluded from being cached. This dialog box allows you to indicate such sites and/or subbranches. An asterisk can be used here as a wildcard to indicate sites (for example, www.windows95.com/newfiles/*).

Clicking the Add button (or the Edit button to alter an existing filter) will allow you to indicate a site for special filtering. Figure 12.3 shows this Cashe Filter Properties dialog box.

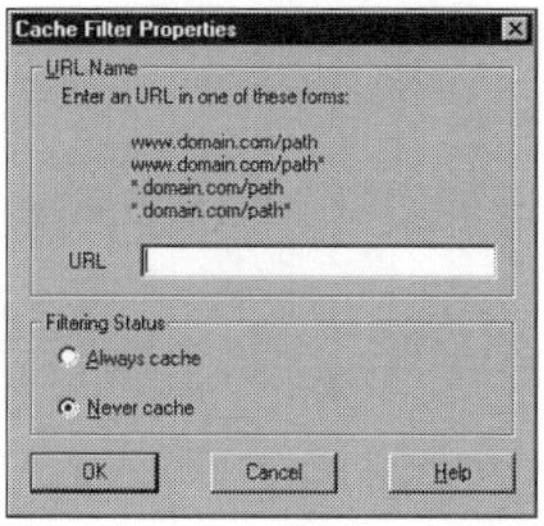

Figure 12.3.
*Adding a special filter
condition in the Cache
Filter Properties
dialog box.*

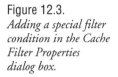

To complete a filter, simply indicate the site to filter and indicate whether the site is to be expressly filtered or not. The general cache policy for the Web Proxy server can be to cache or not cache any data. By default, the Web Proxy will cache all HTTP data it can. If the general cache policy is for no caching, the sites indicated here would be for special caching. As you can see in the figure, wildcards can be used to indicate partial branches.

Methods of Caching

When the Enable Caching check box is checked on the Caching tab, caching will take place. If it is unchecked, the only data that will be cached will be from those sites expressly indicated for caching in the cache filter.

There are two forms of caching that Microsoft Proxy Server uses. The first is passive caching and the second is active caching. These two caching methods are significantly different.

Passive Caching

Microsoft Proxy Server uses passive caching most often. This form of caching requires no extra activity on the part of Microsoft Proxy Server. When objects are originally requested from the Internet by client applications, Microsoft Proxy Server retrieves them and first places a copy of the object in the cache (and sets a TTL for the object) and then passes the object on to the client requesting the data. This is done only if the object is cacheable at all. The following criteria must be met before an object or HTML document can be passively cached:

- The HTTP document request line cannot contain any keyword elements.
- The object had to be requested with a GET command from the client. GET is the primary form of document retrieval used by Web, FTP, and gopher browsers.
- The document header cannot contain user authentication data or data that expressly forbids caching of the page or object.
- The server sending the information must respond with a result code of 200 (success). Any other result code will prevent objects from being cached.
- The page expiration date (contained within the document) must exceed the value of the page expiration date field returned by the Internet server. If the two values match, the object will not be cached.

■ The page or object cannot be encrypted or protected by the Secure Socket Layer protocol (SSL).

The sequence of events when a client requests an Internet object through the Internet proceeds like this:

1. The client requests a page or object from the Internet.
2. Microsoft Proxy Server intercepts the request.
3. Microsoft Proxy Server checks the cache to see if the object is present.
4. If the object is present, Microsoft Proxy Server checks to see if the object's TTL has expired. If it has, the object is again retrieved from the Internet, and the TTL is updated. If the object's TTL has expired but the object has not changed on the Internet site, Microsoft Proxy Server simply updates the TTL of the object. The object is then passed to the client.
5. If the object is not in the cache, Microsoft Proxy Server retrieves it and, if it can be cached, stores it and then forwards it to the client.

If the Internet server returns an error of 403 or 404, the error condition response is stored in the cache. This is referred to as *negative caching* because Microsoft Proxy Server is storing the negative result from the server. Error 403 is returned when a client is attempting to access a page that the user does not have authorization for. Many sites on the Internet are now requiring paid membership for access. When non-authorized users attempt to access information on such sites, the server will often respond with a result code of 403. Result code 403 is a standard result code indicating that the request URL cannot be found.

Many sites use something known as *cookies* to personalize the data they send to clients. Cookies can vary Web pages and make a site seem more dynamic. They can also be used as a form of simple authentication. Cookies will be ignored by Microsoft Proxy Server, and pages with cookies in the header will be cached as long as none of the non-cacheable situations apply.

Passive caching only caches objects when a client requests them. The opposite of passive caching is *active caching*, which is when Microsoft Proxy Server takes an active role to ensure that the objects within the cache are current.

Active Caching

The Caching tab of Web Proxy properties allows you to control how Microsoft Proxy Server handles object TTL and the active caching policy. By default, Microsoft Proxy Server will perform some active caching (when the Enable Active Caching check box is checked). The active caching policy can be increased so that Microsoft Proxy Server will work harder at ensuring the objects in the cache are current.

Active caching allows Microsoft Proxy Server to update cache objects on its own during certain times without having to rely on clients to request objects before they can be verified. Microsoft Proxy Server will perform active caching according to the following guidelines:

- Popularity of an object: The more times an object has been requested by clients on a LAN, the more likely Microsoft Proxy Server is to actively make sure that object is current.

- Server load: Microsoft Proxy Server will automatically verify objects when Internet traffic is low. This helps to make sure that Microsoft Proxy Server is not compounding a high stress load during peak times by adding to the Internet traffic itself.

- Object Expiration: Microsoft Proxy Server will verify objects which are closer to passing their TTL than it will objects that have a longer time to live.

When Microsoft Proxy Server performs active caching, the objects in the cache are more likely to be current. This helps to increase performance for clients because Microsoft Proxy Server is less likely to have to go out to the Internet to retrieve data when current copies of objects are present in the cache. Non-peak times are used to update cache objects so active caching spreads the workload out somewhat by using time when the connection is less stressed.

Figure 12.4 shows the Caching tab of the Web Proxy properties dialog box.

Figure 12.4
The Caching tab of
Web Proxy properties.

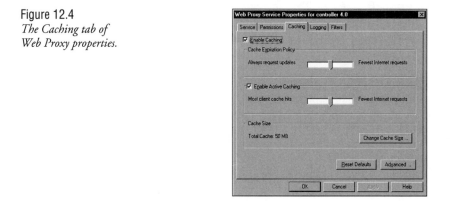

The Cache Expiration Policy slider controls the TTL value assigned to objects. The further to the right the slide is set, the longer objects can live in the cache before they will be updated. All the way to the left on this slider indicates that objects will always be retrieved from the Internet, which effectively nullifies the cache.

The Enable Active Caching slider controls how energetically Microsoft Proxy Server actively caches. When the slider is to the right, Microsoft Proxy Server will perform little active caching and only during off-peak periods. When the slider is to the left, Microsoft Proxy Server will actively cache a greater number of cache objects and will do so during periods of higher Internet accessing by clients.

Cascading Proxy Servers

In the 1.0 release of Microsoft Proxy Server, cascading Web Proxy servers are not supported. This doesn't mean that users can't access a chain of Web Proxy servers is succession, but this is done through a name server, such as a DNS or WINS server. It's not an ability that is internal to Microsoft Proxy Server. Future releases of Microsoft Proxy Server will have built-in Web Proxy cascading, which will allow multiple Microsoft Proxy Servers to share a common cache. Currently, when DNS or WINS is used to group a set of Microsoft Proxy Servers for daisy-chained access, each server maintains its own cache and operates completely independently. Chapter 9, "Concepts and Realities of Name Resolution with Proxy Server," contains detailed information on setting up a name server to perform chained access to a group of Web Proxy servers.

Summary

The Microsoft Proxy Server cache is neither complicated nor difficult to maintain, but it is a vital part of the proxy process. Without it, Internet client performance through a small connection will be poor for many users. Because the intent of Microsoft Proxy Server is to provide inexpensive Internet access to a LAN through a smaller connection, the cache is an important part of the equation. If you can spare the hard drive space, it would be a good idea to double or even triple the available cache space that Microsoft Proxy Server can use. If there are many Internet users on your LAN accessing many different sites on the Internet, increasing the cache size can greatly help Microsoft Proxy Server's performance.

CHAPTER 13

Monitoring Proxy Server Directly and Via SNMP

There are two primary methods to monitor the activity of Microsoft Proxy Server. The first and more common is activity logging, which can be done through standard comma delimited text files, or to a qualified database through ODBC drivers (Open DataBase Connectivity). The second method, and one which will be available to a small minority of network administrators, is monitoring through SNMP (Simple Network Management Protocol). SNMP is a protocol service that can be installed in Windows NT. The purpose of SNMP is to serve out monitoring and sometimes controlling data to a remote workstation(s) so that services running on an NT server can be monitored and controlled from an outside location.

Utilizing SNMP requires client software on the workstation monitoring the SNMP data stream. Several companies make SNMP software, but it's normally pretty expensive stuff. This chapter doesn't delve too deeply into the realm of SNMP. Its primary focus is to explain the structure of the Microsoft Proxy Server logs and also explain the principles of how to connect Microsoft Proxy Server to a database server engine so that log information can be saved to a database file via ODBC.

Microsoft Proxy Server Logs

Microsoft Proxy Server can log information to a text file or to a database through ODBC drivers to engines, such as an Access Server or an SQL Server. Logging to a text file is a very simple process and will give a network administrator a quick way of seeing what transactions have transpired through both Microsoft Proxy Server components (the Web Proxy and the WinSock Proxy). The logs (in either text format or database format) can then be used to generate reports of daily, weekly, or monthly activity.

Text File Logs

By default, Microsoft Proxy Server is configured to log all transaction information to text file logs. The default location of these files will be:

- Web Proxy logs: `c:\winnt\system32\w3plogs`
- WinSock Proxy logs: `c:\winnt\system32\wsplogs`

Normally, a new log file is created automatically every day, although this can be changed to weekly or monthly. A new log file can also be created when the current log file reaches a specific size.

In the Properties sheets of both the Web Proxy and WinSock Proxy services, there is a Logging tab. This tab is identical for both services (except for log file location values) and controls all logging settings for each server. Figure 13.1 shows the Logging tab of the Web Proxy.

Figure 13.1.
*The Logging tab of
Web Proxy Properties.*

Chapter 6, "Configuring Proxy Server," covers in detail all of the settings found on this tab. To ensure that logging is enabled for both proxy servers, make sure the Enable Logging check box is checked on both Logging tabs.

When a log file is created, its name is based on the current date. For example, a log file created on December 5, 1996, would have the filename: w3961205.log. Log files can be in one of two formats: regular and verbose. *Regular logs* are shorter format logs that do not contain all available data elements, and *verbose logs* contain a complete set of all available log data. Figure 13.2 shows a sample of a regular log file generated by the WinSock Proxy. The format of the log files created by both proxy servers is identical.

Figure 13.2.
A regular log file sample.

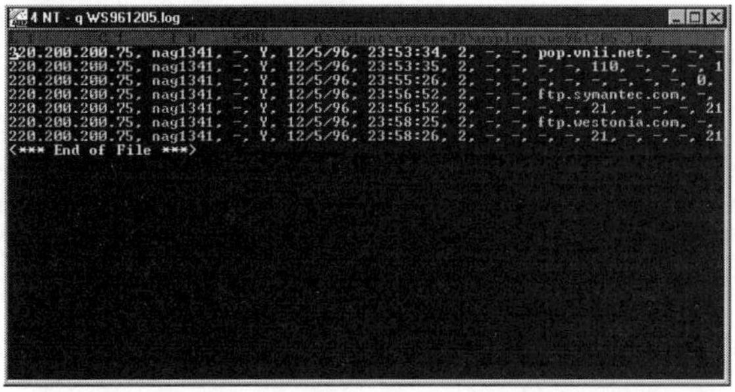

Figure 13.3 shows a sample of a verbose log file.

Figure 13.3.
A verbose log file sample.

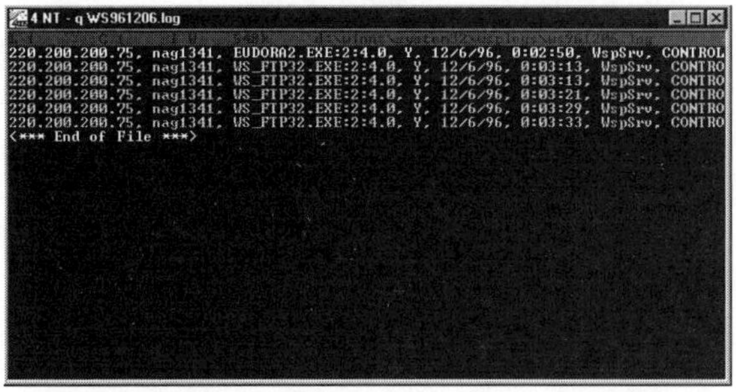

I have purposely tried to access the same sequence of sites in both log files so you can see a side-by-side comparison (well, as close as possible since I did the first log file sample just before midnight and the second sample just past midnight).

As you can tell, each line of the log file is one record. Fields within the record are separated by commas. In the regular log file sample, the sequence of fields within a record is still the same; however, because a regular log is a reduced version of the verbose log, some of the fields are simply represented by a dash (-). This helps to cut down the size of the log files in busy proxy conditions. If you are the administrator for a network of 100 or more proxy users, you might find that daily logs files exceed 10 megs, depending on the amount of traffic that passes through the proxies.

Data Field Definitions

In order to understand the contents of the log file, the following is a definition of each field in the same order you will find in the log files themselves. Remember that log files from the Web Proxy and the WinSock Proxy are identical in format, and regular logs will not omit any data fields, just replace some information with a dash.

Figure 13.4 shows a more complicated log file example.

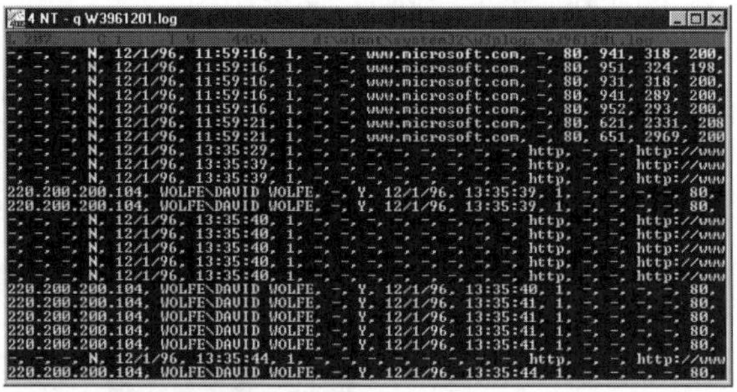

Figure 13.4.

A full example of a Web Proxy log file.

1. Client Computer IP—This field is the IP address of the client connecting to the proxy. When the Web Proxy performs an active caching session (where it goes out to the Web on its own to refresh the contents of its cache), it will log an entry into the log as itself, and this field will be the IP of the Web Proxy server.

2. Client Username—If the name of the user of the proxy client is known, it will be displayed in this field. If it is an anonymous client, the word "anonymous" will be used as a field value.

3. Client Agent—This field is the agent the client user is using to access the proxy server. With Web Proxy clients, the client application will send this information to the Web Proxy in the connection header. With WinSock Proxy clients, the WinSock client software on the workstation will determine the actual name of the program running and pass that along to the WinSock Proxy through the control channel for logging. This field also contains important client operating system information, separated from the agent name by a colon. With Web Proxy clients, this information may or may not be passed to the server in the connection header. With WinSock clients, this information is always passed to the server by the WinSock client software. An example of operating system information passed to the Web Proxy by a client may look like this: compatible; MSIE 3.0; Windows 95. Operating system information passed to the WinSock Proxy by the WinSock client software will look like this: 2:4.0, which is the version code for Windows 95. The following table details the operating system codes logged by the WinSock Proxy:

Logged Code	Operating System
0:3.1	Windows 3.1
0:3.11	Windows for Workgroups
0:3.95	Windows 95 (connection made by a 16-bit client application)
1:3.11	Windows for Workgroups (connection by a client using the Win32s extensions)
2:4.0	Windows 95 (connection made by a 32-bit client)
3:3.51	Windows NT 3.51
3:4.0	Windows NT 4.0

A full example of the field value of this data bit logged by the Web Proxy might be: Mozilla/2.0 (compatible; MSIE 3.0; Windows 95). A full example of the field value of this data bit logged by the WinSock Proxy might be: WS_FTP32.EXE:2:4.0. The exact value of this field when logged by the Web Proxy will vary according to the header information sent to the Web Proxy by the client application making the proxy connection.

4. Authentication Status—This field indicates whether the client is connected with an authenticated connection. A Y value will indicate the client has been verified against the NT security database.

5. Date Logged—The date when the proxy server created the log entry.

6. Time Logged—The time when the proxy server created the log entry. This is given in 24-hour format.

7. Server Name—The name of the server that entered the log record. When Verbose logging is selected, this will be WspSrv for the WinSock Proxy and it will be W3Proxy for the Web Proxy. When Regular logging is selected, this field will be a numeric value of 1 for the Web Proxy and a 2 for the WinSock Proxy.

8. Proxy Name—The name of the NT server running Microsoft Proxy Server. This will be the NetBIOS name given to the machine via the Network Control Panel.

9. Referring Server Name—This is currently a reserved field. In later releases of Microsoft Proxy Server it will be used to indicate the name of the downstream proxy server that referred the connection to the current proxy server. This will be helpful when dealing with cascaded proxy servers that operate in concert with each other. In the current version of Microsoft Proxy Server (1.0) this field will simply contain a dash.

10. Destination Name—This field indicates the domain name the client connected to through the proxy server. This is not always the name the client requested a connection to because some sites on the Internet perform automatic connection forwarding. If the information was pulled from the cache (only when dealing with the Web Proxy), this field will contain a dash.

11. Destination IP Address—This field indicates the IP address the client connected to though the proxy server. As with the previous field, this information may simply be a dash if the data was obtained from the Web Proxy cache.

12. Destination Port—The TCP/IP port connection made between the proxy and the target site. With the Web Proxy, this will always be 80. The WinSock Proxy will log a wide range of ports for this field.

13. Processing Time—The time it took (measured in milliseconds) the proxy server to obtain the requested information once the request was received from the client. The clock stops once the proxy server receives the result code from the target Internet site. If the information was retrieved from the Web Proxy cache, this field indicates how much time it took to locate the information and send it to the client.

14. Bytes Sent—The number of bytes sent to the client by the proxy server. This field may be a dash if no data bytes where sent to the client. This field is only used by the Web Proxy. The WinSock Proxy only enters a dash in this field.

15. Bytes Received—This field represents the number of bytes received by the proxy server from the client. This size is the size of the request line sent by the client to the proxy. As with the previous field, this field is not logged by the WinSock Proxy (it uses only a dash). If this field is a dash in a Web Proxy log, it may mean that the client sent no data or that it did not provide the size information.

16. Protocol Name—In Web Proxy logs, this field will be HTTP, FTP, Gopher, or Secure, depending on the type of protocol used by the client. In WinSock Proxy logs, this field will be the commonly used numeric protocol of the client connection (for example, 110 for SMTP connections).

17. Transport—The method of transport used between client and proxy. Web Proxy connections will always be TCP. WinSock Proxy connections will be TCP, UDP, or IPX/SPX.

18. Operation—Indicates the transport operation performed by the proxy server. The Web Proxy can log GET, PUT, POST, and HEAD. The WinSock Proxy can log Connect, Accept, SendTo, RecvFrom, and GetHostByName.

19. Object Name—This field indicates the name of the object retrieved by the Web Proxy. The WinSock Proxy always logs a dash in this field.

20. Object MIME—This field is used only by the Web Proxy (the WinSock Proxy simply logs a dash here). This field indicates the Multi-Purpose Internet Mail Extensions type for the retrieved object. This field may be a dash if the target Internet server is not defined or supported on the target server. The field can contain the following strings:

MIME Type	Definition
application/x-msdownload	Application
image/gif	GIF Image
image/jpeg	JPG Image
multipart/x-zip	ZIP Archive
text/plain	ASCII Text File

21. Object Source—Only used by the Web Proxy, this field indicates where the object came from. The following value may be logged:

Field Value	Definition
Unknown	Proxy Server could not determine where the object originated.
Cache	Object found in cache.
Rcache	Object found on Internet. Object was added to cache.
Vcache	Object found in cache. Object was verified against target object on Internet.
NVCache	Object found in cache, but could not be verified against target object on Internet. Object was still returned to client.
VFInet	Object found on Internet. Object could not be verified against source.
PragNoCacheInet	Object found on Internet. HTTP header indicates that the object should not be cached.
Inet	Object found on Internet. Object was not added to the cache.

22. Result Code—This field is the result code returned by the target Internet site concerning the retrieval of the object. This field can be a wide range of values. The Web Proxy and the WinSock Proxy log different values for this field. In the Web Proxy log, values under 100 indicate Windows error codes. Values between 100 and 1,000 are HTTP status codes. Values over 10,000 are Wininet or WinSock error codes. The three most common codes logged by the Web proxy will be 200 (Successful Connection), 10060 (Connection Timed Out), and 10065 (Host Unreachable). In WinSock Proxy logs, this field will be one of the following codes:

Code	Definition
0	Successful Connection.
1	Server Failure.
2	Rejection by Proxy due to filtering.
3	Network unreachable due to no DNS service available.
4	Host unreachable because no DNS entry could be found for the host.
5	Connection refused by target Internet site.
6	Unsupported client request (perhaps the client is using a non-compliant TCP/IP stack or the WinSock call is from a non-supported version).
7	Unsupported Address type.

Verbose Fields and Regular Fields

When regular logging is selected, some fields will simply be represented with a dash. Verbose logging will log all known data to all the previously listed fields. Regular logging will log only the following fields:

- Client Computer IP
- Client Username
- Authentication Status
- Date Logged
- Time Logged
- Server Name
- Destination Name
- Destination Port
- Protocol Name
- Object Name
- Object Source
- Result Code

Reading the logs can sometimes be very confusing, because it appears that the proxies sometimes do not log the correct information. The important thing to remember is to keep the order of the fields right, and pretty soon you'll be able to understand them correctly.

Log Cautions

Because the Web Proxy runs as a sub-service of the WWW Server, you can turn off all WWW logging and let the Web Proxy log all connection information. Enabling the WWW log is a redundant action that will only eat up disk space.

Speaking of disk space, keep in mind that log files can grow to a very large size when there are many people accessing Microsoft Proxy Server. This is due to the fact that each object returned from the Internet or cache generates a record. Web pages can contain five, ten, or more objects. Every time such pages are accessed, a large number of log records are created. To make matters worse, some clients will issue the same command over and over again when they receive an error retrieving requested data. This can make the log files huge. It's an excellent idea to only keep a few days worth of logs active and archive the remaining ones you want to keep. If the log disk becomes full, Microsoft Proxy Server may stop operating.

Keeping a log will make sure that you as network administrator are maintaining a high security environment for your company. Without logging, your network users may be bogging down Internet access, and you'll have no way of knowing who or what is causing the problem.

Database Logging

If you have access to a database engine such as SQL Server or Access, you can use ODBC drivers to let Microsoft Proxy Server interface with these engines to log the same information that will be logged to text files. The benefit of logging to a database is that the data is already in an easily manipulated form and is often stored in a more compact manner.

When Microsoft Proxy Server is installed, it will prompt you to install ODBC drivers. The ODBC drivers for interfacing with SQL and Access are provided with Microsoft Proxy Server. If ODBC drivers are already installed on your NT server for some other purpose, you will not need to reinstall them. ODBC drivers operate in a universal manner, and as such are not specific to any certain piece of software (except for the database they are designed to interface with). ODBC was designed to be a generic interface method that applications could use to open a database to write or retrieve data without having to know the specifics of the database engine or format of the data files themselves. Applications make generic calls to the ODBC driver, and the ODBC driver knows how to perform the requested action with the database engine.

Preparing the Database

The first thing to do if you are planning on using a database to log Microsoft Proxy Server information is to prepare a database file to hold the data. This is done through the database itself. This should be a fairly straightforward operation of creating the file with the required fields of sufficient length to hold any possible data. The following table details the exact field names and types Microsoft Proxy servers need in a table or database to correctly log information.

Table 13.1. Microsoft Proxy Server field names and types.

Field Name	SQL Data Type	Access Data Type	Length
ClientIP	varchar	text	50
clientUserName	varchar	text	50
ClientAgent	varchar	text	100
clientAuthenticate	char	text	5
LogTime	datetime	datetime	n/a
Service	varchar	text	25
ServerName	varchar	text	50
ReferredServer	varchar	text	100
DestHost	varchar	text	255
DestHostIP	varchar	text	50
DestHostPort	int	Long Integer	n/a
ProcessingTime	int	Long Integer	n/a
BytesSent	int	Long Integer	n/a

continues

Table 13.1. continued

Field Name	SQL Data Type	Access Data Type	Length
BytesRecv	int	Long Integer	n/a
Protocol	varchar	text	25
Transport	varchar	text	25
Operation	varchar	text	255
URI	varchar	text	255
MIMEType	varchar	text	25
ObjectSource	varchar	text	25
ResultCode	int	LongInteger	n/a

Once the table is constructed, the logging tab of both proxy properties can be used to config-ure the proxies to log in to the correct database engine and pass log information. Chapter 6 covers setting up the logging tab in greater detail.

DSN

DSN stands for Data Source Name. It is a naming convention used by ODBC drivers 2.5 and above. When applications make DSN calls to an ODBC driver, those calls will include vital information, such as the standard name of the ODBC driver being called, the name of the database to open, and the target server to contact. Without DSN, ODBC drivers will be un-able to correctly open the target database and begin logging information. A database can be assigned a Data Source Name, and it is by this name that Microsoft Proxy Server will reference the target database. Make sure that the DSN you give to an SQL or Access database matches the DSN name you indicate on the logging tab of the proxy properties.

DSN is primarily configured through the ODBC Control Applet in the Windows NT Con-trol Panel. Refer to the online help in that applet when configuring DSN for a particular database/engine.

Other Log Files

Microsoft Proxy Server uses other logs for its own internal data. When Microsoft Proxy Server is installed, it logs its setup information to `c:\mspsetup.log`. This is a text log you can refer-ence if setup did not go correctly.

When the WinSock Proxy client software is installed on workstations, it will create a log file called `c:\mpcsetup.log`. This log can be used to help track down installation problems work-stations might be having with the WinSock Proxy client software.

The Windows Event Viewer found in the Administrative Tools folder is the best way of tracking down operational problems with Microsoft Proxy Server. Any application error Microsoft Proxy Server may be encountering will be logged through the Event log. Each event related to Microsoft Proxy Server will be tagged with one of the following source names:

Event Source Name	Definition
WebProxyServer	Web Proxy Server generated
WebProxyLog	Web Proxy log generated
WebProxyCache	Web Proxy cache generated
WinSockProxy	WinSock Proxy Server generated
WinSockProxyLog	WinSock Proxy Server log generated
MSProxyAdmin	Microsoft Proxy Server Administrative interface generated

SNMP

SNMP is a communication protocol designed to allow remote control of a server or server application from an external workstation (or other NT server). In order for SNMP to work, the SNMP protocol must be installed on the server with the application that is to be remotely controlled, and any controlling server or workstation must have the SNMP protocol installed as well as SNMP client software. SNMP client software isn't cheap, nor is it simple to understand.

Most server applications that can be remotely controlled or monitored through the SNMP protocol will come with Mibs or Management Information Base files. *Mibs* are information files that tell SNMP client software how to interface with the server application they are designed for. SNMP client software will compile Mib files into part of its own code so the software will understand how the target server application operates.

The Microsoft Proxy Server Mibs are not installed when Microsoft Proxy Server is installed. If you purchased Microsoft Proxy Server and have an installation CD, the Mibs can be found in the \Alpha\Perfctrs, \I386\Perfctrs, \Mips\Perfctrs, and \Ppc\Perfctrs directories (for the four system architectures that NT supports). The Mib for the Web Proxy service is w3p.mib. The Mib for the WinSock Proxy service is wsp.mib.

Compilation and usage instructions for SNMP control and monitoring is beyond the scope of this book. If you are interested in learning how to use the SNMP protocol and SNMP client software, you may have a hard time finding any demo or shareware clients. SNMP client software is not the kind of software companies put out for use on a try-before-you-buy basis.

Summary

For a large number of network administrators, using Microsoft Proxy Server will be the best way to control company-wide access to the Internet. Using the logging and SNMP monitoring capability of Microsoft Proxy Server, a network administrator can ensure that an Internet link will be used properly and efficiently.

Appendixes

Troubleshooting

This appendix covers some basic scenarios you might encounter when working with Microsoft Proxy Server. Keep in mind that it is impossible to write troubleshooting instructions for every conceivable system design. For the most part, Microsoft Proxy Server is a very smooth running service, requiring very little if any administrator intervention once the service is installed and properly configured.

For my tastes, I can usually find all the information I need by asking fellow network administrators for help on the Microsoft Proxy Server newsgroup. This is a private newsgroup supported only by Microsoft and can be found by linking to their newsgroup server at msnews.microsoft.com. The name of the Microsoft Proxy Server newsgroup is microsoft.public.proxy. Microsoft operates a private newsgroup server that does not share its newsgroup feed to the rest of the Internet on a global basis. However, the public is free to access their newsgroup server, and you will find over 200 newsgroups dedicated to various Microsoft software topics.

Error Messages

Both the Web Proxy and the WinSock Proxy will generate different kinds of errors. The Web Proxy is able to communicate more easily with the client through return HTTP documents when an error is encountered. When an error is encountered by the WinSock Proxy, it is often impossible to determine the exact cause of the error because the WinSock Proxy has no direct way of communicating with the client.

The errors listed for the Web Proxy will be found displayed in a client's browser window unless otherwise noted. The errors listed for the WinSock Proxy can also be seen in the display area of client browsers, if the browser is not set to perform CERN proxy communication and must rely on the WinSock Proxy for its Internet connection. Errors may also be logged through the Event Viewer on the NT server running Microsoft Proxy Server.

Not all possible error messages are listed in this chapter. I have chosen the ones that you are most likely to encounter. If you would like to view a complete list of error messages for Microsoft Proxy Server, you can do so through the online HTML documentation in Appendixes I and J (of the online documentation).

Most error messages are given as a verbose string and a numeric error code. The error code will be listed at the end of the verbose string. Obviously, most network administrators prefer reading a verbose string rather than a cryptic error code.

Web Proxy Messages

Table A.1 is a short list of common error messages you might see as pop-up dialogs displayed on the NT server running Microsoft Proxy Server. These are server-based messages, not user-based messages.

Table A.1. Common error messages displayed on NT server.

Error Message	Definition
The server was unable to load `ODBC32.DLL` for SQL logging due to the following error: *number*. The data is the error code.	Most likely ODBC is not properly installed on the NT server running Microsoft Proxy Server. Reinstall a valid ODBC32 driver into the system or check to ensure that `ODBC32.DLL` is present in the `c:\winnt\system32` directory.
The server was unable to log on the Windows NT account *accountname* due to the following error: *number*. The data is the error code.	This error occurs when a client is attempting to pass a username to Microsoft Proxy Server that is either not present in the NT user database, or is present but the password is incorrect. This is a standard logon error message. Double check to make sure that the client has submitted the correct credentials.

Error Message	Definition
The server was unable to open ODBC Data Source *sourcename*, Table: *tablename*, under User Name *username*. The ODBC Error is: *number*. The data is the error code.	This error occurs when one or both of the proxy servers is configured to log active information to a database, and Microsoft Proxy Server cannot find the correct DSN entry for the given database. Double check the ODBC Control Applet in the system Control Panel to make sure that the DSN name has been correctly configured.
W3PCache corrected a corrupted or old format URL cache by removing all or part of the cache's contents.	If a disk error occurs on your NT service, you may see this error message. It indicates that at least some portion of the cache has become corrupt. It is unlikely that an old format URL will be present because the Web Proxy qualifies all cache data as valid before it stores it in the cache. Scan the system hard disk that holds the cache directory for physical errors.
W3PCache failed to initialize the URL cache on disk.	This message indicates that the Web Proxy cache has become extremely corrupt. Because the Web Proxy stores cache items in a coded format, corruption of the reference file may result in the entire contents of the cache being wasted. Delete the cache directory or attempt to reset the cache defaults from within the Web Proxy properties. The Web Proxy server will not start when the cache is corrupt. You will need to restart the NT server after correcting the problem, or manually start the Web Proxy server on its own.
W3PCache initialization failed due to incorrect configuration. Please use the administration utility or manually edit the Registry to correct the error and restart the service.	It's unlikely that the NT Registry will become corrupt (NT protects the Registry pretty darned well). If this error occurs, examine the Registry settings involved with Microsoft Proxy Server and see if they look OK. It's often difficult to tell correct Registry settings from bad ones. Refer to the "Registry Entries" section later in this chapter for details on Registry entries that might help.

Table A.2 is a list of error messages the user might see when attempting to connect to the Web Proxy server. These messages will be shown in the display area of the browser the user is using.

Table A.2. Error messages when connecting to the proxy server.

Error Message	Definition
`A connection with the server could not be established.`	If clients are receiving this message, it means that the proxy server could not be contacted. Check to see if the Web Proxy service is running and if the workstation can see any other server resource or service. If no other server service can be seen, check the actual network cabling or setup.
`Access is denied.`	This message is by far one of the most common error messages. This message indicates that the client is requesting access to a site or protocol which he does not have access to (as defined in the permissions list of the Web Proxy). Alter the permissions list or explain the security restrictions to the user. This is also referred to as HTTP error 5.
`The access code is invalid.`	This error usually means that there is an error in the LAT file. Copy the server version of the LAT down to the workstation having trouble, and see if that takes care of the problem. Try using another browser and see if the same error occurs. If it does not, reinstall the first browser that was having trouble. If the error does occur, check to make sure the network connection between the workstation and server is stable.
`The connection with the server was reset.`	This error means that the client lost connection with the proxy server and then regained the connection. The server may have rebooted or the service may have been shut down and restarted.
`The connection with the server was terminated abnormally.`	This error means the client's connection with the proxy server has died and has not been regained. This does not mean that the connection with the outside Internet host has been terminated. Check to see if there is an operational problem with the NT server or the Web Proxy server.

Error Message	Definition
`The login request was denied.`	This error means that a client workstation was trying to present logon credentials to the Web Proxy and the credentials were not accepted. This will only occur when authentication is required. Check the NT user account to make sure the workstation is presenting the correct information. Check to make sure the account is not disabled.
`The operation timed out.`	This is the most common user error encountered. It means the target Internet site did not respond to the Web Proxy server's access request. The target name was resolved to an IP, but the IP did not initially respond, or has stopped responding. This error could mean that the Web Proxy's connection to the Internet has been suddenly disconnected after an initial contact to the target site has been made. This error will not be received if the connection to the Internet is down before initial contact, because the target name will not have yet been resolved into an IP address. Check the Web Proxy server's connection to the Internet or try contacting the site directly from the NT server running Microsoft Proxy Server. It is unlikely that there is a problem with the Web Proxy server.
`The server name or Web address could not be resolved.`	This error means that the client is referencing the Web Proxy server by a name that cannot be found in the name resolution server's database. If you want clients to reference the Web Proxy server by a name, there must exist some form of name resolution on the network (see Chapter 9, "Concepts and Realities of Name Resolution with Proxy Server"). If name resolution services are available on the network, check to see if the workstation's TCP/IP settings are correct.
`The URL is invalid.`	The URL entered by the client is not formatted correctly. Resubmit the request in the correct manner.

By far, the previously listed client errors will be the ones most commonly received by clients. Most of the time, errors will be related to a down Internet connection. Keep in mind that ISP's lose their Internet connections, too. Just because your NT server is connected to the ISP does not mean you still have a valid connection to the rest of the Internet. If workstations cannot connect to target sites, yet the NT server is connected to an ISP, check with the ISP to inquire about their situation.

WinSock Proxy Messages

Table A.3 shows a list of server-based WinSock Proxy error messages. These messages will be displayed as pop-up dialogs on the server itself, or can be found through the Event Viewer. These are not user-based messages.

A.3. Server-based WinSock Proxy error messages.

Error Messages	Definition
`Incorrect network configuration. None of server's addresses is internal.`	This error means that the LAT file is not constructed properly. The WinSock Proxy cannot determine which addresses are local and which are remote. Reconstruct the LAT manually or by letting the WinSock Proxy (of Web Proxy) do it automatically. This is done via the Edit LAT Table button on the General tab of either proxy property sheets.
`User username at host hostname has timed-out after number seconds of inactivity.`	This error means that the client did not respond to the WinSock Proxy within the time out period defined through the RAS connection settings. RAS connections can have inactivity periods defined for them on the NT side. If clients do not keep the connection active for the required period, RAS will close the Internet connection. To fix this error, extend or disable the time out value for the RAS connection to the Internet.
`WinSock Proxy server failed to determine network addresses.`	This error generally means that the workstation copy of the LAT does not match the server copy of the LAT. Makes sure both LAT files match.
`WinSock Proxy server failed to initialize. The data (if any) is the error.`	This is one of the most irritating error messages. It means almost anything could be wrong. The WinSock server needs to be reinstalled to ensure that all necessary data and application files are present on the server.

Error Messages	Definition
WinSock Proxy server failed to initialize because of bad Registry. The data is the error.	The Registry entries for the WinSock Proxy are incorrect. Have you been messing with them? Feel free to edit the Registry but always export the branch you are working on to a saved file before making any changes. If you can't remember whether the Registry settings for the WinSock Proxy have been reset to the correct values, you will need to reinstall the WinSock Proxy.
WinSock Proxy server NT failed to initialize the network. The data is the error.	Something is wrong with the network on the server running the WinSock Proxy. Reset the server or try stopping all network services and restarting them through the Service Manager. Many times the NT server will come back to life after a bum service is restarted. Make sure you know in what order to stop and restart services though.
WinSock Proxy server failed to load security DLL.	In order for the WinSock Proxy to be able to communicate with the NT security layer, the file security.dll must be present in the c:\winnt\system32 directory. Without this file, the WinSock Proxy cannot submit logon credentials to NT. Make sure this file is present. If not, reinstall the WinSock Proxy.

Table A.4 shows some possible WinSock Proxy errors users may see. These error messages may be displayed as pop-up dialog boxes generated by the WinSock Proxy client software or the user's Internet client application(s) may report the numeric version of a given error. For example, if a client cannot connect to a target Internet site, it may simply report error 10060.

Table A.4. Possible WinSock Proxy errors that users might encounter.

Error Message	Definition
Connection refused.	This is a common error encountered by many Internet clients, typically FTP clients more than others. It usually means that the target site has no available connections, and the user will have to retry the connection later.

continues

Table A.4. continued

Error Message	Definition
Connection timed out.	This error means that there is a DNS entry for the site name the user is trying to connect to, but it is not responding to the access request. The target site could be down, or the Internet connection between your network and the target site could be severed. This is error 10060 in standard Internet parlance. It is unlikely the error is with the WinSock Proxy. Wait and try the connection in a little while.
Current version is not supported.	This is a WinSock Proxy client software generated error, and it means that the workstation Internet client application has made a WinSock call that does not fall within the 1.1 WinSock standards. Find a client application that is WinSock 1.1–compliant if you want to use the current version of Microsoft Proxy Server.
Host was not found.	This error means that a workstation client has submitted a DNS request that could not be resolved by any known DNS servers. Check the address and try again.
Permission denied.	This error indicates that the workstation client does not have permission to access the requested protocol. Check the WinSock Proxy permissions list to ensure that the affected user has permission to use the protocol desired.
System is not ready.	This error means that the workstation client has attempted to contact the WinSock Proxy during startup or shutdown. If the NT server running Microsoft Proxy Server was just restarted, retry the operation in a few minutes. This error will not be reported.

Since the WinSock Proxy client software runs as a service on workstations, it can also report errors related to normal network operation. If things seem flakey between the workstation and the WinSock Proxy, check to see if the workstation's network settings are correct.

Using the WinSock Proxy Status Program

Located in the c:\mspclnt directory created by the WinSock Proxy client software installation routine is a small program for testing the WinSock Proxy connection between the workstation and the WinSock Proxy server. This application is chkwsp32.exe. Run this application through a DOS shell, not by using the Run command on the Start menu. You will need to see the results it displays.

Run chkwsp32.exe with the -f parameter to see a detailed report about the status of the WinSock client software and the server status. The following is an example of the results of using the chkwsp32.exe application:

```
********************************************************************
****    Winsock Proxy Diagnostic Information    ****
********************************************************************

WAIT...

CONFIGURATION:
  Winsock Proxy Service - Configuration Location: C:\mspclnt\
  Proxy Name (IP Addr):
    Addr1: 220.200.200.1 ( pandyloc.com )
  Proxy IPX Addr:
    Addr1: 02020202-00400526bfe8
  IP: Installed
  IPX: Installed

WAIT...

16-bit RWS CLIENT:
  Winsock Name: C:\WINDOWS\winsock.dll
  Version: 1.0.193.3
  Description: Microsoft Remote Windows Socket 16-Bit DLL

32-bit WSP CLIENT:
  Winsock Name: C:\WINDOWS\SYSTEM\wsock32.dll
  Version: 1.0.193.3
  Description: Microsoft Remote Windows Socket 32-Bit DLL
  Version Type: FREE
  Client version of control protocol: 9

WSP SERVER:
  Testing against server: 220.200.200.1 ( pandyloc.com )
  Version: 1.0.193.3
  Version Type: FREE
  Server version of control protocol: 9
  Windows version: 4.0
  Windows build number: 1381

-----------------------------------------

Client control protocol version MATCHES the server control protocol
```

As you can see, the chkwsp32.exe utility displays quite a bit of information about the current WinSock client version, the WinSock Proxy server version, and the status of the current connection. Keep in mind that the WinSock Proxy client software must match the WinSock Proxy server version running on the NT machine. If you upgrade Microsoft Proxy Server, all network workstations using the WinSock Proxy client software will need to be updated accordingly.

The chkwsp32.exe utility will tell you if the WinSock Proxy server is able to be contacted and if the WinSock Proxy client files are installed correctly.

A little bit of personal advice here: I have found that changing almost any network settings on workstations when the WinSock client is installed will make it so the WinSock Proxy server cannot be contacted, even if every configuration setting is correct. I don't know what to attribute this to. After altering network settings for such things as protocols and network clients, the WinSock Proxy client software just seems to die. I have been unable to get it to come back from the grave without doing a full reinstallation of Windows 95. My advice to you, if you have to alter workstation network settings, first uninstall the WinSock Proxy client software, make the necessary network changes, and then reinstall the WinSock Proxy client software. I have messed up three of my home machines in testing. I might be the only one who has had this problem, but I felt obligated to mention it here.

Installation Errors

As with any piece of software, installation errors can occur. Most errors are minor, but some will prevent you from installing Microsoft Proxy Server and the WinSock Proxy client software. The following sections detail some of the errors you might encounter.

Server Installation Errors

One of the most common errors you may encounter when installing Microsoft Proxy Server is the presence of two or more of the same DLL files in the \WINNT and \WINNT\SYSTEM directories, or along the system search path. This will affect both Windows NT and Windows 95 client workstations. If the system finds a DLL in more than one place in the system, you will experience buggy performance and possible corruption of data. Many TCP/IP applications these days want to do things their own way. Applications such as the America Online client for Windows 95 and the CompuServe client for Windows 95 might decide to add their own directories to the search path and add their own winsock.dll and wsock32.dll files into the Windows system area. This could cause more problems than I can count. You should have a clear understanding of what any Internet application will install before you actually begin installing. Yes, this may mean a little RTFM action, but it'll save you some headaches down the road.

Another common problem encountered when installing Microsoft Proxy Server is the need of having Administrator privileges on the NT server you want to install the software on. In order to correctly install Microsoft Proxy Server you must be logged on with a user account that has Administrator privileges.

Locked files are another common problem. Sometimes it is impossible to install the server software because another application has locked open the system files Microsoft Proxy Server needs to overwrite. When installing the server software, make sure all extraneous software is shut down. Default Windows NT service applications should not cause any files to be locked open.

If you have an NT 4.0 server installation that came right out of the box, you may need to contact Microsoft (via their Web site—www.microsoft.com) to get the latest service pack for NT 4.0. Almost immediately after NT 4.0 was released, a service pack was released that is required before Microsoft Proxy Server will install. This service pack fixes several bugs directly related to Microsoft Proxy Server. Microsoft Proxy Server's installation routine will check to ensure the service pack has been applied and will not continue unless it has been.

Client Installation Errors

Client workstations will normally install the WinSock Proxy client software by connecting to the shared resource name MSPCLNT on the server running Microsoft Proxy Server. This shared resource is created and shared by default and should be used for all client installations.

Personally, I have had a lot of problems getting the WinSock Proxy client setup to run correctly over the network. I have encountered errors related to the setup routine being unable to open the necessary files. I have had to go so far as to copy the entire contents of the MSPCLNT share and all sub-directories down to a temp directory on the local workstation and running the WinSock Proxy client setup from that temp directory. This will not cause any setup problems with mis-pointed file locations or anything of that nature.

If you find you are having similar problems, your only alternative may be to copy the setup files to the local workstations and run the setup routing from there. In theory, you should be able to run the WinSock Proxy client setup routine directly from the Network Neighborhood without even having to map a drive letter to the shared resource. If this approach doesn't work for you, try mapping a drive letter to the resource, and then running the setup routine from the mapped drive. If that still fails, your only alternative may be to copy down to the local workstation.

As already mentioned, making changes to workstation network settings while the WinSock Proxy client software is installed may render the WinSock Proxy client unusable. If you find your workstations are suffering from this apparent bug, follow the uninstall routine for the WinSock Proxy client, reboot, and then make any necessary network setting adjustments.

If you have set the WinSock Proxy client setup routine to automatically set workstations for Web Proxy interface, you should already have Internet Explorer 3.0 or higher installed on all target workstations. Remember that the Internet Control Applet is not present in the Windows 95 Control Panel until Internet Explorer 3.0 or higher is installed. In order to reduce the amount of setup work you may have to do to workstations later on, it is best to have the Internet Control Applet present in Windows 95 for the WinSock Proxy client setup routine to adjust. The WinSock Proxy client setup routine will also make automatic proxy changes to standalone clients like Netscape Navigator (all versions) and Internet Explorer 1.*x* and 2.*x*.

If the NT server running Microsoft Proxy Server has a space in its name like mine does (Controller 4.0), you might find that the WinSock Proxy client installation routine does not correctly set up Web Proxy clients if you have indicated clients should reference the Web Proxy server by name, rather than IP address. Clients may only reference the first or last part of the server name. To try to remedy this, edit the `MSPCLNT.INI` file in the `\MSP\CLIENTS` directory on the NT server, and enclose any server name references in double quotes (as in `Controller 4.0` or `\\Controller 4.0\MSPCLNT`). This should take care of this problem. If it does not, create a static mapping in the WINS server database (for example—`PROXY`) to reference Microsoft Proxy Server Web Proxy by and then edit the `MSPCLNT.INI` file on the server to reference this static mapping name (edit only the `WWW-Proxy=` line to reference the Web Proxy server name; do not alter any NetBIOS names (names starting with `\\`). This is often the best approach because you can segregate the name used to reference Microsoft Proxy Server Web Proxy completely from any specific server name. This WINS database entry can then be easily adjusted, should the location on Microsoft Proxy Server Web Proxy change.

When the WinSock Proxy client software is installed, you should understand how DNS is affected. Any TCP/IP traffic that originates from a workstation will automatically be routed to the WinSock Proxy server, should it be destined for the outside world. This generally means that DNS resolution will take place on the NT server running the WinSock Proxy. I have seen some funky workstation behavior concerning DNS name resolution when the WinSock Proxy client software is installed. In Chapter 9, I talk about how to use DNS and WINS together to resolve all possible network names. I also talk about how to create a zone in the DNS server (for example `pandy.com`) and then use DNS to reference the WINS server for specific name resolutions (for example, `ftp.pandy.com`).

This is done by simply creating a static entry in the WINS database for the host name of FTP. Normally, when DNS receives a request for a name such as `ftp.pandy.com`, if it does not find the host FTP listed in the zone for `pandy.com`, it will pass the host name (FTP) along to the WINS server that should be referenced in the `pandy.com` zone. WINS would just receive the resolution request for FTP, and it would respond to the DNS server with the IP. Then the DNS server would respond to the client with the IP address it was given by the WINS server.

This doesn't always seem to work. It appears that sometimes the DNS server does not pass host resolution requests to the WINS server. I can't tell if this is a workstation-related issue or a server-related issue. In either case, you may need to set up DNS host entries in the zone for your network for most resolution requests. This is a pain (IMHO) because the WINS server is a much more powerful name resolution service in a Windows-based environment.

LAT file errors can cause parts of the Internet to become inaccessible. All addresses found in the LAT file will be referenced as though they were part of the local network. This means that should your network IP subnet not be one of the reserved subnets set aside by the InterNIC, you may be unable to contact the sites on the Internet that validly have IP addresses used by your own private network. To ensure this does not happen, read Chapter 4, "Planning Your Installation and Configuration," carefully.

Registry Settings

It's unlikely you will have to edit Registry settings for Microsoft Proxy Server yourself, but just in case, I'll cover some of the important ones.

On Windows NT there are two Registry editing utilities. One looks like the Windows 95 Registry Editor, and the other is native to Windows NT. Figure A.1 shows the Windows 95 version of the Registry Editor, and Figure A.2 shows the Windows NT native version of the Registry Editor.

Figure A.1.
The Windows 95 version of the Registry Editor.

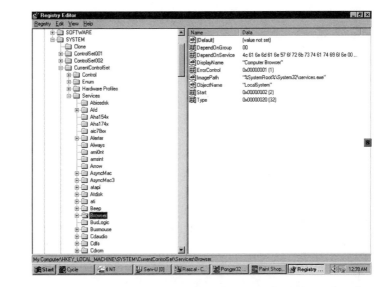

Figure A.2.
The native Windows NT version of the Registry Editor.

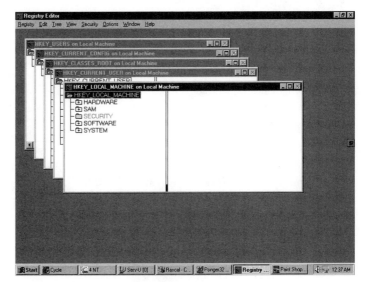

The Windows 95 version of the Registry Editor is started by running REGEDIT.EXE and the native Windows NT version is started by running REGEDT32.EXE. In my opinion, the Windows 95 Registry Editor is the easier one to use, but the native Windows NT version has all of the features necessary to change some advanced Registry keys. This next section covers using only the native Windows NT version of the Registry Editor.

Most of the Microsoft Proxy Server Registry settings can be found off of the following Registry branches:

WinSock Proxy Settings

```
HKEY_LOCAL_MACHINE
 SYSTEM
  \CurrentControlSet
  \Services
   \WSPsrv
```

Web Proxy Settings

```
HKEY_LOCAL_MACHINE
 SYSTEM
  \CurrentControlSet
  \Services
   \W3Proxy
```

Web Proxy Cache Settings

```
HKEY_LOCAL_MACHINE
 SYSTEM
  \CurrentControlSet
  \Services
   \W3PCache
```

WWW Service Settings

```
HKEY_LOCAL_MACHINE
 SYSTEM
  \CurrentControlSet
  \Services
   \W3Svc
```

When making changes to the Registry through the Registry Editor, keep in mind that the changes you make might not take effect immediately. You should always stop and restart any service after making changes to its Registry settings. Changes made through the Internet Server Manager, however, will be immediately effective.

And, as always, edit the Registry at your own risk. Making changes to the wrong settings could make it impossible to start Windows NT and only a reinstallation will remedy the situation. However, none of the settings dealing with Microsoft Proxy Server should affect how NT itself starts up. The wrong settings may cause the service to not start, but not NT itself.

Keep in mind also that most of the key values are set by hexadecimal notation, which is base 16 notation. If you are not familiar with hex notation, it's a pretty simple thing to grasp. For example, hexadecimal 20 equals 32 in standard notation ($2 \times 16 = 32$). The hexadecimal value of 14 equals 20 in standard notation ($16 + 4 = 20$). And you didn't think all that fancy calculus you took in college would come in handy.

Most of the Registry settings are simply the configuration settings you set on the property sheets of both the Web Proxy and the WinSock Proxy. Site filtering settings are common between both the Web Proxy and the WinSock Proxy. These settings are held in the Registry branch:

```
HKEY_LOCAL_MACHINE\SYSTEM\CurrentControlSet\Services\W3Proxy\Parameters\DoFilter
```

Table A.5 shows a list of useful keys in this branch:

Table A.5. Useful keys in the Registry branch.

Key	Definition
FilterType	0 = No site filtering enabled. 1 = General site deny policy set. 2 = General site grant policy set.
NumDenySites	Can be set to any number. When set to a non-zero value, Microsoft Proxy Server will deny access to the first x number of sites listed in the DenySites key (not created by default). Sites will be separated by a space.
NumGrantSites	Can be set to any number. When set to a non-zero value, Microsoft Proxy Server will grant access to the first x number of sites listed in the GrantSites key (not created by default). Sites will be separated by a space.)
DenySites	Can be set to any string value, for example, `www.pandy.com ftp.xyz.com *.netscape.com`. The sites listed here will be excepted from the general site grant policy and access to them will be prohibited through Microsoft Proxy Server.
GrantSites	Can be set to any string value, for example, `www.pandy.com ftp.xyz.com *.netscape.com`. The sites listed here will be excepted from the general site deny policy and access to them will be granted through Microsoft Proxy Server.

A short list of important Web Proxy Registry keys is shown in Table A.6. These keys are found in the Parameters folder off of the main Web Proxy branch (see above).

Table A.6. Important Web Proxy Registry keys.

Key	Definition
DnsCacheSize	Can be set to any hex number in the range of 12c–7530. The default is bb8. This refers to the cache size in bytes. This key sets how large the DNS cache size will be for Microsoft Proxy Server. When client access the outside Internet, Microsoft Proxy Server stores the most recently accessed IP addresses. Increasing this value on busy networks may speed up name resolution somewhat.
DnsTTLInSecs	Can be set to any hex number in the range of e10–8ca0. This refers to the time to live in seconds. The default is 5460 (24 hours). This sets the time to live value for DNS cache entries. When their time to live expires, cached DNS entries will be flushed.
MaxFtpThreadsFactor	Can be set to any hex number in the range of 8–24. The default is 8. This refers to the number of processor threads Microsoft Proxy Server will start for FTP sessions. Once the thread limit has been reached, Microsoft Proxy Server will begin sharing threads for FTP sessions.
RequestTimeoutSecs	Can be set to any hex in the range of 10–1000. This value is in seconds. The default is 3c. Determines what the time out factor is when Microsoft Proxy Server is attempting to contact an Internet site.

Table A.7 shows a list of important Registry key values that affect Web Proxy caching. These keys are found in the Parameters folder of the Web Proxy Cache primary branch.

Table A.7. Important Registry key values affecting Proxy caching.

Key	Definition
CleanupFactor	Can be set to any hex number in the range of 0–64. The default is 19. This number represents the cleanup percentage. When a cache clean up is performed, this key determines what percentage of the cache is cleaned up. By default, only the oldest 25 percent of the cache is cleaned.

Key	Definition
CleanupInterval	Can be set to any hex number in the range of 0–93a40. The default is 15180. This number represents number of seconds. This determines how often the cache is cleaned. By default, it is set to 86,400 seconds, or once every 24 hours.
CleanupTime	Can be set to any number in the range of 0–23. This number indicates the hour of the day. By default it is set to 0 (12 a.m.). This key determines when cleanup occurs (by default at midnight).
Persistent	Can be set to 0 or 1. By default it is set to 1. Determines whether or not the cache is cleared when the Web Proxy Service is stopped. A 0 value indicates the cache will be completely cleared every time the Web Proxy Service stops (which will happen when NT shuts down to reboot).

Some important Registry keys which control how the WinSock Proxy server operates are shown in Table A.8. They are found in the Parameters branch off of the main WinSock Proxy server branch.

Table A.8. Registry keys controlling the operation of the WinSock Proxy server.

Key	Definition
Authentication	Can be set to 0 or 1. By default it is set to 1 (authentication enabled). If this key is set to 0, the WinSock Proxy will not demand NT Challenge/Response Authentication from workstations, which will in essence grant access to everyone.
TcpBufferSize	Can be set to any hex number 600 or higher. By default it is set to 800. This number refers to number of bytes. By default, this key defines the number of buffer bytes allocated to each TCP/IP connection.
UdpBufferSize	Can be set to any hex number in the range of 600–ffff. By default it is set to 1000. This number refers to number of bytes. This key controls what the largest UDP packet size is that will be passed through the WinSock Proxy server. UDP packets that exceed this size will not be passed from client to server and vice versa.

Obviously, there are many other keys involved with each element of Microsoft Proxy Server; however, these other keys are more easily set through the property sheets of both proxy servers. Remember to stop and restart the proxy servers after making changes to their Registry settings.

Troubleshooting Tips

When trying to figure out a problem that seems to involve Microsoft Proxy Server, try to first determine if it is a general network problem or a problem that is specific only to clients trying to access Microsoft Proxy Server. For what it does, Microsoft Proxy Server is a very simplistic service.

If clients are having trouble connecting to Microsoft Proxy Server, check to see if the TCP/IP protocol is loaded correctly. Many times workstations are set to receive their IP setup from a DHCP server, but sometimes they can't contact the DHCP server on startup. If workstations have disabled the DHCP server error message, they may never know they do not have an IP address. To test to see if this is the case, try pinging the name localhost. If TCP/IP is loaded correctly, Windows 95 will respond to the local ping request. If TCP/IP to not loaded correctly, the ping command will display an error message.

If workstations are set to use DHCP for their startup IP configuration, but they are not getting it and you are certain their are no physical errors with the network or the DHCP server itself, try deleting the following folder out of the Windows 95 Registry:

```
HKEY_LOCAL_MACHINE\System\CurrentControlSet\Services\VxD\DHCP
```

When Windows 95 workstation first contacts a DHCP server, its location is logged for future reference. Sometimes Windows 95 seems to get confused about where the DHCP server can be found and no longer broadcasts a DHCP location request. This will prevent the workstation from obtaining an IP address even after it has booted many times and successfully contacted a DHCP server. Deleting the folder mentioned will force Windows 95 to rebroadcast a DHCP location request on the next boot up. This folder will be recreated once a new (or possibly the same) DHCP server is located (or relocated as the case may be).

If you are using IPX as your exclusive network protocol, the Web Proxy server will not be used at all. Only the WinSock Proxy client and server can communicate over an IPX connection. If workstations are having trouble contacting the WinSock Proxy over an IPX link, make sure that the frame type defined for IPX on both the NT server and workstation(s) match. Do not trust Windows 95 to automatically determine the frame type used by a network. I have found that this rarely works, and you'll save yourself a lot of headaches by manually indicating which frame type to use.

Ping can be used on workstations to attempt to ping a server on the Internet through the WinSock Proxy server. Only the first half of the ping command will work, though. Ping should be able to get as far as resolving the host name to an IP address; however, the ping negotiation after that point takes place using ICMP, which is not supported through the WinSock Proxy.

Ping can therefore be used to simply test to see if workstations are getting proper name resolution through the WinSock Proxy server.

If you are using RAS to make the Internet connection from your NT machine running Microsoft Proxy Server to an ISP, but the connection keeps timing out, you might need to find a utility that can run on the NT machine to simulate network activity through the RAS connection to the ISP. Most ISPs will disconnect after a certain number of minutes of inactivity. There are several shareware programs, such as Ponger and Rascal, that are designed to help keep a connection to the Internet open. Search your favorite Internet file depository for such a utility if you would like to ensure that your Internet connection remains open as long as possible. Rascal (which can be found on `www.windows95.com`) is very nice because it will actually redial an ISP should the connection be broken.

Summary

Hopefully, you won't have too many problems with Microsoft Proxy Server. It's a pretty stable package and should not cause you too much grief. Before installing, make sure your network is running properly and you have considered as many eventualities as possible. This will save you some work down the road. With more and more companies turning to proxy servers to control employee access to the Internet from the office, applications such as Microsoft Proxy Server will become more common. Hopefully, this appendix gave you the mental tools necessary to track down most of the common problems you may encounter.

Auto Dial

If you are like the majority of Microsoft Proxy Server users, you will most likely be using a periodic dialup connection to gain the Internet connection used by LAN users. Most Internet Service Providers offer many online hours for a flat fee. Some even offer "unlimited" access. If you put them to the test by keeping your computer on and online all the time, they tend to get testy. Therefore, you need a way of automatically connecting the NT server running Microsoft Proxy Server to the Internet when a proxy client makes an Internet request. The Auto Dial configuration utility, found in the Microsoft Proxy Server folder, is the application that will allow you to set up the RAS entry to dial and the number of times which the Microsoft Proxy server is permitted to dial out. Figure B.1 shows the location of the Auto Dial utility.

Figure B.1.
*The location of the
Auto Dial utility.*

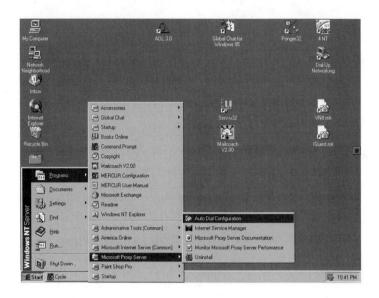

The Auto Dial utility is very easy to configure. You need to indicate which hours Microsoft Proxy Server is permitted to dial out to the Internet and which RAS account should be dialed. This necessitates that you have RAS installed and at least one ISP account configured within RAS.

WinSock Proxy client requests will always force Microsoft Proxy Server to initiate a dial-out to the Internet if Auto Dial is enabled. Web Proxy client requests will only initiate a dial-out if the requested information cannot be found in the Web Proxy cache. Some clients may time out before Microsoft Proxy Server can finalize the Internet connection. A dial out connection can take up to a full minute to negotiate. However, most of the time Microsoft Proxy Server should simulate a successful connection to a target server until the Auto Dial connection is established. This means that if the connection cannot be made, the client application will not respond with a Site Not Found error, but rather a No response from server error.

Figure B.2 shows the Auto Dial utility.

To enable Auto Dial, simply check the Enable Dial on Demand check box. By default, all times are permitted for Auto Dial. If you need to remove certain time slots from Auto Dial, simply click a time block, hold down the left mouse button, and drag the pointer to the end time. Blue indicates allowed Auto Dial, and white indicates when no Auto Dial is permitted.

Clicking the upper left-hand corner of the time chart allows you to select all times. You can also click on the days or the hours to enable/disable entire blocks at once. The Credentials tab allows you to select a RAS entry to dial when Internet requests are received and what logon name and password to use. Figure B.3 shows the Credentials tab.

Figure B.2.
The Auto Dial utility.

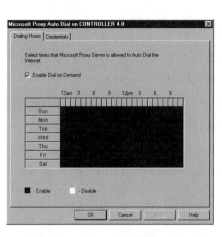

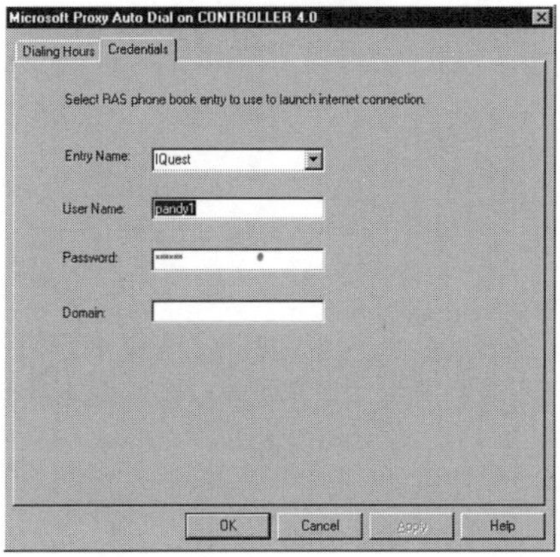

Figure B.3.
The Credentials tab.

Any RAS phone book entry can be selected from the Entry Name drop-down list. The User Name and Password fields can be used to indicate the username and password to use when logging on to the selected provider. If the selected provider is another NT system, the Domain field can be used to indicate which domain on the target network the logon credentials should be presented to for validation. This field should be left blank if the selected entry is a traditional UNIX host.

Once you have completely configured the Auto Dial settings, you can click OK (or Apply). The WWW service and the WinSock Proxy service should be stopped and then restarted in order for Auto Dial to be enabled. Stopping the WWW service also stops the Web Proxy service because the Web Proxy service runs as a sub service to the WWW service. The WinSock Proxy runs on its own without any reliance on the WWW service. To start and stop these services, use the Internet Service Manager, which can be found in either the Microsoft Internet Server or the Microsoft Proxy Server folders. The WinSock Proxy service and the WWW service can be stopped and started in any order.

Auto Dial allows the Microsoft Proxy Server to establish connections to the Internet when needed and can help keep costs down without LAN users ever knowing that the network does not have a constant connection to the Internet. Most providers will disconnect a connection after 10 to 15 minutes of inactivity. Auto Dial will reestablish the Internet connection when needed.

Summary

Auto Dial is a necessary element of any proxy server. Many UNIX-based proxy servers do not have the Auto Dial capability, and they do not have the capability to support non-CERN-compatible clients. Microsoft Proxy Server will help keep your connection costs down while providing full-time Internet access.

Index

MACMILLAN COMPUTER PUBLISHING USA

A VIACOM COMPANY

Technical

Support:

If you need assistance with the information in this book or with a CD/Disk accompanying the book, please access the Knowledge Base on our Web site at **http://www.superlibrary.com/general/support**. Our most Frequently Asked Questions are answered there. If you do not find the answer to your questions on our Web site, you may contact Macmillan Technical Support **(317) 581-3833** or e-mail us at **support@mcp.com**.

Designing and Implementing Microsoft Index Server

Mark Swank and Drew Kittel

Tripoli is an index server that allows companies to automate their indexing of crucial data. Its integration with Windows NT and Internet Information Server opens the doors to a large market of corporate NT and IIS users who will want to automate their indexing. This book shows readers how to use Tripoli. Everything from installation to implementation is discussed in detail.

Shows readers how to organize and maintain large amounts of information

Teaches ways to integrate the server into existing systems

Covers maintenance, administration, and security issues

$39.99 USA/$56.95 CDN　　　　*User Level: Accomplished*
1-57521-212-9　　　　　　　　*350 pp.*
7 3/8 x 9 1/8　　　　　　　　*12/01/96*
Internet—Networking/Servers

Designing and Implementing Microsoft Internet Information Server 2

Arthur Knowles and Sanjaya Hettihewa

This book details the specific tasks to setting up and running a Microsoft Internet Information Server. Readers will learn troubleshooting, network design, security, and cross-platform integration procedures.

Teaches security issues and how to maintain an efficient, secure network

Readers learn everything from planning to implementation

Covers Microsoft Internet Information Server

$39.99 USA/$56.95 CDN　　　　*User Level: Casual–Expert*
1-57521-168-8　　　　　　　　*336 pp.*
7 3/8 x 9 1/8　　　　　　　　*07/01/96*
Internet—Communications/Online

Apache Server Survival Guide

Manuel Alberto Ricart

As one of the most popular servers on the Internet, Apache Server is an inexpensive, secure alternative to other Web servers. This book is an excellent resource that addresses diverse networking and configuration issues.

Provides all of the knowledge needed to build and manage an Apache Web site

CD-ROM includes source code from the book, utilities, and demos

Covers the latest version

$49.99 USA/$70.95 CDN　　　　*User Level: Accomplished*
1-57521-175-0　　　　　　　　*650 pp.*
7 3/8 x 9 1/8　　　　　　　　*11/01/96*
Internet—Networking/Servers

Netscape Server Survival Guide

David L. Gulbransen, Jr.

With the recent reduction in the price of its server technology, Netscape's marketability is increasing. Both current and migrating Netscape administrators alike will need the comprehensive coverage found in this book.

Teaches the reader how to install, configure, and maintain a Netscape server

Discusses third-party products, commonly used Netscape utilities, and an extensive troubleshooting guide

CD-ROM contains software demonstrations, sample configuration files, and exotic logon scripts

$49.99 USA/$70.95 CDN   *User Level: Accomplished–Expert*
1-57521-111-4   *800 pp.*
7 3/8 x 9 1/8   *10/01/96*
Internet—General/WWW Applications

Microsoft BackOffice 2 Administrator's Survival Guide, Second Edition

Arthur Knowles

This all-in-one reference describes how to make the components of BackOffice version 2 work best together and with other networks. BackOffice is Microsoft's complete reference for networking, database, and system management products.

Contains the fundamental concepts required for daily maintenance, troubleshooting, and problem solving

CD-ROM includes product demos, commercial and shareware utilities, and technical notes from Microsoft vendor technical support personnel

Covers version 2.0

$59.99 USA/$84.95 CDN   *User Level: Accomplished*
0-672-30977-7   *1,200 pp.*
7 3/8 x 9 1/8   *11/01/96*
Client/Server

Microsoft BackOffice 2 Unleashed

Joe Greene, et al.

An instrumental tool for anyone in charge of developing or managing BackOffice. It covers the individual pieces of BackOffice as well as key phases in the development, integration, and administration of the BackOffice environment.

Contains coverage on using BackOffice as the infrastructure of an intranet or the Internet

Instructs readers on integrating individual BackOffice products

CD-ROM includes source code, third-party products, and utilities

Covers BackOffice

$59.99 USA/$84.95 CDN   *User Level: Accomplished–Expert*
0-672-30816-9   *1,200 pp.*
7 3/8 x 9 1/8   *11/01/96*
Client/Server

Microsoft SQL Server 6.5 Unleashed, Second Edition

David Solomon, Ray Rankins, et al.

This comprehensive reference details the steps needed to plan, design, install, administer, and tune large and small databases. In many cases, the reader will use the techniques in this book to create and manage his own complex environment.

CD-ROM includes source code, libraries, and administration tools

Covers programming topics, including SQL, data structures, programming constructs, stored procedures, referential integrity, large table strategies, and more

Includes updates to cover all new features of SQL Server 6.5, including the new transaction processing monitor and Internet/database connectivity through SQL Server's new Web wizard

$59.99 USA/$84.95 CDN
0-672-30956-4
7 3/8 x 9 1/8
Databases

User Level: Accomplished–Expert
1,100 pp.
10/01/96

Microsoft Internet Information Server 2 Unleashed

Arthur Knowles, et al.

The power of Microsoft Internet Information Server 2 is meticulously detailed in this 800-page volume. Readers will learn how to create and maintain a Web server, integrate IIS with BackOffice, and create interactive databases that can be used on the Internet or a corporate intranet.

Readers learn how to set up and run IIS

Teaches advanced security techniques and how to configure the server

CD-ROM includes source code from the book and powerful utilities

Covers Microsoft Internet Information Server 2

$49.99 USA/$70.95 CDN
1-57521-109-2
7 3/8 x 9 1/8
Internet—Networking/Servers

User Level: Accomplished–Expert
800 pp.
09/01/96

Add to Your Sams.net Library Today
with the Best Books for Internet Technologies

ISBN	Quantity	Description of Item	Unit Cost	Total Cost
1-57521-212-9		Designing & Implementing Microsoft Index Server	$39.99	
1-57521-168-8		Designing & Implementing Microsoft Internet Information Server 2	$39.99	
1-57521-175-0		Apache Server Survival Guide (Book/CD-ROM)	$49.99	
1-57521-111-4		Netscape Server Survival Guide (Book/CD-ROM)	$49.99	
0-672-30977-7		Microsoft BackOffice 2 Administrator's Survival Guide, Second Edition (Book/CD-ROM)	$59.99	
0-672-30816-9		Microsoft BackOffice 2 Unleashed (Book/CD-ROM)	$59.99	
0-672-30956-4		Microsoft SQL Server 6.5 Unleashed, Second Edition (Book/CD-ROM)	$59.99	
1-57521-109-2		Microsoft Internet Information Server 2 Unleashed (Book/CD-ROM)	$49.99	
		Shipping and Handling: See information below.		
		TOTAL		

Shipping and Handling: $4.00 for the first book, and $1.75 for each additional book. If you need to have it NOW, we can ship product to you in 24 hours for an additional charge of approximately $18.00, and you will receive your item overnight or in two days. Overseas shipping and handling adds $2.00. Prices subject to change. Call between 9:00 a.m. and 5:00 p.m. EST for availability and pricing information on latest editions.

201 W. 103rd Street, Indianapolis, Indiana 46290

1-800-428-5331 — Orders   1-800-835-3202 — FAX   1-800-858-7674 — Customer Service

Book ISBN 1-57521-213-7